CUCINA DI CALABRIA

CUCINA DI CALABRIA

*Treasured Recipes
and Family Traditions
from Southern Italy*

MARY AMABILE PALMER

FABER AND FABER, INC.
BOSTON   LONDON

Library of Congress Cataloging-in-Publication Data

Palmer, Mary Amabile
Cucina di Calabria / by Mary Amabile Palmer
p.   cm.
ISBN 0-571-19918-6 (cloth)
1. Cookery, Italian—Southern style.   2. Cookery—Italy—Calabria.
I. Title
TX723.2.S65P35   1997
641.5945′78—dc21   97-13177
                                                                CIP

Jacket design and interior illustration by Jane Mjølsness
Book design by Will Powers and Wendy Holdman
Typesetting by Stanton Publication Services, Inc.
Printed in the United States of America

I am dedicating this cookbook
to the past with gratitude
and to the future with hope.

To the past— to my parents,
Jennie (Giovanina Marino)
and Frank (Francesco) Amabile
and to my sister,
Margaret (Domenica) Amabile De Marco,
for the past is our heritage.

To the future—
to my two sons, John and David;
to my grandchildren, Katherine, Jennifer, and Spencer;
and to all future grandchildren and great-grandchildren
forever and ever, for the future is our challenge.
I give this book to them and their families with my love.

CONTENTS

ACKNOWLEDGMENTS

There are many, many people to whom I owe an enormous amount of gratitude for their help and encouragement. Special thanks go to my parents, Jennie and Frank Amabile; my sister, Margaret De Marco; my sons, John and David; and my three grandchildren, Katherine, Jennifer and Spencer, all to whom I have dedicated this book. Special thanks also to my dear daughters-in-law Amy and Diane, for their help and faith in me; to Janet Clair Box; and my relatives in Bova Marina, Bova Superiore, and Reggio Calabria who fed my body and soul, who contributed many recipes and information about the customs, folklore, holidays, feasts, and history of Calabria. Sincere and special thanks to my dear friend Rosemary Huang for her encouragement and her help in researching some recipes and Calabrian history. To my many old and new friends, near and far, who volunteered to taste and sometimes retaste many dishes, who came to my Calabrian dinner parties and luncheons, who advised and encouraged, I offer a special note of appreciation.

Along the way, I was fortunate to meet many people who provided invaluable information. Special recognition goes to my newly made Calabrian friends, especially in the greater Boston area, who contributed much of their time in assisting me with my search for recipes and for historical and cultural data; to Calabrian restaurateurs who generously shared with me their prized recipes; and to the many Calabrian people I encountered at outdoor food markets and in bakeries, shops, restaurants, libraries, and bookstores, who willingly gave me recipes and offered invaluable information about the history, folklore, and customs of Calabria. With apologies to any whom I have inadvertently overlooked, I want to list those who helped in one way or another:

Karen Andreas; Janet Andrews; Lena Antinucci; Steve Ariantha; Jim and Claire Bailey; Domenica, Madalena, and Mary Barletta; Linda Bassett; Barbara Beatty; Jessica Biondi; Antonio Bonaccorso and the staff of Bonaccorso's Ristorante, Reggio Calabria, Italy; Janet and Jim Box; Molly and Maggie Box; Rozalyn Brooks; Michael Burke; Francesca Calabro; Joy and Nick Cann; Mario Sabello and Pasquale D'Angelo and the staff of Il Cantinone Ristorante, Paestum, Italy; Joyce Carbonelli; Evelyn and Julian Carey; Jenny and Phil Carey; Mary Ellen Carroll; Helen Chen; Lillian and Marie Christopher; Sally A. Cleary; Elie and Merrill Cohen; Bill Connell; Ann Connors; Doe Coover of the

Doe Coover Agency; Shirley Corriher; Deborah Costen; Angela and Giovanni Creseo; Culinary Historians of Boston; Antonella, Andrea, and Valeria Cuppari; Maria and Enzo Cuppari; Fortunato, Giuseppe, Silvio, Sergio, and Maria Chiarra Cuppari; Dottie and Bob Curran; Delores Custer; Steve DiFillipo and staff and Chef Paul King of Davio's Restaurant, Cambridge, Massachusetts; Theresa Delfino; Jane DeLorenzo; Arnold De Marco Sr. and Arnold De Marco Jr.; Maureen and Rudy Di Carlo; Giovambattista and Lucretia Dieni; Antonina, Giuseppi, and Simone Dieni; Rosario and Lena Dieni; Giuseppe and Enrico Dieni; Teta and Giuseppe Dieni; Nona Dryer; Dino Leone and the staff of Due C Ristorante, Luzzi, Calabria; Nino D'Urso; Lamoyne and Jerry Ebner; John and Karen Erickson; Virginia C. Evans.

Faber and Faber, Inc.; Mimma and Nino Favasuli; Giuseppe and Massimo Favasuli; Kristine Fayerman-Piatt; Renie and Fran Federighi; June Ferris; James A. Fiore; Alyn Fiorini; Edie Francesconi; Donald Fry; Mitra Gazinuri; Guy Giarroffa; Rick Goodell; Janet Green; Maria Guarnaschelli; Concetta Gullo; Mike Hebdon; Kerson and Katherine Huang; Mary Ann Hurd; Ludmilla Ivonavitch of Iggy's Bread, Marblehead and Watertown, Massachusetts; Angela and Fortunato Iriti; Anna and Giovambattista Iriti; Pasqualina and Francesco Iriti; Jackie Jackson; Judy and Ron James; Nancy Harmon Jenkins; Stuart and Randee Kaplan; Fran Keefe; Nan Kelley; Patricia Kelly; Rita Kohn; Bob Grillo Lane; Annette Lapont; Dinnaro and Isabella di Dellavilla and Pasquale of La Primula Ristorante, Bova Marina, Italy; Sally Larhette; Nancy and Ralph Lewis; Gail and Henry MacLaren; Montell McBroom; Judy McLaren; Pat and Rich Malone; Roy Goldstein of Martignetti's Liquors, Boston; Ellen Marden; Doris and Pat Mauriello; Marie and Marlene Mauriello; Mickey, Mickey, Jr., and Katherine Mauriello; Gene Marra; Patrice and John Mciver; Sue and Steve McHugh; George Minesteri; Angela; Ganna and Giovanni Minniti; Ellenia and Rocco Minniti; Manilla and Giuseppe Minniti; Paulette Mitchell; Theresa Montera; Maria Giaconda Motta; John Mozzone; Sally and Frank Nass; Al Natale; Tony Navarro; Mary Nebolini; JoAnn Newby; Betty Niland; Nunzia, Laura, and the staff of Nunzia's Ristorante, Benevento, Italy.

Elaine and Obie O'Bryant; Cassidy and Emily O'Bryant; Ana Ortins; Stanton (Tony) Orser; Stella Mauriello Palmer Palleschi; Amy Palmer; Diane Palmer; Bert Parisi; Ramona and Joe Pascucci; Debra and Kirk Pasquinelli; Beanie Petro; Linde Piette; Amelia and Giuseppe Pirri; Patricia Prell; Rosa Rasiel; Fran Reisinger; Linda Reynolds; Pat and Ralph Richwagon; Marissa Rizzi; Rick Rodgers; Michael Roman; Jean and Roger Rotundi; Stephen Russo; Mike Samet; Linda Saraco; Ron Sarni; Linda Saulnier; Muriel Schroeder; Cristina Blasi and Gabriella Mari of Scuola di Arte Culinaria Cordon Bleu, Florence, Italy; Janet and Terry Smart; Pat Stafford; Staci and Tom Stager; Sesa

Sternback; Gay Talese; Barbara and Fred Tassinari; Martha B. Taylor; Janet Claire Thorpe; Gail Tighe; Mary Toohey; Laurel and David Treweek; Sam and Steven Treweek; Priscilla and Dincer Ulutas; Frank and Sally Valentour; Catherine van Orman; Pauline and Pat Verducci; Bruce C. Wallace; Paul and Denise Weber; Fraffie Welch; Donna Wolfe; Women's Culinary Guild of New England; Betty and Roy Woodrow; Bill Wrinn; Harriet Zabusky-Zand; Mimma, Domenico, and Maria Zavattieri; Chuck Zegelbone; June Zeiff; Mildred and Herb Zimmerman; Betty and Art Zinc.

Finally, but in no way least, I must thank two very important people: my agent, Jane Dystel of Jane Dystel Literary Management for her faith in my book and in me; and my editor, Valerie Cimino of Faber and Faber for her judgment, attention, and kind assistance.

To everyone, everywhere, my sincerest and deepest thanks for your help in making this book a reality.

Mary Amabile Palmer

INTRODUCTION

You don't have to be Calabrian or even Italian to make good use of *Cucina di Calabria*. All you need is the desire to enjoy good food. And for those who love Italian cooking, this book will introduce the exciting and until now largely overlooked cuisine of Calabria, the southernmost province of Italy and home of my ancestors. An Italian-American woman with a culinary background, a propensity for cooking, and a love of family and tradition, I have devoted this cookbook exclusively to the cuisine of Calabria. It is a celebration of a cuisine I know intimately and love. When my research failed to unearth any English-language cookbook devoted solely to Calabrian cuisine, I wrote *Cucina di Calabria* to fill that gap.

Most Italian cookbooks include a limited number of southern Italian recipes and few Calabrian recipes, even though 80 percent of Italian-Americans are from the *Mezzogiorno*—the provinces south of Rome, which include Calabria, Basilicata, Campania, Abbruzzi, Molise, Apulia, and Sicily. This is not because Calabrian cuisine isn't adventurous or delicious. On the contrary, Calabrian cuisine is all of that. It is because few recipes traveled beyond villages or even family circles, and few were documented.

Furthermore, from medieval times to the early 1900s, southern Italian cooking was virtually unknown in northern Italy, and northern Italian cooking was unknown in the south. Traditionally, the art of Calabrian home cooking had mostly been handed down orally, from mother to daughter in the kitchen, and given to others reluctantly, almost in whispers. It is as though for centuries, the cuisine was jealously guarded from the rest of the country. To some extent, the American experience has broken down that chain. Consequently, many of these unrecorded recipes are in danger of being lost, and others are becoming Americanized. Thus emerged my calling to correct this oversight by quickly and authentically recording, preserving, and celebrating these priceless recipes. I could not bear to see these old culinary treasures fade away.

With the encouragement of my family and friends, and especially the encouragement and help of my dear friend Rosemary Verducci Huang, I began researching and writing this cookbook. Immediately the task of finding recipes began. The collection from American-based sources, including family, relatives, and friends of Calabrian descent, near and far (some themselves in the culinary world), was exciting but quite limited. It soon became apparent that I would have to go to Calabria to seek out the bulk of the recipes.

During my first trip to Calabria in 1993, I acquired many exciting recipes and fascinating information about Calabria's culture and history. After a year of writing and testing recipes, I returned to Calabria in 1994 in search of more recipes and data on traditions, folklore, customs, and celebrations. That trip took me deeper into the heart of Calabria and into more small villages. I also returned to Bova Superiore, where my parents were born, and to Bova Marina and Reggio Calabria, where most of my relatives now live. Although I had traveled to Italy several times previously, those two trips to my ancestral homeland were like no others; both exceeded my expectations.

Libraries, bookstores, people on the street, restaurateurs, my Calabrian relatives and friends, and last but not least, my mother and sister, all contributed ideas for this book. All of them also shared information about holidays and festivals, as well as historical information. Later, my cousin Angela (who teaches high school English and French) and her mother, Giovanina (named after my mother), mailed me additional recipes. Although some of my older relatives do not speak English, no one would have trouble understanding that kind of hospitality and kindness. They taught me new lessons in love.

Everywhere, everyone I approached for recipes and historical data was more than willing, even eager, to share their knowledge. One Calabrian woman, however, was skeptical. When my cousin Mimma proudly told her I was writing a Calabrian cookbook, in Italian she asked, "But does she know how to make *petrali*?" a favorite Calabrian cookie, which to me spelled the equivalent of, "Can she bake a cherry pie, Billie boy?" Thus, the recipes and other fruits of my research set the tone for the book.

Cucina di Calabria is more than a cookbook. It interweaves recipes with stories and anecdotes on "Cuisine," describing the role food has played in the family as a means of bonding and as a daily expression of love; on "Scenes," taking the reader on an armchair tour evoking the beauty of Calabria; and on "Memories," providing information about Calabrian culture, traditions, customs, folklore, holidays, festivals, and daily life both in Italy and in the United States. I think of it affectionately as a cookbook, a story, and a history.

The more I learned, the more passionate I became about ensuring the recording of these recipes for posterity. With intense dedication, I set out to introduce and share these exciting, delectable, and sometimes hidden recipes with everyone and to do it before they become Americanized. For when comparing recipes obtained in Calabria with recipes given me by second- or third-generation Calabrians in America, I found that some recipes from the Americans were already so affected that indeed some were not Calabrian at all. Checking each American-derived recipe for its authenticity took on primary importance. Preparing recipes given to me in Italy required many testings for exact proportions of ingredients, since many recipes lacked precise measurements. And of course, I had to adapt all of the recipes in this book to the American market and kitchen. Nonetheless, these jewels are as authentic as possible. In the interest of today's knowledge about nutrition, however, I have substituted olive oil for lard when lard was called for and have reduced the amount of oil without sacrificing full Calabrian flavor.

On a personal level, writing this cookbook has been enormously challenging and immeasurably rewarding. I wish to ensure that my children, grandchildren, and future generations have authentic recipes for the dishes served by their forebears, collected and recorded in one place. I hope that the recipes will enrich their lives and that they will want to perpetuate this important aspect of their heritage.

The book is also timely. In America, the favorite ethnic food is Italian, and recently a food magazine reported that southern Italian is the "in foodie." Also in vogue is the highly acclaimed Mediterranean diet. Calabrian cooking fits the bill on all counts! The recipes will intrigue and delight Italian food devotees and pasta lovers. Fast-food enthusiasts and working couples will find a variety of quick-to-fix sauces, most prepared in less time than it takes for the pasta to cook or to buy a prepared jar at the market, and other quick and tempting dishes that look and taste as though they took hours to prepare but are ready in less than thirty minutes. Serious cooks and members of the culinary world will discover new dishes to explore; inveterate cookbook collectors will find a "first;" and vegetarians will be pleased with the many vegetable, pasta, and soup recipes. As an added bonus, most recipes are low in fat and cholesterol and high in nutrients.

Calabrians prepare food in ways that preserve natural flavors and nutrients and respect its intrinsic goodness. Their cuisine is more creative, more diversified, and more daring than that of most other parts of Italy. Perhaps this is because the Calabrians took the best from the cuisines of their numerous invaders, interweaving them with their own to create a wonderful blend of tastes and textures. They have devoted many generations to perfecting these dishes. To be Italian, rich or poor, is to celebrate food; food is the centerpiece of Italian culture.

While working on this book, I often reminisced how my mother prepared delicious, nutritious meals day after day, how she planned holiday dinners weeks in advance, and how with love and patience she tended to every detail. Besides wishing to feed her loved ones traditional dishes, my mother knew that food kept the family close. Eating together was a means of bonding, focusing on, and maintaining family ties throughout life. All meals were treated with reverence. Every day the family ate together and talked, strengthening their love. I have sought to maintain those same family ties with all family members, parents, children and grandchildren. We are all still very much connected to our Calabrian roots—its culture, food, and traditions—and are proud of that. Preparing Calabrian dishes helps us to maintain that connection.

Recently, fourteen members of our family came together to celebrate the Christmas holidays, some from as far as California and Florida. In advance, I planned menus for five days, paying particular attention to selecting traditional Calabrian dishes for Christmas Eve and Christmas Day. A special touch on Christmas was provided by two Italian musicians who played and sang Calabrian and other southern Italian folk songs, delighting us all, especially my mother who sometimes joined in the singing of songs such as "Calabrasella." The treasured thank-you notes are reflective of this special time. Those preserved notes are my reward and, at the same time, my contribution of memories to my family.

I have had numerous Calabrian dinner parties at my home for up to fifty friends, all of whom willingly tasted new recipes and gave me their honest opinions. While visiting the homes of my sons and their wives—John and Amy, David and Diane—and my sister Margaret and brother-in-law Arnold, I am easily enticed into the kitchen to create for them a labor of love.

Extra special thanks go to my sons, John and David. David is the excellent cook in the family and delights me when he calls for recipes. He has tested many. He and Diane include many Calabrian recipes at dinner parties and other special occasions in their sparkling new home in Salem. Diane is modest about her kitchen skills, which are better than she professes. She loves to quote Barbra Streisand in *The Prince of Tides*. "I may not know how to cook but that doesn't mean I don't know how to eat." Early on, John helped to edit some portions of my cookbook proposal. He and Amy let me serve traditional Calabrian dinners for them, my grandson Spencer, and sometimes their friends when I visit in California. Janet and Jim Box also give me carte blanche whenever I visit them and my granddaughters in their lovely lakeside home in Orlando, Florida. In turn, early on they edited a passage in my proposal. My granddaughters often help with meals. I have also happily served as "chef" in the homes of other family members and many friends.

Whenever I am with my granddaughters, I try to pick recipes they will enjoy cooking and eating. A few years ago, Katherine, Jennifer, and I made four different pizzas "from scratch," as Katherine proudly reported in school as one of the fun things she did that summer. Jennifer's thank-you note for Christmas said, "Everything was so delicious, Nana, and so . . . Italian." They help their dad, David, make homemade pasta, sauce, and meatballs. Spencer is already my helper in the kitchen.

I am aware that my children and grandchildren's lives are different from the lives of my mother and my ancestors. Today's lifestyle is busier and more frenetic, and many people cannot devote as much time or energy to cooking as they might wish. However, as previously stated, you will be delighted to know that many recipes in this book can be prepared in less than thirty minutes. This should entice you into the kitchen and promote family dining. The rewards last a lifetime. For although changes in lifestyle are inevitable, we should not lose the art of home cooking. You may not cook some time-consuming dishes every day, but you will be able to explore them on weekends and especially on holidays. That wish is extended to all who buy this book.

A Brief Look at the History of Calabria

Calabria's multicultured, multilayered history resembles nothing so much as one of the region's most exceptional dishes, *Sagne Chjine*, dialect for a special Calabrian lasagne consisting of layers upon layers of thinly sliced, distinctive foods, painstakingly constructed into a whole that is far more than the sum of its parts (page 104). Each tier maintains its own taste and texture, yet melds into a complete experience that is far richer because of its diversity.

A kaleidoscope of regimes in Calabria, previously called Bruttium, and southern Italy rose and fell from the eighth century B.C. onward, for rarely did conquerors not see something of value there, even while their motives were unknown to those conquered.

Sufficient visual history remains to testify to the passing parade in southern Italy of Greeks, Byzantines (who named the area Calabria), Etruscans, Romans, Saracens, Normans, French, and Aragonese, each of whom helped form Calabria and southern Italy's character. Customs from Greece, Albania, and Provence that originated centuries ago are still practiced in some mountain villages. Calabria is, in fact, a mosaic of cultures drawn from the various people who invaded it over the centuries, resulting in a delightful southern Mediterranean rhythm. Despite the layering of cultures, one after another in a continuous cycle of conquest and oppression, this mosaic did not prevent the remarkable Calabrians from preserving their collective soul.

Calabria, a peninsula of 5,822 square miles about 150 miles long and 20 miles wide at its narrowest, is separated from Sicily by the Straits of Messina. In ancient times, it encompassed the whole of the foot-shaped section of Italy. Today, the province occupies only the toe and part of the instep. Within the province of Calabria are three subprovinces: Catanzaro, Cosenza, and Reggio di Calabria, the latter known as Rhegium in ancient times. Referred to as the Switzerland of the south because of its majestic and magnificent mountains, Calabria is sandwiched between the sparkling turquoise and azure waters of the Ionian Sea to the east and the Tyrrhenian Sea to the west. Calabria's 485 miles of wraparound white-sand coastline contrast vividly with the beautiful, tumultuous mountains that dominate it. And Calabria is blessed with mild weather that prevails most of the year.

The dramatic Pollino Mountains in the northeast separate Calabria from Basilicata and rise to almost 7,500 feet; the beautiful, dense Sila Massif are in central Calabria; and the Aspromonte, a massif of towering heights, stand close to Reggio Calabria at the very toe of Italy. All have been shaped by centuries of earthquakes and rock slides into formidable and beautiful terrain.

Those very mountains to a certain extent shut off Calabria geographically from the rest of the Italian land mass. Its rather isolated patriarchal society of the past has been changing slowly, and although much economic progress has taken place in the past half-century, there have been few changes in traditions. The poverty of the region has to some extent helped to preserve its past.

Southern Italy is vastly different in character, custom, and appearance from northern Italy. It certainly is not as rich—it never has been—and its people are frugal of necessity. Frustrated for centuries by the injustice of Italy's uneven economic development, southern Italians know themselves to be victims. Ironically, it is felt that it is the northerners who have caused the southerners' status, toward which northerners show undeserved prejudice.

Tombs, graves, and manmade grottoes, primarily the Grottoes of Rosita and Scalea, give testimony to the prehistoric habitation of Calabria. But the true history begins with the mass Greek colonization of the region in the eighth century B.C. The Greeks brought the Etruscans, Romans, and southern Italians in contact with their civilization. Legends tell of the oracle of Delphi directing the Greeks to sail westward to a green land. Greek mythology describes how Italos, grandson of Odysseus and Penelope, leading characters of Homer's ancient Greek epic *The Odyssey*, conquered the toe of the Italian peninsula. The Greeks established themselves in cities such as Locri, Sibari, and Crotone and in villages such as Bova Superiore (home of my ancestors), intermixing with an already developed culture. At one time, Sibari was the most opulent center of all Magna Graecia. Today, although still a charming city, little evidence of its grandeur and wealth remains.

The Greeks brought with them their civilization and political skill as well as the art of the vine and the olive. Indeed, wines from the Calabrian city of Ciro were so prized by the ancient Greeks that they were served in celebration at some of the earliest Olympic games, for the Greeks, like the Romans, had a passion for fine food and wine. Ciro wine still ranks high with southern Italians, and olives and olive oil are indispensable to southern Italian cooking.

Ancient Italian history between the period fifth century B.C. and fifth century A.D. was largely that of the Roman Empire. Although Etruscans came to Calabria sometime during the ninth century B.C. and Greek rule began to decline by the sixth century B.C., it was not seriously challenged until Rome began its southern expansion during the long Samnite Wars of 342 to 290 B.C. Roman legions chased Hannibal, the Carthaginian general known for his military genius, through Calabria's mountains and forests during the Second Punic War about 200 B.C. They returned more than a century later to capture Spartacus, leader of the most famous of the slave insurrections during the Roman Empire. Calabria's rugged terrain enabled Spartacus to evade the Roman legionnaires for several years before his inevitable capture and crucifixion.

After the collapse of the Roman Empire about 476 A.D., Italy fell under foreign rule. This was followed by a series of epidemics and earthquakes and what was termed the Dark Ages. It was not until a second wave of Greeks from the Byzantine Empire settled in Calabria that some measure of stability and well-being was restored. Peace was short-lived, however. As trade between Greece and Italy increased and flourished, Calabrians began to leave their mountain villages and move to the sea. But when in 827 A.D. the Saracens began attacking the Calabrian coastline, Calabrians returned to the safety of the mountains.

At the end of the Dark Ages about the tenth century, the Arab world, greatly influenced by Greek culture, possessed exotic spices, herbs, sugar cane, and coffee. Spices were valued as money. Local cuisine was enriched by the Arabs, who brought a variety of hitherto unknown fruits, vegetables, and spices from the Orient, such as citrus fruits, eggplants, hot red peppers, pine nuts, cloves, and nutmeg. The Arabs established numerous bases, and trade with the East flourished. The Byzantine Empire controlled the heel and toe of southern Italy while involved in continual warfare. Traces of this Arab influence still linger today in southern Italian cooking, especially in Sicily.

Norman conquest, begun in 1057 A.D. by Robert and Roger de Hauteville, continued for more than a century. Under Roger II, the Normans established the Kingdom of Naples and Sicily. Unlike the contemporaneous Norman invasion of England, domination of southern Italy was more the work of errant knights seeking individual spoils and glory rather than a single planned invasion dominated by one leader. As a result, Norman rule in southern Italy and Sicily was haphazard and uneven. Eventually some order and uniformity evolved through the introduction of large feudal holdings. However, this system of large landed estates held by Norman overlords and worked by increasingly impoverished, landless peasants devastated Calabria's economy so thoroughly that it took centuries to recover.

In addition, a lapse in the succession of Norman kings created a political vacuum, and southern Italy was drawn into the conflict between the German emperor and the Holy Roman Empire. This created a need for additional revenue, which led to repressive taxation that was devastating to southern Italy. As a result, local discontent again flared into periodic uprisings.

The reign of the relatively enlightened Emperor Frederick II (1194–1250), German king and king of Sicily, restored order and a certain level of prosperity. He instituted a new code of laws, bringing a measure of justice to the area. In spite of those reforms, however, southern Italians resented the financial and military burdens imposed on them by his imperial ambitions. Dynastic rivalries among the successors of Frederick II further weakened the grip of the Holy Roman Empire's influence on southern Italy, and as imperial power waned, the local nobility's power increased.

At the end of the fifteenth century, Italy became the battleground of French, Spanish, and Austrian imperialism. The deep shadows of poverty and oppression became even more unbearable as Italy fell to the exploitive Spanish, perhaps the harshest of all of Calabria's invaders. As a result of their oppressive rule, the light of the Italian Renaissance of the fifteenth and sixteenth centuries barely touched Calabria. Creativity was stifled. Time indeed was standing still in the south. Although the Spanish Inquisition failed to take hold in Sicily, it was fiercely imposed in Calabria. Minorities such as the Waldensians, considered heretics, were persecuted and massacred by the Spanish in the mid-1500s. Evidence of this remains in the town of Guardia Piemontese in the form of two ancient doors inscribed *Porta del Sangue* (Bloody Door) and *Porta dei Valdesi* (Door of the Waldensians).

Calabrian philosopher Tommaso Campanella of Stilo led an uprising, but local resistance was quickly wiped out, and he was imprisoned. Liberation from Spanish rule came about in 1700 only through the defeat of Spain by the Austrians at the end of the Spanish Succession, but little change took place. Calabria and the rest of southern Italy continued as pawns in larger European upheavals.

In 1734, Naples and Sicily were ruled by Charles of Bourbon, son of Philip V of Spain, thereby founding the Neapolitan House of Bourbon. In 1759, Ferdinand IV of Naples (third son of Charles III of Bourbon) became king of the Kingdom of Naples and Sicily. As a result, Calabria reached the lowest point in its history. Strongly influenced by his wife, Maria Carolina (sister of Marie Antoinette), Ferdinand used repressive military measures to secure his throne. Local discontent was fanned by news of the French Revolution, and partisan revolutionaries rebelled. Ferdinand retaliated by ordering a military campaign against the political insurgents in Calabria and brutally killing them.

In 1805, Napoleon sent his brother Joseph to the Kingdom of Naples and Sicily to punish Ferdinand IV for violating the neutrality Naples had pledged in the Treaty of Florence four years earlier. Soon Joseph left to assume the Spanish throne, and the crown of the Kingdom of Naples was given to Joachim Murat, brother-in-law of Napoleon and Joseph Bonaparte. Murat began a series of reforms: He abolished feudal law and began to build roads and other public works. Although Murat had broken with Napoleon in an attempt to maintain his holdings, their fates were too closely linked for Murat and his reforms to survive Napoleon's downfall. In 1815, Murat was captured at Pizzo on the Calabrian coast, imprisoned and executed, and is buried there.

Heretofore, southern Italians preferred the restraint of the Greeks to the extravagances of the Romans. But now, the eternally patient peasants felt compelled to rebel. Insurrections in Calabria and Sicily in 1837 and 1844 were punished by widescale executions; those spared the firing squad were banished to galleys or imprisoned for life. Corruption, persecution, and terror reduced southern Italy to a state of fear and misery. Survival in a land stripped of hope became increasingly difficult, and the suffering imposed by the Bourbons sowed bitter seeds of discontent.

Tired of being forgotten by the national government, of being treated as inferiors and wounded to the core, secret political societies were formed in reaction. At first, the members were weak and disorganized and even vague in philosophy and goals. However, as they gradually affiliated with liberal groups forming in other parts of Italy, they became stronger in purpose and organization. They eventually adopted the program "Italy, one free, independent republican nation" a slogan proclaimed by Giuseppe Mazzini (1802–1872), founder of *Giovane Italia* (Young Italy). In 1831, Nicholas Giuseppe Garibaldi (1807–1882), an early advocate of Mazzini's philosophy, became involved in the *Risorgimento* (uprising) against ruling Austria.

Reforms began to evolve amid the volatile politics of the 1830s and 1840s— reforms that would lead to a united Italy. Ready for a hero after so many centuries of exploitation, Garibaldi was regarded with hope as the one who could not only unify the country but also improve living conditions for all. In this endeavor, he traveled throughout Italy, stopping off in Melito di Porto Salvo, about twenty miles from Reggio Calabria, and for the first time ate pasta with tomato sauce. At that time, tomatoes were confined primarily to southern Italy. So impressed was he with the sauce that when he and his soldiers returned north, they took the recipe with them, thus making Melito famous.

Soon, Garibaldi relieved the Bourbons of their command and helped create the unification of Italy. In 1861, the parliament of a newly united Italy met for the first time in Turin, which became Italy's capital. Florence replaced Turin as Italy's capital in 1865 and was subsequently replaced by Rome in 1870. In 1871, the proclamation of the Kingdom of Italy completed the unification of Italy. This kindled hope for change, but conditions did not improve in the *Mezzogiorno*; for the most part, life remained unchanged. Tax monies continued to flow out of the south to the north, and poverty continued unabated. Many southern Italians felt that the new republic was merely a variation of a familiar theme of foreign exploitation. They realized that they had been addicted to hope. Mistrust of the new government took hold.

By 1892, so outraged at the injustice they and their ancestors had endured for centuries with no change in sight and so resentful of the severe living conditions and the enduring caste system, these heretofore gentle, passive, and resigned folk, perhaps feeling an unconscious stirring in them of the spirit of the old brigands, began thinking of emigrating. It was not long before they became convinced that only emigration offered release from the grinding poverty and despair that gripped Calabria. The deep dissatisfaction that had now grown to enormous proportions erupted in the form of mass migration. By the end of 1924, almost five million had left their beloved ancestral homes in search of a better life. Sadly, Italy was then a country to leave rather than one to enjoy. Italy's population was reduced by about one-third. Of this, 80 percent were from the *Mezzogiorno*.

Italy entered World War I in 1915 on the side of the Allies. After the war, social and political unrest was fertile ground for the growth of fascism. In 1919, Benito Mussolini came onto the national stage. He organized a group of nationalistic followers called the "black shirts," two years later was elected to Parliament, and soon became Italy's prime minister He founded the National Fascist Party and in October 1922 seized power and marched into Rome. Called *Duce* (leader), in 1928 he dissolved Parliament and created a dictatorship. Fascism did little to solve any of the country's problems. In fact it caused as much harm as had been inflicted by any foreign predecessor. The middle classes by now had taken over and busied themselves with their own fortunes. Once gain, the poor were ignored.

In 1936, Mussolini aligned himself with the Germans, and in 1940 the country entered World War II. A rebellion by the people took place, and in 1943 Italy gladly surrendered to the Allies. Mussolini was removed from power and in 1945, following the collapse of Germany, was captured by partisans and executed. In 1946, Italy ended the monarchy and became a republic. In 1948, it established a constitution and a parliamentary republic.

The south was still trapped in deep poverty until about 1950, when it began to realize its potential. Even with the chronic weakness of government, Italy's economy grew faster than many other European countries due to little more than the people's own ingenuity and dynamism. Despite this, southern Italians still have a lower per-capita income than their northern cousins. Although the state began to recognize and agree that it had long neglected the south, this view was oversimplified. Few were truly aware how complex the southern problem was, not only from an economic standpoint but also from a social and agricultural one. There was disagreement about how to resolve the multiple problems: Some saw only economic problems; others saw an enclosed society that would require lengthy remedies and would take generations to solve; and still others thought of southerners as inferiors and took no interest in any reform.

Exceeded only by the Japanese, in the 1960s all of Italy's economy surged, including the south where considerable progress has been made. Although the south still lags behind the north, conditions have improved beyond the most imaginative expectations. Funds from the government trickled down to the south. The work of *Cassa per il Mezzogiorno*, Italy's work relief for the south, resulted in improvements in Calabria.

In the 1970s, inflation and unrest made major Italian goods such as automobiles less competitive. But the smaller firms run by hardworking owners and nonunion workers surprised all when they were able to compete internationally. By the 1980s, they were most responsible for the country's successes. At the same time, workers and big business combined forces to renew their earlier competitiveness not only in machinery, but also in clothing and textiles. Road building, expanded ports, and some sporadic industry brought some measure of prosperity to the region. In addition, the people were given health care and other social benefits. Finally, southerners began to feel that their government cared.

Schools received more funds, and education denied to most people in the *Mezzogiorno* during centuries past has been available to all for some time now. The heavy dialect of the south is disappearing. Calabrians are redefining themselves. They are talking, dressing, and traveling in ways unknown a few generations ago. Television, motorbikes, trains, and buses have made even more striking differences in the Calabrian lifestyle. Tourism was and is of major importance to Italy's economy. And more and more, southern Italy with its natural beauty and its outstanding food is working toward getting its share.

Calabria has seen many regimes rise and fall throughout its long history. As one considers the many centuries of almost continuous hardship, poverty, and exploitation imposed on southern Italy, the extraordinary courage, endurance, and resilience of these people is remarkable. To their credit, those southern Italians who refused to emigrate or who returned survived all of those hardships, invasions and exploitation, earthquakes and extreme poverty.

Yet despite those hardships, Calabrians remain a kind, affectionate, and generous people. The source of their strength always was and is love of family, which for them and all southern Italians is the whole—it is everything. That love coupled with tenacity is what enabled them to endure and survive, whether they remained in Italy or emigrated to America or elsewhere.

The Immigrants

Calabrians are survivors. When conditions became unbearable, their will to survive was so great that they, and many southern Italians, were willing to uproot their families, leave their beloved relatives, lifelong friends, homes, and simple but beautiful villages and face a new, unknown, and even alien world in search of a better life for themselves and their children. This took enormous courage.

Century after century, southern Italians had endured an excessive wave of invaders and withstood the neglect and mistreatment of the north and the "State," all the while hoping conditions would improve. It was only when that hope was irrevocably shattered, when the reasons for leaving mounted, when the Americas beckoned, that they decided to leave. They left because they were oppressed, because they were poor, because they were hungry, because they were treated like chattel in the lingering feudalism of large landed estates that were controlled by negligent, abusive *padrone* (landowner, master, owner, boss). They left because they were politically oppressed; because the north instituted harsh economic conditions, including a tax system that took advantage of them while benefiting the north; because prejudice against them was widespread. Finally, they left because even after the *Risorgimento* (uprising and revival), which they believed would improve their status at last, the "State" passed laws that adversely affected them.

The *Risorgimento* was supposed to unify the country and improve living conditions for all. It began in the north with four men, Giuseppe Garibaldi, King Victor Emanuel II, Giuseppe Mazzini, and Count Camillo di Cavour. While the roots of the *Mezzogiorno's* contempt and deep suspicion for the "State" had been entrenched for centuries, they adulated Garibaldi as a liberator and admired Mazzini as an active revolutionary who also fought hard for unity. They dared to hope that conditions would improve. But Garibaldi's influence and Mazzini's efforts lost out to the structure approved by Cavour, and the south was left to stagnate in a near-colonial state. Those in power and the north had little knowledge of, and even less concern for, what life was like for southern Italians. So when Italy became a State in 1871, conditions did not improve in the *Mezzogiorno*. In fact, conditions worsened. Calabrians and southern Italians felt as though they were being subjected to a new kind of invader. Italy was united in name only.

Widespread rebellion erupted and continued for five years after the unification. In the 1880s and 1890s, dissatisfaction grew into rebellion of enormous proportions. Southern Italians' pleas for justice had gone unheeded, making it almost impossible for them to feel allegiance to their country. The future held no hope for change; the next chapter had already been written. After being addicted to hope for centuries, many now admitted that their hope and that of their predecessors had been misplaced; they had to break that addiction.

Lured to the Americas by dazzling promises of work and wealth, many decided to leave, putting an end to their dark, hopeless, and desperate epic. The dream of coming to America became a reality, and this time rebellion erupted in the form of mass migration. The saying of the day was "*Dami cento lire e mi ni vaiu a La Merica*." Give me a hundred lire and I will go to America.

A few far-sighted statesmen warned of the dire consequences of so many workers leaving the country, but their warnings went unheeded. As feared, much of the land went uncultivated. Some tried to obscure the cause for the mass migration, blaming it on steamship recruiting agents from other countries, mainly the United States. Truth is, the cause was the central government's unwillingness to acknowledge the intolerable living conditions in the south and to change them.

In its more distant history, southern Italians were neither allowed a voice in the formation of the government, nor permitted an education or allowed to travel. But even when travel restrictions were lifted, they did not leave their villages; they felt irrevocably rooted to their country. Parents did more than just raise their children—they were their teachers and role models. Though not formally educated, they were innately shrewd and insightful. That wisdom and astuteness was passed on by word of mouth from generation to generation. Proverbs were plentiful and useful and at one time were the only form of education. Often rhyming, sometimes amusing, they provided important moral lessons.

The majority of the peasants were *giornalieri* (day laborers); others were servants employed by the gentry. Still others, called *contadini*, were farmers who often owned a little land, a house, and perhaps a donkey, the sole means of transportation. Their houses were mostly small, single-story dwellings. In some parts of the south, such as in the province of Basilicata just north of Calabria, people and animals alike lived in a one-room cave. Indoor plumbing did not exist for most until into the twentieth century, and most homes were still illuminated with kerosene lamps. Irrigation existed only in the north. It was only through the southern Italian's motivation and persistence that farmers and tenant farmers were able to produce ample vegetables and fruits to feed the nation even while left with little enough for themselves. The few admired educated, such as artisans and shopkeepers, held honorary titles of *Mastro* or *Don*.

The family primarily, and to some extent religion, provided a sense of security, unity, and faith. The family stood together, side by side, from the first breath to the last, totally committed. Through days of laughter and nights of fear and pain, they were always there for each other, for better or for worse, unconditionally. Their faith, after all, had never been in their government, it had always been in the family. It was family loyalty and caring that had nurtured them and sustained them over the years. They did not exist in a state of depression, however—life was celebrated in many ways. They had their festivals, their beloved music, storytelling, and many forms of family celebrations. Much was made of weddings, religious feasts, and visits with relatives and friends.

Prior to emigrating, Calabrians and southern Italian peasants had limited choices for survival. They could accept their lot stoically, become priests and receive free education and travel, or become brigands. The vast majority chose to accept their lot (until the seed of migrating was planted), wishing to become neither priests nor brigands. The brigands waged a war of revenge against the central government and lost. Desperate for heroes, these gentle, sorrowful people with centuries of resignation and repression behind them, while repulsed by the brigands, also felt a tinge of pride—some dramatically dared to rebel. But in 1865, nonsustainable brigandage came to an end.

As author Gay Talese stated in his compelling epic *Unto Thy Sons* about his Calabrian ancestors and the millions of southern Italians who emigrated from Italy, "So from hill towns and fishing villages young men planned their departure. The economy of southern Italy was then at a starvation level, and most of the emigrants in the 1880s were men abandoning their villages, bearing heavy valises made of wood . . . en route to the rail terminal to await the Naples-bound train that would take them to the trans-Atlantic ships headed for the promised land of the United States."

Often wives and children did not accompany men on their initial trip to America. Ever the patriarch, the husband alone decided when, or if, to go. Women were generally opposed to emigrating and often resented not being included in the decision. Some women refused to go, certain they would never see their parents or relatives again. Talese noted that some such women were labeled "white widows" and criticized because they dressed in the same light-colored clothes as eligible young women. The female community looked upon this as unseemly, suggestive, and even threatening. Women with children left behind had a difficult time. Often they had to supplement the money sent to them by their husbands, and this usually meant working on the farm, an uncommon practice for women. All prayed their husbands would send for them, and most husbands did. But a few women were abandoned, never to hear from their husbands again, contrary to the country's culture and tradition. Although in some countries women live in fear of abandonment, this is rare in Italy where family is of utmost importance.

At first, many Italians migrated to Latin America. A siege of yellow fever caused destinations to shift to the United States. They left from the ports of Naples, Genoa, and later from Palermo. The journey from a little village to a port city involved much maneuvering; the journey from Italy to America was long and tedious, lasting three weeks or more. There was mass seasickness, sanitary conditions aboard ship were deplorable, and the food was abominable.

There was little or no privacy or opportunity to bathe. Stricter sanitary and overcrowding regulations were ordered, but often these were not enforced. However, they made the best of it, singing, telling stories, and playing cards to help pass the time.

Privileged first- and second-class passengers were processed aboard ship. The masses, however, pale from being in sunless, crowded steerage for most of the crossing, underwent the frightening process of immigration on Ellis Island, America's main gateway, a quarter of a mile away from the Statue of Liberty. Wearing name tags, the immigrants were sent to the Great Hall, a large room about 170 feet long and 100 feet wide, with a 60 foot ceiling. As many as 1,200 ate in the giant dining room, amid the buzz of many different languages. Apprehension mounted with the knowledge that there would soon be an inspection and a medical exam. If they passed, they were free to go; if the doctors found something wrong, their clothes were so marked with chalk and they could either be detained for several days until the matter was resolved or deported. Families worried about being separated, as sometimes one member did not pass the exam. The decision then had to be made whether all should return to their native land or only the one who did not pass. It must have been an extremely wrenching choice. Tears and heartbreak were inevitable. Perhaps this is why Ellis Island was sometimes called the Isle of Tears.

Those rejected could appeal, but there was often a long wait. Even if they were turned away for whatever reason and had to return to their native land, many tried again, irrespective of the now known ordeal of the voyage, so desperately did they wish to become American citizens. Most passed, bravely ready to face the strange new world, stamped card in hand with the magic word "Admitted."

By 1924, sixteen million immigrants had come to America, the largest migration in the history of the world, of which almost five million were Italians. Most were illiterate, but all were eager to learn, to work, and to build. That figure might have been greater had not the United States imposed stricter immigration laws at that time and, almost simultaneously, had not the Fascist Regime come into power, prohibiting almost everyone from leaving Italy. In 1923, my parents successfully emigrated from Bova Superiore to Schenectady, New York.

In honor of my immigrant parents, I was proud to have *The Frank Amabile Family* imprinted for all time on the Wall of Honor. A Certificate of Registration is sent to donors, and I sent copies to all family members. In July, 1995, I took my granddaughters, Katherine and Jennifer, to New York City. We saw the usual interesting sights the big city offers, including the Statue of Liberty and Ellis Island. A photograph taken of them standing in front of a collage of immigrants is priceless to me. I look forward to bringing my grandson Spencer and future grandchildren there as well.

Sometimes the immigrants' passage money was loaned to them by yet another exploitive kind of *padrone*; this new boss, hustler, con man, or pimp was little different from the old ones. The fare and interest charged was often exorbitant. Other forms of exploitation included lower salaries or poorer housing than was promised. On occasion, exploiters were their own *paesani* (fellow countrymen). Those seeking work on their own had similar problems. Organizations were formed to prevent such exploitation; one was headed by Sister Frances Cabrini, who later became known as Mother Cabrini.

The immigrants settled mostly in the industrialized northeastern states, especially New York, with New York City having the most. Later, they would spread out across the country. Many went to California and the far west, although San Francisco had more northern Italians than southern. The Dakotas and Arkansas have the smallest number of Italian immigrants. The largest ethnic group in Toronto, Canada are Calabrians. And even Alaska is home to approximately 40,000 Italian-Americans.

When they immigrated, they brought with them their traditions, their hopes, and their dreams for a better standard of living. However, immediately great waves of cultural shock rocked them—transitions from tiny villages to the big city; from warm, sunny climates to cold, blustery, snowy winters; from farming to mostly factory work; from donkeys and mules to cars and trains; and from the safety of their native culture to a different culture and a different language. In addition to these adversities, they encountered anti-Italian sentiment. Soon they became aware that they were not accepted and were considered of low status. Although the United States had generally applauded the unification of Italy, a country perceived as friendly, this was not reflected in the tacit acceptance of prejudicial treatment endured by the immigrants.

Life between the two cultures was not easy. In order to afford high rents, many were forced to live in crowded tenements that were cold in winter and unbearably hot in summer. Eventually, as conditions improved, they moved to better quarters or bought their own homes. Although they brought their frugality with them, they began to eat better. Still, nothing was wasted. Many wrote to their compatriots, exaggerating favorable conditions in America in the hope of luring them to emigrate. And if they returned to Italy to visit family or to choose a wife, as was common, they wore their best American clothes giving the impression of prosperity, further hoping to influence them to emigrate.

Many immigrants found work in factories that were called sweatshops—hot and oppressive buildings, often with no windows, for long hours and little pay. Others helped build the railroads, the subways, the skyscrapers, or helped feed and clothe the nation. They were hard working, gave an honest day's work, and took pride in what they did. Proud and honest, no matter the hardships, only the very destitute applied for welfare. Better they should take on outside extra work, as did my father. As the number of Italian immigrants increased, so did intolerance. Earlier immigrants perceived them as an economic threat, and many name-callers were people who themselves had endured prejudice when they came. Foreigners tended to be scapegoats for all crimes.

In an effort to alleviate some of this prejudice, well-intentioned social workers and educators encouraged immigrants to change their last names by removing the vowels. In truth, their lack of knowledge and understanding of Italian traditions and culture contributed to feelings of inadequacy among the immigrants. Forcing these and other changes on them was in direct conflict with those traditions. Many parents objected to these changes, believing them to be a denial of self. So strong were their roots that many of them never really assimilated. These proud people who had come from a rather isolated society where traditions seldom changed, clung to their traditions until they died, sometimes leaving their children even more confused about their identity.

As they had in Italy, the family, neighborhood (which now replaced the village), and the Roman Catholic Church continued to govern their behavior. Immigrants from any country tend to cluster with their fellow countrymen, who give them a sense of acceptance and safety as well as provide them with a ready community with which to socialize. Italians tried to find *paesani* from their same village since each province had its own dialect and its own traditions. It was the security of *la via vecchiata* (the old way) that helped them during the transition between two cultures—leaving behind the customs of the native land for the unfamiliar and puzzling ones of the new world.

Nevertheless, because many Italians felt mistreated by some Americans, they developed feelings of inferiority. These prejudices no doubt contributed to the willingness of some insecure second-generation Italians with tenuous connection to their new country to denounce their culture in favor of assimilation, making the white Anglo-Saxon Protestant ethic their ultimate goal. This was to become a permanent decision for some, but only a temporary one for others, who in time regained pride in their ancestry. Yet, despite the discrimination and prejudice encountered, Italian immigrants were loyal to their adopted land.

The typical dark-eyed southern Italian-American father was a totalitarian who ruled strictly and totally. He tended to make decisions without consulting his wife or children. But beneath the bravado of manliness, he often endured the hardship of everyday life alone, unable to express his fears or feelings even to his wife. However, his love of family and those close to him gave him the will to survive, and he made decisions for the family based on those instincts.

Nevertheless, the patriarchal father produced mixed feelings among first-generation children, especially girls, with restrictions on dating, for example, and the practice of prearranged marriages. In addition, at that time, women had little hope of becoming handsome heroes as men did. Often, their only lot was to marry one, be his exclusive property, serve him, and give him sons. As women became exposed to more liberal views in the United States, became educated, and held responsible positions, they rebelled, even to the point of denying their Italian roots. Slowly, as more and more successful women became accepted, many of those rebels reconnected with their roots.

Meanwhile, those who stayed behind in Italy were shocked at those who left. The continuity of family was deeply ingrained in these people: You stayed together on hallowed ground no matter what. So when in desperation thousands emigrated, many who did not leave viewed the emigrants' decision with concern and sadness. They thought them doomed to a life of nostalgia.

For some, this prophecy came to pass, so hauntingly expressed in a song: "*Calabria mia . . . lo cianciu pi 'ttia*" ("My Calabria, I cry for you"). Some immigrants returned to Italy to stay. However, they would no longer tolerate inadequate housing and lack of schooling. They demanded and got improved human rights. It is believed that when the immigrants learned that conditions had improved somewhat back in the old country, a large number permanently returned. Families who returned also had their problems, though different from those encountered in the United States. A certain amount of resentment existed between those who stayed behind and those who returned and had amassed even modest wealth. Resentment was already in place against those who were receiving money from their American relatives. Furthermore, children of those who returned had their own difficulties adjusting to the change. They did not like the simple village life and felt more American than Italian.

Despite prejudice, Italian-American men and women have won the respect of many, distinguishing themselves in every facet of American life. They have successfully entered the fields of politics and law, have contributed vastly to music, literature, the arts, theater, the sports world, and the business world as founders of banks and heads of giant corporations. Their traditions—love of family, family values, kindness, and generosity—are admired and emulated. Most would agree that those solid, old-fashioned values are badly needed now.

We Italian-Americans take great pride in our fellow countrymen's accomplishments. Although we are grateful to all of them for giving us immeasurable pride in our heritage, it is to our predecessors, the immigrants, that we owe our deepest admiration and eternal gratitude.

Their enormous courage in leaving the only world they knew, their determination, hard work, and sacrifices to overcome all cultural obstacles, including prejudice, are what have made success possible for their offspring. It is therefore to all Italian-American immigrants, including my dear parents, Frank and Jennie Amabile, that I dedicate this essay, with admiration, gratitude, and a multitude of thanks! "*Mille grazie!*"

LA CUCINA DI CALABRIA

THE CALABRIAN KITCHEN

Always on hand in the Calabrian kitchen are olives, olive oil, herbs, spices, and cheese of one kind or another. No meal can be prepared without at least one of these essentials. Because of their importance to the Calabrian cuisine, I must give them their due.

Erbe, Spezie, e Condimenti
Herbs, Spices, and Seasonings

One cannot exaggerate the importance of herbs and spices in Calabrian cooking. The growing and use of fresh herbs has held a primary place in Calabria for centuries. The greatest secret to a successful sauce, vegetable dish, or entrée is the clever, skillful blending of fresh herbs and seasonings in proper proportion. Calabrians have uncovered that secret. They regard herbs highly and use them well, instinctively sensing that they bring new dimensions to food.

One of their most popular herbs is basil. Tomatoes and basil are lovers, seemingly made for each other. The tangy aroma of a tomato sauce with fresh basil and garlic is incomparable. As a salad, tomatoes and basil combined with fresh mozzarella creates a miracle of sorts. And adding basil to vegetable dishes enhances them considerably. Other widely used seasonings are parsley, rosemary, bay leaf, fresh or dried hot red pepper, oregano, and sage. Italy owes the import of oregano and sage to the Greeks and cloves and nutmeg to the Arabs. Of supreme importance to Italian cooking are onions and garlic, which appear in many recipes.

Southern Italian cuisine is not inhibited in the use and proportion of spices. Thus the food is famous for being robust and spicy. Hot pepper is used frequently in varying amounts, depending on the dish. My father grew long, thin green and round, red hot peppers. He would cut the green ones into tiny pieces and add them to a fresh tomato salad or a vegetable dish. Mom made her own dried crushed red pepper. While I was researching this book in Calabria, my relatives gave me some whole, dried rainbow-colored hot peppers, which I shared with family and friends. Now authentic Calabrian hot peppers grow in the O'Bryant's garden in Orlando.

The history of herbs is interesting. For example, historically, the principal forms of exchange were spices and food; in addition to their culinary usage, many were used for medicinal or superstitious purposes. Some were used for fragrances. Fortunately, herbs are plentiful almost all year-round in sunny southern Italy. In the United States, most herbs can be bought year-round in supermarkets. Whenever possible, use fresh herbs and spices. If you must use dried, substitute one teaspoon of the dried for every tablespoon of the fresh. The following list includes the most popular Calabrian herbs, spices, and seasonings.

Anchovy A flat, strongly flavored fish that appears in many Calabrian dishes, it is often used as a seasoning or accent. *Alici* melts and blends with other ingredients. Abundant in the Mediterranean for thousands of years, ancient Romans ate them fresh and fermented them (or other fish) into an essence called *garum* to "salt" their food when salt was heavily taxed. Underrated in the United States, many Americans are familiar with them only when added to pizza and are unaware of the subtle but important zip and flavor they add to many dishes. Fresh anchovies, much appreciated by Italians, must be imported from Europe, and because of the high cost of importing and the long list of regulations are not widely available.

Aniseed A Middle Eastern herb, the fruit *anaci* contains seeds called *semi-di-anaci*, for which the plant is grown. The seeds were used by the ancient Romans in pastries and wedding cakes and were also prized by the Egyptians and ancient Greeks. They are used primarily as a flavoring in desserts, pastries, and liqueurs such as *anisette*.

Basil A Calabrian staple, *basilico* is considered of great importance in southern Italian cooking. A highly pungent, aromatic herb, minty and clove-like, it is added to tomato sauces, served alongside fresh tomatoes and mozzarella, and added to soups, vegetables, and salads. It is said to have grown at the foot of the cross on which Jesus was crucified and was mentioned in Boccaccio's *Decameron*. Ancient Greeks called it *basilicum* (royal plant); Greek women gave sprigs of it to friends to ward off the "evil eye." It is said that the smell of fresh basil is good for the heart, making man merry and glad. Basil can be preserved under oil or frozen, but fresh is a joy and is far superior. Dried basil is a poor substitute; taste and character are lost in the process.

Bay leaf An evergreen, bay leaves are available year-round in Calabria. Dried are adequate, however. Aromatic, added to soups, stews, and vegetables, *alloro* was considered sacred by the ancient Greeks and Romans.

Capers Italy has the reputation of having the best capers in the world. These tiny green flower buds of a southern Italian shrub are pickled in brine or preserved in salt; only the bud is eaten, not the flower. *Capperi* are picked at precisely the right time and dried in the sun. Rinsed or not, their distinguished flavor enhances sauces and soups. Use sparingly.

Cinnamon This spice, often used in cookies and pastries, is variously said to have been brought to Europe by the Arabs, or from India, or from the Spice Islands, or from China.

Clove This spice, used in baking, is believed to have been introduced to Europe by the Arabs.

Fennel seed An important ingredient in Calabrian sausage, *semi di finocchio* is also used in breads and main dishes. The seeds are collected from wild fennel in autumn. Cultivated fennel is sometimes called anise in American markets.

Garlic One of the first foods ever cultivated and the oldest known, *aglio*, a member of the lily family, is said to have been found first in Asia Minor. The Chinese began using garlic about 4000 B.C., and it was venerated in ancient Egypt as a source of strength. The superstitious in much of the world wore it to ward off the "evil eye." Ancient manuscripts dating to 500 B.C. referred to it as a cure for many illnesses, since it was thought to possess antiseptic properties. Pliny of Rome recommended it as a cure for several ailments, a belief that continued for centuries. Today, its allium compound and strong antiseptic and antibacterial properties are said to help the body's natural enzymes defuse potential carcinogens and lower cholesterol and blood pressure. It is essential and invaluable to Mediterranean and Asian diets. Baking or roasting garlic, rendering it sweet, is gaining popularity in the United States. Garlic powder and garlic salt taste awful and should be banned! Only firm, fresh garlic captures its true essence. Sautéing it brings out the most flavor. Remove the sprout for easier digestion and never overbrown; it turns bitter. Store garlic in a dry, cool place.

Honey The Romans and the Greeks used honey as a sweetener, and today it is universally used.

Marjoram Marjoram has a romantic history. It is said that Venus, the Roman goddess of love, first planted it on Mount Olympus and that its fragrance was a reminder of her beauty. Ancients used *maggiorana* as bath perfume and in nosegays. It was a necessary ingredient in all love charm recipes. Shakespeare spoke of it in his writings. Said to be a native of Portugal, its use as a seasoning is still popular.

Lemon juice   Used in many fish dishes and in place of vinegar in some vegetable dishes, lemon juice enhances flavor, and thus less salt is required.

Mint   An aromatic perennial, easy to grow, mint is used in vegetable dishes, desserts, and drinks. A favorite of the Romans, it was used in baths, for medicinal purposes, and later in tea and other drinks. Of the many varieties, most popular are peppermint, spearmint, and apple mint.

Nutmeg   This baking spice was introduced to Europe by the Arabs.

Onions   Onions are both vegetable and seasoning! A necessity in Italy, they play a major role in many dishes. Onions originated in Western Asia and were cultivated in Egypt nearly 4,000 years ago. Once used for medicinal purposes, they were always respected for their flavor and versatility. The white onion is sweet, the red onion is mild and sweet, and the yellow onion has a stronger taste. Onion skins can be rinsed and used in making stock.

Oregano   A strong, pungent plant with a robust, aromatic flavor, oregano belongs to the mint family and dries well. It is added to sauces, salads, and meats. The Greeks introduced it to Italy, and it is highly valued in both countries. It was served as a tea, eaten for medicinal purposes, and used to crown married couples, as it was believed to bring happiness. Overused by Americans, this potent herb, especially when dried, should be used sparingly.

Parsley   The flat-leaf plant is one of the most widely used Calabrian staples. It adds much flavor and depth to sauces, soups, and vegetable dishes and is also lavishly used as a garnish. It is native to Sardinia and has an unusual history. Ancient Greeks used it to decorate tombs, to crown victorious athletes with wreaths, and in wedding celebrations. In medieval England, parsley was associated with black magic. In later centuries it gained favor as a curative. Italian parsley is more flavorful than the curly variety and is the favorite of most cooks. It is available fresh year-round. Its Italian name is *prezzemolo*, but I knew it as *petrosino* as a child.

Pepper, black   Freshly ground black peppercorns are used extensively in soups, stews, sauces, meat, and vegetable dishes. It was introduced to Europe from the Spice Islands, India, and China.

Pepper, fresh, hot   Fresh hot peppers are often chopped finely and passed at the table. Some say that they help to keep cholesterol in check and to stimulate one's metabolism.

Pepper, crushed red   *Peperoncino*, crushed red pepper, is common to Calabrian cooking and used in many sauces, vegetable, and meat dishes.

Rosemary Throughout history, rosemary has been honored for its scent, which was thought to enhance knowledge and aid memory. An aromatic perennial, *rosmarino* is used in roasted poultry and meat, in stuffings, and on flat breads. Greek students wore crowns of rosemary in their hair. The Latin *ros maris* translates as "sea dew" because it grew near the sea. It was also believed that *maris* referred to the Virgin Mary. A symbol of remembrance, it is used at celebrations such as Christmas, weddings, and funerals. Because of its reputation as a symbol of fidelity, it has also graced burial bouquets and centerpieces. Medicinally it is said to stimulate circulation and help relieve coughs and headaches. Rosemary is an herb that dries successfully, but fresh is always best.

Sage *Salvia* is sometimes combined with rosemary to season meat, poultry, vegetables, and hearty soups. Ancient Greeks introduced it to the Romans; southern Italians and Sicilians quickly adopted it. It has a musty mint taste. Dried sage is not very effective; fresh is much better.

Salt Italians use coarse salt, *sale grosso*, in preserving meat, fish, and herbs. Fine salt, *sale fino*, is used in cooking. Sea salt is preferable to table salt, which has chemicals added to prevent caking.

Sesame The plant, native to India, was brought to Italy by Arabs. The seeds are nutty and flavorful and are used in breads, cookies, and vegetable dishes. Store sesame seeds in the refrigerator.

Sugar Sugar was introduced to southern Italy and Calabria by the Arabs in the ninth century. Desserts have sprung forth in all their glory ever since.

Vanilla Prized fruit of the New World, it was brought to Spain by the conquistadors in the early 1500s. Vanilla extract came into use in the United States after its manufacture began in the 1800s. It is used in many desserts.

Vinegar Red wine vinegar is the favorite of Calabrians and southern Italians. White wine vinegar is used only occasionally. Increasingly, the popular artisan-made balsamic vinegar, a product of northern Italy, has been winding its way around the globe.

Olive e Olio d'Olive
Olives and Olive Oil

It is said that silvery olive trees dotted the hills of Sicily as far back as 10,000 years ago, brought there by the Greeks. Olives were in fact Greece's first great export crop. The Romans discovered olives at about the same time as the

Greeks and brought them to northern Italy and to their colonies. A few thousand years later they were cultivated in Turkey, where they still grow in abundance. The Arabs introduced them to Spain, and in forthcoming centuries, all Mediterranean countries were enjoying the pleasures of olives.

Referred to in the Bible nearly 100 times as "King of Trees," references to olives also appear in the Koran and in Greek and Roman writings. In ancient times, olive branches were distributed on Palm Sunday. Later, they became peace offerings. Hercules was said to have brought them with him on his travels (for added strength?). Oil also served purposes other than culinary. Moses spoke of using olive oil for holy annointing; it provided light in oil lamps; and drops of warmed oil were used to reduce ear aches. Oil is still used to anoint the dying, babies at baptism, children at confirmation, and monarchs at coronations. It is also still used in soaps and cosmetics.

Olive trees grow in dry places quite well. Gnarled, slow growing trees live for centuries without dying for lack of water. Their average age is said to be between 300 and 600 years. The hillsides of southern Italy are covered with many contorted olive trees that produce wonderful olives and excellent olive oil, both of major importance to the cuisine.

A favorite of southern Italians as well as of all Italy and the Mediterranean, brine-, oil-, or salt-cured underripe green olives and ripe, ebony black olives always adorn antipasti tables at midday and in the evening, served plain, marinated, or mashed. Olives are added to various Calabrian sauces and vegetables dishes, adding zest and zing, but they are heavenly by themselves. One of Italy's most famous and luscious olives comes from the town of Gaeta, near Naples. Many varieties of olives are available to us, primarily from Greece, Italy, and some Middle Eastern countries. But in some specialty ethnic stores, olives can also be found from France and North Africa. So appreciated is the olive in Italy that festivals are held in its honor.

Olive oil is the preferred fat in Mediterranean countries, where nearly all the world's olives grow. More and more, it is becoming the more fashionable international fat, although its use has been in vogue in all Mediterranean countries for thousands of years. Others who primarily used butter in cooking began converting to olive oil when they learned how highly praised it is by nutritionists and medical researchers as being very high in monounsaturated fats. Italy has led the way in producing the best quality oil, and southern Italy produces more oil than any other region. Not surprisingly, California is beginning to produce fine quality olive oils.

There are four main types of olive oil and several color variations from light yellow to a dark green hue. In general, the greener the color, the fuller the flavor. Like a fine wine, fine oil should have a full, fragrant bouquet.

- Extra-virgin olive oil is produced from the first pressing—cold pressed without heat, it has a dark green hue and is the most expensive. It has a full bodied taste and aroma that enhances any dish. It is often called the "flower of the olive," with no solvents or chemicals added. It contains no more than 1 percent acidity. (The lower the acid, the more flavor and aroma are imparted to the food.) If a recipe calls for fruity olive oil, choose either extra-virgin or virgin olive oil. Extra-virgin olive oil is best appreciated in salads or when drizzled over fresh vegetables or pizza. It is a must for dunking crusty Italian bread, seasoned with salt and crushed red pepper.
- Virgin olive oil comes from the second pressing and is quite good. It too is not treated with chemicals. Not as readily available as extra-virgin oil and olive oil, it is used in cooking and in salads.
- Olive oil comes from the third pressing and is treated with chemicals to extract flavor. It is a pale yellow and can be used for frying or sautéing. It does not compare with extra-virgin olive oil in flavor or bouquet, nor does it compare with virgin olive oil.
- The fourth pressing is subjected to further chemicals to obtain the remaining bits of flavor. Highly acidic with a somewhat bitter taste, it is not recommended.

Containers should clearly identify the type of oil. If you can afford it, use extra-virgin or virgin oil at the table and for cooking. It has the best rich and fruity taste. Kept in a cool place away from light and heat and not refrigerated, it will keep for up to two years without turning rancid.

Formaggio
Cheese

Originally made as a means of preserving milk, cheese became popular on its own early in history. It is made from the milk of the cow, ewe, buffalo, goat, camel, mare, or llama, depending on the part of the world. Italy has been blessed with a large variety of cheese since ancient times. The ancient Romans had at least thirteen different cheeses.

Every section of Italy has its own cheese specialties. Some cheeses are for eating and others are for cooking, although that line is often crossed depending on the age of the cheese and whether it is served in the course of the meal—in the dish, alongside it, or on top of it—or with dessert.

Cheese, in fact, is a very versatile Italian commodity. It can be a part of every course of the meal. It is often one of the choices on an antipasti table; it is served at midday and evening meals; it is added to soups, sauces, pizza, vegetables, and frittatas; it is stuffed into pasta and pastry. It becomes a seasoning when grated and sprinkled on top of soups, pastas, and vegetables; it also combines comfortably with fruit for a simple dessert.

If you haven't tried some of the more exotic cheeses, you are missing something close to greatness. Find an Italian specialty store and inhale the breath of Italy.

The most commonly used Calabrian and southern Italian cheeses include:

Caciocavallo   Similar to provolone or gouda; when young it is a compact eating cheese, a fine accompaniment with fruit. Left to dry, it is grated over soups, pasta, and vegetable dishes. Its name is derived from *cacio* (cheese) and *cavallo* (horse) because the roundish cheeses were strung together in pairs and dried suspended over a pole, the way saddle bags are draped over a horse.

Gorgonzola   Gorgonzola is considered one of the best blue cheeses in the world. It is younger, sweeter, and milder than other blue cheeses, preferred by many over salty versions, and often served with fruit for a simple dessert. A stronger, more aged form is also available, however. It is great in pasta dishes, in salads, and on pizza.

Incanestrato   When aged, this spicy cheese is used for grating; when fresh, it is an excellent eating cheese, often served with fruit. *Incanestrato*, "placed in a basket," usually comes in a reed basket and takes the shape of the container. It is available in many Italian specialty stores.

Mozzarella   A fresh, soft, rindless white cheese, traditionally mozzarella is made from water buffalo milk. Most mozzarella comes from Naples, and it is considered one of southern Italy's great contributions to the world of cheese. The *ovalini di bufala* (little buffalo eggs) are getting scarce, but Italian specialty stores and some supermarkets in the United States carry them. Used primarily for eating, not cooking, the difference between this mouthwatering, freshly made mozzarella and the prepackaged kind is enormous. Pairing it with fresh, ripe tomatoes, basil, and lightly drizzled with extra-virgin olive oil creates a dish fit for royalty. Most mozzarella in the States is made with cow's milk and is quite good.

Parmigiano   This cheese, developed by the Etruscans, has been in existence for more than 2,000 years. Made from cow's milk and known primarily as a grating cheese, the inner soft part is good for eating. A very hard cheese with a thick crust, it comes in a large wheel that is generally aged for two to three years. A specialty of the city of Parma, in Italy, and once more common in northern Italy, today it reaches every corner of the country and has become indispensable in many Italian and French kitchens. It should be grated as needed for best flavor.

Parmigiano Reggiano   This exclusive, golden colored, aged vintage cheese comes in a giant wheel that is branded to denote that its milk, of the highest quality, comes from cows from Parma and Reggio nell' Emilia. It has a distinctive, nutty, sweet taste. If possible, try to use this brand over other Parmesan cheeses; it is one of Italy's best and is considered one of the finest cheeses in the world. It should be grated only as needed.

Pecorino   Pecorino is made by every shepherd from sheep's milk, although some may contain a small amount of cow's milk. It has been in existence since before the founding of Rome. It is especially popular in Calabria and southern Italy. Some varieties of pecorino cheese aged for only a few months are eaten as snacks or with desserts. When aged, it is grated as needed, and it can be used in place of parmigiano. More assertive than parmigiano, the most notable sharp and tangy flavored pecorino is pecorino Romano.

Provola   Similar to mozzarella, it is a soft, fresh cheese; *provola affumicata* is smoked.

Provolone   When provolone is young, it is a mild slicing yellow cheese, creamy and piquant to the taste. It originated in and is still produced in southern Italy, is very popular in Calabria, and is readily available in the United States. An excellent eating cheese, it appears in sandwiches and on antipasti tables. This is the cheese you see hanging in bunches in Italian specialty stores. As it ages, it becomes more flavorful and is added to sauces and vegetable dishes. When hardened, it can be grated—nothing is ever wasted—but this is not its primary use.

Ricotta   Made throughout all of Italy, Calabria and Sicily are reputed for having the best. Ricotta is a fresh, light cheese made from milk that has been cooked twice (*ricotta* literally means recooked). It is traditionally made from ewe's milk but can also be made with cow's milk. It is similar to cottage cheese but smoother, creamier, and with a sweet milk flavor. It is extremely versatile. It is used in lasagne, stuffed into ravioli and other pastas such as tortellini, and sweetened for use in desserts. In Italy it is commonly spread on bread for break-fast or as a snack. Calabrians also sprinkle it with crushed red pepper and eat it with crusty bread.

Ricotta Salata   This young, mild but flavorful cheese, imported from Italy, is sometimes substituted for pecorino. Very low in fat and contrary to its name, only lightly salted, it keeps longer than fresh ricotta. It can be used in lasagne dishes (omit any extra salt), appears on antipasti tables along with other dishes, and is crumbled onto pasta and vegetables.

Scamorza   Available in many Italian specialty stores, pear-shaped scamorza is made from cow's milk. Its flavor is enhanced by immersing it in a brine solu-tion. A soft cheese, it is eaten as is and added to sauces and vegetable dishes.

ANTIPASTI

APPETIZERS

Antipasti are designed to create a climate of anticipation for the rest of the meal and to stimulate one's gastric juices. *Antipasto,* "before the meal," dates back to Roman times. The main meal was divided into *antipasto, primo piatto* (pasta or soup), *secondo piatto* (meat or fish), and *contorni* (vegetables and/or salad). Gracing Roman tables were familiar foods such as fish, sausages, vegetables, eggs, olives, and lettuce. In his book *De re Coquinaria* (*Concerning Cooking*) Roman gastronome Apicius devoted an entire chapter to antipasti.

Many more foods have since been added to the antipasti list. Depending on the season, Calabrian antipasti include a seemingly endless variety of seasonal vegetables, usually home grown or bought that day in the noisy, fragrant outdoor markets. Eggplant is especially popular and usually featured in one or more interesting dishes. Sweet, long, light green Italian peppers, called *friarelli* in some parts of Calabria, are lightly sautéed or stuffed; red and green peppers are roasted or fried with tomatoes and onions. Calabrian antipasti tables also include variously prepared fresh fish, creamy fresh cheeses, olives, salami, prosciutto, and particularly the famous Calabrian *sopressata* (dried, seasoned sausage), all artistically displayed.

Having said all that, those numerous antipasti are served in restaurants. In most homes, lavish antipasti are reserved for holidays, feast days, or special celebrations. If served at all at other times, usually only one antipasto is chosen. It can be as simple yet agreeable as a few thin slices of prosciutto with melon or fresh figs, or it can be as interesting and impressive as *Melanzane al Forno* (Baked Eggplant with Two Cheeses, Ham, and Tomato Sauce, page 45). But for those special occasions, the sheer abundance and variety of Calabrian antipasti are a sign of the lavish hospitality and exuberance for which Calabrians are noted.

Restaurants, however, formal or informal, have no such restrictions. As you enter, you see a well-appointed *tavola di antipasti,* with a burst of colorful, creative, and contrasting dishes designed to invoke anticipation for the rest of the meal. They are at once varied and imaginative, simple and elaborate, all totally designed to captivate you with the first bite.

The old rule of serving hot antipasti before a light meal and cold antipasti prior to a hearty, substantial meal is often superseded by serving a combination of both, particularly on special occasions. What has not changed is that anti-pasti must harmonize with the rest of the meal and, of course, must have visual appeal. An elaborate array of antipasti can be followed by a pasta dish alone, omitting the meat or fish course altogether. Not unheard of is an entire meal of several contrasting antipasti only, many of which require little time to assemble, making a true meal of varied tastes. Add a glass of wine, some fresh crusty bread, and in no time dinner is served.

As with other parts of the meal, antipasti in Italy vary from region to region. Traditionally antipasti are eaten at the table. I prefer to serve them that way at a sit-down dinner party. It is easier on guests and the hostess. For a large group, however, the various antipasti dishes can be placed on a serving table, a buffet, or the dining room table.

Many of the following recipes easily double as vegetables to be served with the meat or fish course. However, several antipasti are as handy as your refrigerator or supermarket and require little or no preparation. They include various meats such as prosciutto, sliced paper thin and served with melon or fresh figs; varieties of salami and capicola, thinly sliced; sopressata, thinly sliced; a variety of cheeses such as fresh mozzarella, provolone, and ricotta salata, thinly sliced; hard-boiled eggs, halved and crisscrossed with an anchovy fillet; canned anchovy fillets, sardines, and tuna; pickled vegetables such as cauliflower, eggplant, and mixed vegetables; sliced raw seasonal vegetables; and finally, a sprinkling of capers in strategic places.

Just remember when selecting a group of antipasti: They are supposed to *grappi 'pittitu* (open up the appetite). Which reminds me, *buon appetito!*

Bruschetta
Grilled or Toasted Bread

Bruschetta has traveled well, not only throughout Italy, but also across the Atlantic, where it has fast become popular. Traditionally, the bread was grilled. However, you can also toast it in the oven or toaster oven. It can be served hot or prepared in advance and served at room temperature. A grouping of toppings with different tastes, textures, and colors is a great beginning for a buffet or dinner party.

6	half-inch slices of full-bodied, thick-crusted Italian bread, halved
1 or 2	cloves garlic, halved
2	tablespoons extra-virgin olive oil

Toast or grill bread for 1 or 2 minutes, or until a light golden brown. Rub one side of each slice of bread with the cut side of garlic and drizzle lightly with olive oil.

Serves 12

Bruschetta con Olive Schiacciate
Bruschetta with Crushed Seasoned Olives

While in Calabria researching this book, I found a wonderful kitchen tool called a *battecarne*, which translates as "pound the meat." Besides doing that very well, the 3-inch-diameter mallet with its short handle does a great job of cracking nuts and olives. Most supermarkets carry succulent Italian or Greek olives, which are readily available at Italian specialty stores. Some recipes suggest grinding the olives, but I prefer them coarsely chopped. If serving them to family, marinate them whole for 3 to 4 hours and serve with the pits. Let everyone do their share.

1	recipe *Bruschetta* (Grilled or Toasted Bread, page 32)
½	pound green or black olives, brine-cured (or a mixture)
3	tablespoons extra-virgin olive oil
2	tablespoons finely chopped white onion
1	tablespoon fresh basil, finely chopped
1	teaspoon fresh lemon juice
¼	teaspoon crushed red pepper

Rinse and drain olives on paper towels. Crack with a mallet or *battecarne* and remove pits. Chop coarsely and put in a medium-sized mixing bowl. Add all other ingredients, except bruschetta, and mix well. Marinate for at least 2 hours, mixing a couple of times.

Put olives in a serving bowl and place in the center of a platter, surrounded by the bruschetta. Serve at room temperature.

Serves 12

TIP: If you choose to grind the olives, put all ingredients except bruschetta in a food processor and pulse until coarsely chopped.

VARIATION: Add 1 or 2 teaspoons capers, drained and finely chopped.

Bruschetta con Pomodori
Bruschetta with Tomatoes and Herbs

I ordered this enticing antipasto at La Primula Restaurant in Bova Marina. It was excellent. Their bread was freshly made, and the tomatoes and herbs were picked from their garden. The charming couple who run the restaurant, Isabella di Dellavilla, the owner's daughter, and Pasquale, her fiancé, were accommodating. They gladly contributed this recipe and simultaneously tucked a loaf of bread under my arm.

> 1   recipe *Bruschetta* (Grilled or Toasted Bread, page 32)
> 2   medium tomatoes
> 2   tablespoons fresh basil, finely slivered
> 1   tablespoon fresh Italian parsley, finely chopped
> 1   tablespoon extra-virgin olive oil
> ¼   teaspoon salt

Wash tomatoes and cut in half. Squeeze out a little juice and as many seeds as possible. Cut into ¼-inch cubes and put into a serving bowl. Add remaining ingredients, except bruschetta, and mix thoroughly.

Place bowl in the center of a platter, surrounded by the bruschetta. Serve at room temperature.

Serves 12

Bruschetta con Tonno
Bruschetta with Tuna Spread

From cupboard to table in minutes, Calabrians transform this nutritious basic into a perky topping with just a little tinkering. It can then leap from a great family treat to an impressive antipasto suitable for guests.

> 1   recipe *Bruschetta* (Grilled or Toasted Bread, page 32)
> 1   6½-ounce can tuna in oil, undrained
> ½   small red or sweet white onion, coarsely chopped
> ½   fresh lemon, juiced
> 1   tablespoon fresh Italian parsley, coarsely chopped
> 1   clove garlic, coarsely chopped

½ teaspoon freshly ground black pepper

⅛ teaspoon salt

Put all ingredients, except bruschetta, in a blender or food processor. Whirl until very smooth.

Spoon mixture into a serving bowl and place in the center of a platter, surrounded by the bruschetta. Serve at room temperature.

Serves 12

VARIATIONS:
- Add 1 tablespoon drained capers.
- Add 2 or 3 anchovy fillets, coarsely chopped.
- Add 8 black or green olives, brine-cured, pitted and halved.

Bruschetta con Fagioli
Bruschetta with White Beans

I discovered this recipe at Nunzia's Ristorante in Benevento, Campania. The restaurant, located in a charming old part of town, has been in Nunzia's family for 67 years; it was first managed by her grandfather, then by her father before her. Gracious and charming, Nunzia and her daughter Laura welcomed me and contributed this recipe. Nunzia did it all: She planned the menu; helped cook, take food orders, and serve; and still found time to chat with everyone.

1 recipe *Bruschetta* (Grilled or Toasted Bread, page 32)

1 16- or 19-ounce can cannellini beans

1 tablespoon extra-virgin olive oil

1 teaspoon garlic, finely chopped

¼ teaspoon salt

¼ teaspoon dried oregano

¼ teaspoon freshly ground black pepper

Drain beans in a colander or sieve, reserving 2 tablespoons of the liquid. Set aside.

In a large, heavy skillet, add olive oil over medium heat. Sauté garlic for 1 or 2 minutes or until light golden brown. Add beans, the reserved liquid, and remaining ingredients (except bruschetta). Lower heat and simmer for 1 or 2 minutes, mixing constantly until beans are heated through.

Put beans in a serving bowl and place in the center of a platter, surrounded by the bruschetta. Serve at room temperature.

Serves 12

Crostini
Toasted Bread

Crostini are thin toasted slices of Italian bread that are served primarily with antipasti, especially the pureed kind that can be spooned on top. If you are toasting a large amount of bread, an easy method is first to cut it into ½-inch slices, then halve them or cut into various small sizes and shapes. Unlike bruschetta, crostini need not be brushed with oil or garlic, and they need not brown. They can also be made ahead of time.

6 to 8   half-inch slices of Italian bread, halved

Preheat oven to 350° F.
Place bread slices on an ungreased cookie sheet. Toast in oven for 2 to 3 minutes on one side; turn and toast for 1 to 2 minutes on the other side.

Makes 12 to 16 crostini

Crostini con Fegatini
Chicken Livers with Anchovies on Crostini

When I served this spread as an antipasto at a luncheon for friends, one of my best friends, Roz Brooks, who is an expert on Jewish chopped liver, said, "How good can it be?" with just the right intonation. Everyone laughed and tasted it and said it was outstanding. Different from the Jewish version, this recipe includes anchovies and capers for an assertive, sassy touch. Don't be too quick to pass this recipe by, even if until now you have not been a liver lover. This is a fine Calabrian culinary delight, appreciated in other parts of southern Italy as well. Most supermarkets sell liver or will take orders for it. It is almost always available at specialty meat markets. This recipe can be made a day ahead.

1   recipe *Crostini* (Toasted Bread, page 36)
2   tablespoons extra-virgin olive oil

½	medium onion, finely chopped
½	pound chicken livers, washed and coarsely chopped
4	tablespoons dry white wine
4	anchovy fillets, mashed
1	tablespoon capers, mashed
2	teaspoons white vinegar
¼	teaspoon freshly ground black pepper
⅛	teaspoon salt (optional)

In a large skillet, add olive oil over medium heat. Sauté onion for 3 to 4 minutes or until translucent. Remove with slotted spoon and set aside.

Raise heat to medium-high and sauté chicken livers for 2 to 3 minutes, turning constantly, until lightly browned. Return onions to skillet. Add wine, lower heat, and simmer for 8 to 10 minutes. If consistency seems too thick, add a bit of water.

Add anchovies, capers, vinegar, pepper, and salt to the skillet and mix well. Let simmer for 1 or 2 minutes to allow ingredients to blend. Remove and put in blender or food processor. Whirl until smooth. Spoon mixture into a serving bowl and refrigerate.

To serve, place bowl in center of a platter, surrounded by the crostini.

Serves 12 to 16

Crostini con Aringhe
Herring on Crostini

Salting as a means of preserving food was practiced in Egypt and Spain prior to Christianity. Because Roman Catholics observed many meatless days, the salting of food, especially fish, became a thriving business. By the twelfth century, the small, oily herring was a staple of the European diet and became the most important salt fish by the fourteenth and fifteenth centuries. Here is a refreshing dish to complement your antipasti table that is easy, quick, and can be made a day ahead. Increase the crushed red pepper if you like it hot!

1	recipe *Crostini* (Toasted Bread, page 36)
1	pound fresh herring
2	tablespoons olive oil
2	cloves garlic, finely minced

1   tablespoon white wine vinegar
1   tablespoon fresh Italian parsley, finely chopped
¼   teaspoon salt
¼   teaspoon crushed red pepper

Slit herrings, remove bones, and wash thoroughly but quickly in salted water. Drain on paper towels and pat dry. Cut into 1-inch chunks.

In a large, heavy skillet, add olive oil over medium heat. Add garlic and sauté for 1 to 2 minutes or until light golden brown. Remove and set aside. Add the herring, turn to coat, and sauté for 3 to 4 minutes. When herring is almost cooked, mash with a fork until smooth. Add the garlic, vinegar, parsley, salt, and crushed red pepper. Mix thoroughly.

Spoon mixture into a serving bowl and put in center of a platter, surrounded by the crostini. Serve immediately, or refrigerate and serve cold or at room temperature.

Serves 12 to 16

VARIATION: For an even quicker, magical version, buy pickled herring. Drain and proceed with the recipe, omitting the vinegar and salt.

Crostini con Ceci
Chickpeas with Garlic and Lemon on Crostini

There are several versions of this recipe throughout the Mediterranean. Some recipes do not require the garlic to be sautéed, which makes this a quick and easy delight. Others call for wine vinegar instead of the more traditional lemon juice. I find lemon juice to be the better choice. This dish is served in some parts of Calabria as one of many antipasti on Christmas Day. It has gained such favor in Calabria and in America that it now appears frequently as an antipasto with drinks. It can be made a day or two ahead.

1   recipe *Crostini* (Toasted Bread, page 36)
1   19-ounce can chickpeas
2   tablespoons extra-virgin olive oil, divided
1   clove garlic, finely minced
2 ½   tablespoons fresh lemon juice
½   teaspoon salt

¼ teaspoon freshly ground black pepper
2 tablespoons fresh Italian parsley, coarsely chopped

Drain the chickpeas, reserving 2 tablespoons of the liquid.

If you wish to sauté the garlic, add 1 tablespoon of olive oil to a small skillet over medium heat. Add the garlic and sauté for 1 to 2 minutes or until light golden brown.

Put chickpeas, reserved liquid, 1 tablespoon of olive oil, garlic, lemon juice, salt, and pepper, in a blender or food processor. Whirl until smooth. Add the parsley and whirl 1 to 2 seconds only; otherwise, the mixture will turn green.

Place mixture in a medium, low bowl. Put bowl in center of a large, round serving platter. Arrange crostini around the edges of the platter. Serve at room temperature for maximum flavor.

Serves 4 to 8

Carciofi Ripieni
Artichokes with Herbed Stuffing

Artichokes were known to the Romans in the fifth century B.C. and are a favorite of Mediterranean countries. Their arrival in America is attributed to the French, who settled in Louisiana. Known in dialect as *carciofi ammudicata,* this dish is almost always included on holidays and special occasions. To eat artichokes cooked this way, peel off one leaf at a time, hold the top edge of the leaf, and put the filled edge in your mouth. With your teeth together against the leaf, pull it slowly away from you. It's fun!

6 fresh, medium-sized artichokes
1 lemon, freshly juiced
1¼ cups fine dried bread crumbs
½ cup grated pecorino cheese
4 tablespoons fresh Italian parsley, finely chopped
4 cloves garlic, finely minced
2 anchovy fillets, finely chopped (optional)
½ teaspoon salt
¼ teaspoon freshly ground black pepper
3 tablespoons olive oil

Remove and discard discolored, tough outer artichoke leaves. Place each artichoke on its side and cut stems back to about 1 inch from where they join the base, so artichoke can stand without tipping. Cut across the top to remove prickly tips and remove the choke that lies on top of the heart. In a pan of cold water, add the juice of one lemon. Put each artichoke in the pan, hold it upside-down, and dunk it up and down to rid it of any debris.

In a large mixing bowl, mix the bread crumbs, cheese, parsley, garlic, anchovy if using, salt, and pepper. Bang each artichoke on a hard surface to loosen its leaves, then spread the leaves apart with your fingers. Divide the mixture evenly among the artichokes, filling spaces between the leaves with as much as you can. Tap gently to settle the mixture and dribble olive oil evenly over the artichokes.

Put artichokes in a heavy skillet, large enough to hold them upright so they will not tip during cooking. Add enough water to reach 1 inch and bring to a boil on top of stove. Lower heat, cover, and simmer for 30 to 35 minutes or until tender, adding more water if needed. Serve hot or at room temperature.

Serves 6

Cavolfiore con Olive Nere e Peperoni Rossi
Cauliflower with Black Olives and Red Peppers

A delightful contrast of colors adds appeal to this savory cauliflower dish. Served on Christmas and New Year's Day, it is a fine addition to an antipasti table and is equally at home as a side dish. It also qualifies as a make-ahead dish. In fact, it should sit for at least an hour after preparation to allow the ingredients to blend.

1   cauliflower head, 1½ to 2 pounds
3   tablespoons extra-virgin olive oil
2   tablespoons red wine vinegar
1   red pepper, raw or roasted, seeded and thinly sliced
2   cloves garlic, coarsely sliced
1   teaspoon salt
½   teaspoon freshly ground black pepper
¼   cup Italian black olives, brine-cured, pitted and halved
2   tablespoons fresh Italian parsley, finely chopped

Wash and cut cauliflower into florets. In a double boiler, steam florets for 5 to 7 minutes or until they are cooked but still crisp. Remove to a deep mixing bowl.

Immediately drizzle olive oil over florets and mix gently until coated. Sprinkle with vinegar and add red pepper, garlic, salt, pepper, and olives. Mix thoroughly. Let stand for one hour. Remove garlic slices. Transfer mixture to a serving dish, sprinkle with parsley, and serve at room temperature.

Serves 12 to 16 as an antipasto, or 6 to 8 as a side dish

Pasticcio di Uova e Prosciutto
Egg, Cheese, and Prosciutto Pie

I warmly remember my mother and my godmother's mother making this traditionally rich, elegant pie every Easter. In ancient times, eggs evoked new and eternal life, good luck, and fertility. We enjoyed this pie as an antipasto on Easter and for lunch the following day. It is so revered that if you were given a whole pie for Easter, you knew you were considered special. Also known as *pizza piena*, it is festive and flavorful. Ham can be substituted for the prosciutto, but it will not have that distinctive taste. This recipe can be made a day ahead.

PASTRY:
- 3 cups all-purpose flour
- ¾ cup butter, at room temperature
- 2 medium eggs, lightly beaten

FILLING:
- 8 or 9 large eggs
- 1¼ pound fresh farmer's (basket) cheese, crumbled
- ⅓ cup freshly grated pecorino cheese
- ¼ pound prosciutto, coarsely chopped
- ¼ pound salami, coarsely chopped
- ½ teaspoon freshly ground black pepper

Preheat oven to 375° F.

To make the pastry, sift flour into a mixing bowl and blend in butter with a pastry blender. Add eggs and mix quickly. Form pastry into a ball, put in a floured bowl, cover, and set aside.

Break 8 eggs for the filling into large mixing bowl and whisk until frothy.

Divide the pastry dough in half. Put half back in the bowl, cover, and set aside. Roll the other half between two pieces of waxed paper. Fit to bottom and sides of a 10-inch pie dish or a 10-by-12-inch baking dish. Do not trim excess.

Distribute the farmer's cheese, pecorino cheese, prosciutto, and salami evenly over the pie shell. Add pepper to eggs and pour evenly over pie mixture. Eggs should completely cover the meat and cheese. If they do not, add an extra lightly beaten egg.

Roll out remaining dough and cut into ½-inch strips. Crisscross strips evenly over the top of the pie, press edges into bottom layer, and crimp. Bake for 45 to 55 minutes, or until eggs are firmly set and top is golden brown. Allow to set for at least 10 minutes before cutting. Serve hot, warm, or cold.

Makes up to 16 pieces or more

VARIATION: You can substitute soft mozzarella for farmer's cheese and Parmesan for pecorino cheese.

Polpette di Melanzane
Eggplant Balls

I knew even before trying this recipe that it that it would be delicious. It is a perfect example of creative Calabrian cuisine. It's best to roll all of the eggplant balls in bread crumbs before starting to sauté them. This allows them to set and lets you give full attention to turning them over slowly. They freeze well or can be made a day ahead. Two of my old friends, Renie and Fran Federighi, attended a large Calabrian buffet party I gave at which I served these eggplant balls. Renie found them delightful. Fran said, "I don't normally like eggplant, so when I eat something with eggplant in it and I like it, it's got to be good!" Eggplant balls sit equally well on an antipasti table or alongside a serving of fish or meat.

- 1   pound eggplant, unpeeled
- 1   cup fine bread crumbs, divided
- 2   slices stale Italian bread
- 2   ounces pecorino or Parmesan cheese, grated
- 3   cloves garlic, finely minced
- 3   tablespoons fresh Italian parsley, finely chopped
- 2   tablespoons fresh basil, finely chopped
- 1   egg, lightly beaten

¾	teaspoon salt
½	teaspoon freshly ground black pepper
5	tablespoons olive oil, divided

In a large saucepan over high heat, bring to boil enough water to cover eggplant. Lower heat, cut eggplants in half lengthwise, and add to pan. Add pinch of salt and simmer for 20 minutes or until tender. Drain well. Chop into ¼-inch cubes or run through a food processor. Put chopped eggplant into large mixing bowl and add bread crumbs.

In a small bowl, soak the bread in water. When soft, squeeze out the water and add the bread to mixing bowl. Add cheese, garlic, parsley, basil, egg, salt, and pepper. Mix well. If it is too moist, add more bread crumbs.

Form the mixture into balls. For an antipasto, use 1 rounded tablespoon for each ball. For a side dish, use 2 rounded tablespoons. Roll each ball in bread crumbs and set aside.

In a large, heavy skillet, heat 2 tablespoons of olive oil over medium-high heat. Add balls to skillet, taking care not to crowd them. Sauté the smaller ones 3 to 4 minutes or the larger ones 5 to 6 minutes, turning constantly until golden brown. Add more olive oil as needed. Remove with slotted spoon onto paper towels to drain. Keep warm until all are cooked.

Place eggplant balls on a serving platter with a container of fancy toothpicks. Serve warm or at room temperature. You may add a small bowl of hot *Salsa Marinara, Pronto!* (Mariner's Style Tomato Sauce—Quick, Easy, and Perky, page 130) in center of platter for dipping.

Serves 12 to 16 as an antipasto, or 4 to 6 as a side dish

Melanzane e Zucchini alla Griglia
Grilled Eggplant and Zucchini

When it's cookout time and you have a grill going for fish or chicken, grill yourself some vegetables at the same time. Eggplant and zucchini are Calabrian favorites and, when grilled, produce a sweet, smoky flavor. Serve them as an antipasto or alongside your entrée. Cooking food over live fire has a primal hold on many of us. If you're not feeling primal, the vegetables may be quite satisfactorily broiled or roasted in your oven as well.

1   small to medium eggplant, ¾ to 1 pound
1   long, slender zucchini, about ½ pound
3   tablespoons olive oil

MARINADE:
2   tablespoons extra-virgin olive oil
1   tablespoon red wine vinegar
1   clove garlic, coarsely sliced
¼   teaspoon freshly ground black pepper
¼   teaspoon dried oregano

Wash and dry eggplants and zucchini. Cut each into ½-inch slices. Place oil in a small bowl. With a pastry brush, brush both sides of slices.

To grill: Place eggplant and zucchini 4 inches above hot coals. Grill for 15 to 18 minutes, turning occasionally, until both sides are a deep golden brown.

To oven broil: Preheat broiler with door slightly ajar for at least 5 minutes. Put eggplant and zucchini on cookie sheet on second shelf from top of oven. Broil for 18 to 20 minutes, turning occasionally, until both sides are a deep golden brown.

To oven roast: Preheat oven to 500° F. Put eggplant and zucchini on cookie sheet and roast for 15 to 18 minutes, turning occasionally, until both sides are a deep golden brown.

Put cooked vegetables in a deep casserole. To a small bowl or jar, add olive oil, vinegar, garlic, pepper, and oregano. Mix thoroughly. Pour marinade over vegetables, refrigerate, and let marinate for several hours. Remove vegetables from refrigerator at least 30 minutes before serving.

Serves 8 as an antipasto, or 4 as a side dish

Melanzane al Forno

Baked Eggplant with Two Cheeses, Ham, and Tomato Sauce

This enticing Calabrian dish is lighter than the more common eggplant parmesan; it contains less cheese. A bit of ham contributes to its success. Present it as an antipasto for a large party, serve it as a fine side dish, or let it be dinner itself! My cousin Maria Dieni Cuppari of Bova Marina contributed this recipe. It was one of the outstanding dishes served at the *festa* given in my honor by Maria and her sister Mimma Favasuli. I have changed only one thing: I broil the eggplant slices instead of frying them. It is easier, takes less time, and reduces the amount of oil substantially.

2	medium eggplants, 1 to 1¼ pounds each
3 to 5	tablespoons olive oil
1	recipe *Salsa Marinara, Pronto* (Mariner's Style Tomato Sauce—Quick, Easy, and Perky, page 130)
8	ounces whole-milk mozzarella cheese, shredded, divided
4	tablespoons freshly grated pecorino or Parmesan cheese
⅛	pound thinly sliced American baked ham, coarsely chopped
½	cup fine bread crumbs
3	cloves garlic, finely minced
½	teaspoon salt
¼	teaspoon freshly ground black pepper

Preheat broiler for 5 minutes, with oven door slightly ajar.

Cut a thin slice off both ends of eggplants and discard. Peel and cut eggplants lengthwise into uniform ⅓-inch slices. Put 3 tablespoons of olive oil into a small bowl. With a pastry brush, lightly brush both sides of sliced eggplant with oil. Add more oil as needed. Place eggplant on broiler pan in a single layer. Broil for 10 minutes, turning once, or until lightly browned. Do not leave unattended.

Set oven temperature to 375° F.

In a medium saucepan over medium heat, simmer the *Salsa Marinara* for 2 to 3 minutes.

In a medium bowl mix 4 ounces of the mozzarella, the pecorino or Parmesan cheese, ham, bread crumbs, garlic, salt, and pepper. Into an 8-by-10-inch, lightly oiled baking dish, spoon a thin layer of tomato sauce. Divide eggplant slices into thirds. Put one-third into the baking dish and cover with half of the cheese and bread crumb mixture. Cover with a thin layer of sauce. Add another layer of eggplant, sprinkle remaining cheese mixture, and add another thin layer of sauce. Add the last layer of eggplant and a final layer of sauce. Sprinkle with remaining 4 ounces of mozzarella.

Bake uncovered for 35 to 40 minutes or until the eggplant is tender throughout and golden brown. Serve hot or at room temperature.

Serves 20 to 24 as an antipasto, 12 to 15 as a side dish, or 6 to 8 as a main dish

Caponata
Sweet and Sour Eggplant

Caponata is a zesty mixture of compatible vegetables that can serve as an interesting antipasto or as a relish to complement a simple dish, such as broiled fish. It also combines nicely with a meat sandwich for lunch, and vegetarians can use it as a sandwich filling. Don't let the number of ingredients scare you—with the help of a food processor, the vegetables are ready in minutes. It can be made several days in advance. Caponata dates back to the seventeenth century and is popular not only in Calabria but also throughout southern Italy and Sicily. This extraordinary dish is traditionally served on Christmas Eve, during Lent, and on special occasions such as New Year's Eve or Day.

2	tablespoons olive oil
2	celery stalks with leaves, cut into ½-inch cubes
1	large onion, cut into ½-inch cubes
1	green bell pepper, seeded and cut into ½-inch pieces
3	cloves garlic, finely minced
1½	pounds eggplant, cut into ½-inch cubes
1	16-ounce can Italian plum tomatoes, coarsely chopped
3	tablespoons tomato paste
⅓	cup Italian green or black olives, brine-cured, pitted and sliced
2½	tablespoons red wine vinegar
2	tablespoons capers, drained
2	tablespoons pine nuts
1	teaspoon sugar
½	teaspoon salt
1	recipe *Crostini* (Toasted Bread, page 36) or *Pizza di Pane* (Flatbread with Rosemary, page 258)

Wash, dry, and cut vegetables as directed, or put through food processor. If using food processor, pulse individually 2 to 4 times, just until chunky, and set aside.

In a large, heavy skillet, heat olive oil over medium heat. Sauté celery, onion, and pepper for 5 to 7 minutes or until onion is translucent. Add garlic and sauté for 1 to 2 minutes or until light golden brown. Add eggplant, tomatoes, and tomato paste. Lower heat, cover, and simmer for 15 to 20 minutes, stirring occasionally. Add olives, vinegar, capers, pine nuts, sugar, and salt. Simmer 2 to 4 minutes, stirring occasionally until all vegetables are tender.

Remove from heat, cool, and refrigerate. Serve at room temperature with crostini or flatbread.

Serves 20 to 24 as an antipasto, or 8 to 10 as a side dish

VARIATIONS:

- If you prefer caponata a little sweeter, substitute 2 tablespoons raisins for sugar or add 1 additional teaspoon of sugar.
- If you prefer caponata spicy, add up to ½ teaspoon crushed red pepper.

Maccu
Fava Bean Puree

Maccu, which means crushed in Calabrian dialect, is an ancient recipe for fava beans, the oldest bean in Europe. This puree is served on March 19, the Feast of St. Joseph, patron saint of the family, children, the Universal Church, and pastry chefs! My mom used to cook them in lightly salted water, slip them out of their jackets, and eat them as is.

1	recipe *Pizza di Pane* (Flatbread with Rosemary, page 258) or *Crostini* (Toasted Bread, page 36)
10	ounces dried fava beans
½	small onion, coarsely chopped
2	tablespoons pecorino or Parmesan cheese
1	tablespoon extra-virgin olive oil
½	teaspoon fennel seeds
⅛	teaspoon freshly ground black pepper

Soak fava beans overnight. Drain and slip off the outer skins.

Put beans and onion in a medium saucepan. Cover with cold water and bring to a boil. Reduce heat, cover, and cook for 3½ to 4 hours or until beans are soft. Put in a food processor and pulse until beans are completely pureed. Add cheese, olive oil, fennel seeds, and pepper. Mix well.

Serve with *Pizza di Pane* or crostini.

Serves 12

Finocchio all'Olio
Fennel with Seasoned Olive Oil

Fennel is a crisp white bulb vegetable similar to celery, but much more flavorful. It always adorns Easter, Christmas Eve, and Christmas Day tables, either sliced and then dipped into a tiny dish of extra-virgin olive oil with salt and crushed red pepper or tossed with a salad dressing. Be sure the fennel is firm and bulbous. If the stalks are spreading, it is not fresh. The feathery plumes, which resemble dill, should be fragrant and not wilted. Fennel and its plumes are added to soups and pasta sauces. Sliced fennel can be added to a mixed salad to give it zip or can serve as a garnish for a second course. The plumes can provide an interesting border garnish for a dish of colorful vegetables.

> 1 large fennel bulb
> 3 tablespoons extra-virgin olive oil
> 1 teaspoon red wine vinegar
> ½ teaspoon salt
> ½ teaspoon crushed red pepper

Cut off plumes from fennel bulb, rinse, and set aside for garnish elsewhere. Cut off top stalks and remove the outer stringy layers. Cut fennel bulb in quarters, then slice lengthwise into thin wedges. Wash in cold water and drain on paper towels.

In a small bowl, mix the olive oil, vinegar, salt, and crushed red pepper. Whisk and set aside. Do not refrigerate.

Put fennel in a salad bowl, drizzle the dressing over it, and toss thoroughly until the fennel is thoroughly coated.

Serves 4 to 6

Funghi Marinati con Olio e Limone
Mushrooms Marinated with Oil and Lemon

It is a rare antipasti table in Italian restaurants here or in Italy that does not include this popular mushroom dish. Mushrooms come alive in this tangy marinade. For an extra zing, substitute red pepper for the black pepper. This recipe can be prepared a day in advance.

1	pound fresh button mushrooms
½	lemon, freshly juiced
3	tablespoons extra-virgin olive oil
2	tablespoons red wine vinegar
2	cloves garlic, cut in thick slices
2	tablespoon fresh Italian parsley, finely chopped
½	teaspoon salt
¼	teaspoon freshly ground black pepper

Wash mushrooms quickly, as they can get waterlogged otherwise. You also can brush them clean if they are not too sandy.

Steam mushrooms in a large double boiler for 3 to 4 minutes or until tender. Drain on paper towels and pat dry.

Meanwhile, combine all remaining ingredients in a small bowl and set aside. Put mushrooms in a medium-sized mixing bowl. Pour liquid over all, cover, and refrigerate for at least 2 hours. Stir occasionally. About ½ hour before serving, remove from refrigerator, discard garlic, stir again, and transfer mushrooms to a serving dish. Serve at room temperature.

Serves 8 to 10

Olive Verdi o Nere Cunzati
Marinated Green or Black Olives

What could enhance and enrich an antipasto table more than glorious, glistening olives, marinated with fruity extra-virgin olive oil?

½	pound green or black olives, oil-cured, rinsed, and pitted
½	small red onion, very thinly sliced
4	tablespoons extra-virgin olive oil
1	tablespoon white wine vinegar
1	clove garlic, sliced
½	teaspoon dried oregano
¼	teaspoon crushed red pepper

Although it is not necessary to pit the olives, the flavor is better absorbed if they are. Crack with a small mallet or *battecarne*. Put olives in a medium-sized bowl with all the other ingredients and mix thoroughly. Put in a glass jar, cover, and refrigerate. Will keep for 2 months. Serve at room temperature.

Serves 8

Peperoni (Friarelli) Ripieni
Italian Peppers Stuffed with Anchovies, Capers, and Cheese

Frugal Calabrians make good use of stale bread. They slip chunks or slices of it under a serving of soup, they toast, grate, and sprinkle it over pasta dishes or vegetables, and they use it as stuffing as in this recipe. Several testings were required before I got the stuffing exactly right. It is no surprise that with slight variations, the dish is also popular in other southern provinces.

8	small Italian light green peppers
2½	cups coarse bread crumbs
5	tablespoons grated Parmesan or pecorino cheese
3	tablespoons fresh Italian parsley, finely chopped
2	tablespoons capers
2	cloves garlic, finely minced
10	anchovy fillets, coarsely chopped
1	egg, lightly beaten
¼ to ½	cup water

¼ teaspoon salt
¼ teaspoon freshly ground black pepper
3 tablespoons olive oil

Wash peppers, drain, and pat dry with paper towels. Leaving whole, cut out stems and remove seeds.

In a medium-sized mixing bowl, combine bread crumbs, cheese, parsley, capers, garlic, anchovies, egg, ¼ cup water, salt, and pepper. If mixture does not seem to stick together, add more water gradually. The exact amount of water required will depend on how dry the bread crumbs are. Mix until moistened. Spoon stuffing loosely into the peppers.

To pan cook: In a large, heavy skillet, heat olive oil over medium high heat. Add peppers and sauté for 6 to 8 minutes, carefully turning until all sides are medium brown. Reduce heat to low and sauté for 12 to 15 minutes, turning occasionally, until peppers are tender.

To bake: Preheat oven to 400° F. Brush 1 tablespoon olive oil on bottom of an 8-by-12-inch baking dish. Add peppers, brush tops with remaining oil, and bake uncovered for 18 to 20 minutes, turning once, or until peppers are tender.

Serve peppers whole or halved, hot or at room temperature.

Serves 8

VARIATION: 12 green olives, brine-cured, pitted, and coarsely chopped can be added to the stuffing.

Peperoni (Friarelli) Fritti
Fried Italian Peppers

These sweet, long, pale green peppers are called *friarelli* in some parts of Calabria. This simple but savory method of serving them adds a special treat to your antipasti table, to a sandwich, or to an entrée. A simple dish like this is capable of conjuring up warm and loving memories of food and family. These peppers were one of the antipasti served at my son David's birthday party. A friend of his, restaurateur Gene Marra, commented that he hadn't seen the dish, one he loved, since he left home. The expression of nostalgic enjoyment on his face was touching. The memory of food is indeed powerful. Don't neglect to sprinkle with the crushed red pepper—it is integral to the taste and appearance of this dish. If your market does not carry *friarelli*, they can be found in any Italian specialty store. A red variety is sometimes available.

12 large Italian light green peppers
4 tablespoons olive oil, divided
¼ teaspoon salt
¼ to ½ teaspoon crushed red pepper

Wash peppers and pat dry with paper towels. Cut out stems, remove seeds, and cut each pepper in half. Heat 2 tablespoons olive oil in a large, heavy skillet over medium high heat. Cook a few peppers at a time without crowding them. Sauté for a total of 8 to 10 minutes, turning once and adding more olive oil as needed, until a light golden brown. Remove peppers with tongs or a slotted spoon and put on paper towels. Keep warm.

Arrange a layer of peppers on a serving platter. Sprinkle lightly with salt and crushed red pepper. Continue layering and sprinkling until all peppers are used. Serve hot or at room temperature.

Serves 16 as an antipasto, or 8 as a side dish

Peperoni Arrostiti
Roasted Peppers

If you have never had the pleasure of tasting roasted or grilled peppers, you have missed something close to regal. There are several ways to cook them. In Calabria, my cousins grill them over wood embers, which they claim is the most flavorful way. However, roasting or broiling in the oven also works quite well. The secret is to char them thoroughly. Red peppers are favored over green for their sweet taste, but for a delightful rainbow effect, also use yellow, orange, and green, and alternate them on the serving dish. It is best to make these at least 1 to 2 hours before serving to allow the flavors to mingle.

8 large mixed red, yellow, orange, or green peppers
3 tablespoons extra-virgin olive oil
2 cloves garlic, halved and coarsely sliced
3 tablespoons fresh Italian parsley, finely chopped, divided
½ teaspoon salt or more, to taste

To grill: Place peppers 4 inches above hot coals. Grill for 15 to 18 minutes, turning several times, until skins are charred and blistered.

To oven broil: Preheat broiler with door slightly ajar for at least 5 minutes.

Put peppers on cookie sheet on second shelf from top of oven. Broil for 18 to 20 minutes, turning occasionally, until skins are charred and blistered.

To oven roast: Preheat oven to 500° F. Put peppers on cookie sheet and roast for 15 to 18 minutes, turning occasionally, until skins are charred and blistered.

Peel peppers and cut lengthwise into 1-inch strips. Put peppers in the bowl with strained juice. Drizzle with olive oil, then add garlic, 2 tablespoons parsley, and salt. Mix thoroughly. Let stand for at least 1 hour at room temperature before serving to allow ingredients to mingle. Remove garlic and arrange on a serving platter, alternating colors. Sprinkle with remaining parsley.

Alternately, refrigerate and remove at least 30 minutes before serving.

Serves 8 to 12 as an antipasto, or 4 to 6 as a side dish

TIP: The easiest way to remove skins from roasted peppers is to put them in a plastic bag, then seal the bag, place it in the sink, and let cool. Put a strainer over a medium-sized bowl, pour juice from the bag, hold pepper upside down over strainer to save juices, and remove stem, and seeds, and skin.

VARIATIONS:
- For a tangy touch, add 1 tablespoon red wine vinegar or balsamic vinegar with oil and seasonings.
- Sprinkle 1 tablespoon capers over arranged peppers.

Peperonata con Pomodori e Cipolle
Peppers with Tomatoes and Onions

This savory vegetable dish is celebrated by the Mediterranean community. The French version contains eggplant and is called ratatouille, and the Greeks and Spanish have their own versions. The Calabrian creation is so appreciated, it adorns antipasti tables, is served at dinner parties, and often shines at family meals, all with equal success and enthusiasm. You can use green, red, or yellow peppers in any combination. The marriage of peppers, tomatoes, and onions is as palatable as it is colorful. The final dish matches up particularly well with pork chops or sausages.

> 3 tablespoons olive oil, divided
> 1 large onion, coarsely chopped
> 2 cloves garlic, finely minced
> 1 16-ounce can Italian plum tomatoes, coarsely chopped

1 tablespoon fresh Italian parsley, coarsely chopped
½ teaspoon salt
¼ teaspoon crushed red pepper (optional)
4 large green, red, or yellow peppers, washed,
   seeded and cut into 1-inch pieces

In a large, heavy skillet over medium heat, add 1 tablespoon olive oil. Add onion and sauté for 3 to 4 minutes or until translucent. Add garlic and sauté for 1 to 2 minutes or until a light golden brown. Lower heat and add tomatoes, parsley, salt, and crushed red pepper. Simmer for 15 minutes.

Meanwhile, in a large heavy skillet over medium heat, add remaining 2 tablespoons olive oil. Add peppers and stir to coat. Sauté for 5 to 6 minutes, turning frequently, until the peppers begin to brown. Lower heat and sauté for 10 to 12 minutes or until tender, turning occasionally.

Add the tomato sauce to the peppers. Mix thoroughly and let simmer for 2 to 3 minutes. Transfer to a serving dish and serve immediately or at room temperature.

Serves 12 to 16 as an antipasto, or 6 to 8 as a side dish

Arancini
Stuffed Rice Balls

Although pasta is preferred over rice in southern Italy, these tempting rice balls are popular not only as an appetizer or side dish, but also at festivals as street food, both in Italy and in the United States. *Arancini* translates as "little oranges" because they resemble golden oranges when fried. However, there is another name not quite so well known that is both charming and descriptive, *Supplì al Telefono* (telephone wires). When the rice ball is pulled apart the mozzarella that is tucked in the middle stretches out between each half, resembling telephone wires. While in Calabria researching this book, I tasted my cousins' distinctive version. They added bits of salami along with the mozzarella. I loved it after the first bite.

1¾ cups chicken stock or water
1   cup rice
½   teaspoon salt
¼   cup pecorino or Parmesan cheese, freshly grated

2 tablespoons fresh Italian parsley, finely chopped
2 tablespoons salami, finely chopped
2 eggs
4 ounces fresh mozzarella cheese, cut into ½-inch cubes
1 tablespoon water
¾ cup finely ground bread crumbs
    olive oil for frying

In a large saucepan over high heat, add stock or water. Cover and bring to a boil. Add rice and salt, and stir. Cover, lower heat, and simmer for 15 to 17 minutes or until the rice is tender but not mushy. Remove from heat, mix, and let air dry, uncovered, for 5 minutes. Add the pecorino or Parmesan cheese, parsley, salami, and one egg, well beaten. Mix thoroughly. Set mixture aside until cool enough to handle.

In a medium-sized bowl, add remaining egg and water and beat well. Put bread crumbs in a flat dish.

Using a scoop or measuring spoon, place 1½ to 2 tablespoons of rice into the palm of one hand. Roll into a ball. Press thumb into the center and tuck in a square of cheese. Roll to seal cheese securely. If rice is too sticky, dredge hands with flour before forming ball. Put rice ball on a cookie sheet and repeat the process until all the rice is used up.

Roll each rice ball in the egg bath and then in the bread crumbs and return to cookie sheet. Repeat until all are coated.

In a large, heavy skillet, over medium-high heat, add about 1 inch of olive oil. Fry the rice balls a few at a time; do not crowd. Turn constantly and cook until golden brown, about 1½ to 2 minutes. Do not leave unattended. Drain on paper towels and serve hot or warm.

Makes 22 to 28 rice balls depending on size.

TIPS:
- For years I have used an ice-cream scoop to form meat or rice balls or cookies. It saves time and makes balls or cookies of uniform size.
- These rice balls can be prepared in advance and refrigerated or frozen before dipping in egg and bread crumbs.

Pastìccio di Spinaci e Uova
Spinach and Egg Pie

Savory Spinach and Egg Pie is a popular choice for a luncheon, light supper, or antipasto. Some recipes call for a crust. This satisfying pie is crustless, reducing calories and preparation time. It is also a great make-ahead dish. It can be baked in the morning, refrigerated, and reheated just before serving. It can also be frozen.

10	ounces fresh spinach, washed, stemmed, and coarsely chopped
3	eggs
¼	cup milk
10	ounces ricotta
4	ounces mozzarella cheese, shredded
¼	cup freshly grated pecorino or Parmesan cheese
½	small onion, finely chopped
1	tablespoon fresh Italian parsley, finely chopped
½	teaspoon salt
¼	teaspoon freshly ground black pepper

Preheat oven to 350° F.

Put spinach a double boiler or steamer. Steam for 1 to 2 minutes—just long enough to wilt. Drain, squeeze dry, and set aside.

In a large mixing bowl, add eggs and beat lightly. Add spinach, milk, ricotta, mozzarella, grated cheese, onion, parsley, salt, and pepper. Mix thoroughly. Pour into an oiled 10-by-10-inch baking pan and bake for 25 to 30 minutes or until set. Serve hot or at room temperature.

Serves 16 to 20 as an antipasto, or 8 to 10 as a side dish

Pomodori e Mozzarella con Basilico
Tomato and Fresh Mozzarella with Basil

Sometimes combining the simplest of ingredients creates a miracle of sorts. Double that if the miracle requires almost zero preparation time. Called *Caprese* in many parts of Italy, the secret to this mini-miracle is *fresh* juicy tomatoes, *fresh* velvety mozzarella (preferably *di bufala,* buffalo milk mozzarella, or a good quality cow's milk mozzarella), and *fresh* fragrant basil. If you have never had this salad with fresh ingredients, you have never had this salad! Prepare close to serving time. Have all ingredients at room temperature and just slice, arrange, and serve. Do not refrigerate—it will dull the taste of the tomatoes and cheese. Serve as an appetizer, side dish, or salad—it works everywhere!

    4   large, ripe tomatoes, cut into ½-inch slices
    ¾   pound fresh mozzarella, cut into ½-inch slices
    1   large bunch fresh basil leaves
    2   tablespoons extra-virgin olive oil
    ¼   teaspoon salt
    ¼   teaspoon freshly ground black pepper
    1   tablespoon capers (optional)
    1   tablespoon red wine vinegar (optional)
        Italian bread or flatbread

Wash and slice tomatoes. Slice mozzarella. Rinse and dry basil. Line a large round platter with alternating layers of tomatoes, mozzarella, and basil until all tomato and mozzarella slices are used. Drizzle olive oil evenly throughout and sprinkle with salt and pepper. If desired, sprinkle with capers or vinegar.

Let stand for at least 5 minutes to allow the flavor of the basil to penetrate the tomatoes. Serve with crusty Italian bread or flatbread.

Serves 10 to 12 as an antipasto, or 6 to 8 as a side dish or salad

Fagioli Bianchi con Pomodori Secchi
White Beans with Sun-dried Tomatoes

Sun-dried tomatoes add an intense, rich flavor to this dish. Calabrians cut plum tomatoes in half to dry in the sun and string cherry tomatoes or lay them on straw to dry. If you are making this dish early in the day, do not add the sun-dried tomatoes until just before serving.

1	cup dried cannellini beans
6	cups cold water
1	teaspoon salt
4	tablespoons extra-virgin olive oil, divided
2	tablespoons red wine vinegar
½	teaspoon freshly ground black pepper
⅓	cup sun-dried tomatoes
2	cloves garlic, finely minced
1	teaspoon fresh sage leaves, finely chopped
1	tablespoon fresh Italian parsley, finely chopped, for garnish

Using the quick soak method, put the rinsed and picked over dried beans in a large pot with twice their quantity of cold water. Cover and boil rapidly for 2 minutes. Remove from heat and let stand for 1 hour or more. Drain and rinse.

Put the beans in a large pot and add the 6 cups of water. Bring to a boil, then lower the heat. Simmer for 40 minutes or until the beans are tender. Add salt and simmer for an additional 10 minutes. Drain, reserving 3 tablespoons of the liquid, and transfer beans and liquid to a mixing bowl. While warm, dress the beans with 3 tablespoons of the olive oil, stirring to coat all the beans. Add vinegar and pepper. Mix well.

Put the sun-dried tomatoes in a small dish and cover with hot water. Let soften for 5 to 10 minutes. (If the sun-dried tomatoes are packed in oil, they need not be soaked.) Drain on paper towels and cut each tomato into ¼-inch thin slivers.

In a large, heavy skillet, heat the remaining tablespoon of olive oil over medium heat. Add garlic and sage. Sauté for 1 to 2 minutes or until garlic is light golden brown. Add this and the sundried tomatoes to the beans and mix gently. Transfer mixture to a serving dish, sprinkle with parsley, and serve warm or at room temperature.

Serves up to 12 as an antipasto, or 6 as a side dish

TIP: Do not add salt to beans during soaking or cooking, as it toughens them. Add it 10 minutes before they are done.

Fagioli Bianchi, Tonno, Uova, e Verdure
White Beans, Tuna, Eggs, and Vegetables

Choices—that's what you have with this healthy salad that can be prepared in about twenty minutes with ingredients you probably have in your cupboard and refrigerator. It's ideal on a day when you forgot to take something out of the freezer and you've had a busy day, and it's a good choice for a light supper or a satisfying lunch. Start cooking the eggs first. Then pick and choose from among the diverse variables, depending on your mood. You can also choose to put some variables alongside the mixture instead of in it. Of course, you can cook dried beans in advance if you like. But even in Calabria, busy families often rely on good-quality canned cannellini beans for dishes such as this.

CONSTANTS:

1 or 2	eggs, hard boiled
2	tablespoons extra-virgin olive oil
1	tablespoon red wine vinegar
¼	teaspoon salt
⅛	teaspoon freshly ground black pepper
1	19-ounce can of cannellini beans
1	6 ½-ounce can Italian tuna in oil, drained and broken into small chunks
1	stalk celery with leaves, thinly sliced
1	teaspoon Italian parsley, finely chopped

VARIABLES:

8	ounces of fresh mushrooms
1	small carrot, thinly sliced
1	stalk fennel, thinly sliced
½	red or green pepper, cut into ½-inch cubes
½	medium onion, coarsely chopped
8 to 10	black or green olives, brine-cured, halved and pitted
2	filets of anchovies, coarsely chopped
1	small tomato, cut into thin wedges
1	tablespoon capers, drained

Peel eggs, halve, slice coarsely, and put in a salad bowl.

In a small bowl add the oil, vinegar, salt, and pepper. Mix well and set aside.

Add drained, rinsed beans, tuna, celery, and parsley to a salad bowl. If using fresh mushrooms, steam in a double boiler for 3 to 4 minutes, drain, slice coarsely, and add to salad bowl. Prepare and add any variables of your choice and mix gently. Sprinkle dressing over all and mix again. Transfer the contents to a serving platter and if desired, garnish with any of the remaining variables. Serve at room temperature.

Serves 4 to 8 as a light supper or lunch

Zeppole con Alici, Uva Secca, o Semplice
Fried Dough with Anchovies, Raisins, or Plain

Zeppole is what they are called in Bova Superiore, the village of my ancestors. In other parts of Calabria and southern Italy they are called *Collari, Crispeddi, Crispelli,* and *Pizzelle.* Serving them on Christmas Eve is a longtime Calabrian tradition, one I recall with warm feelings. The entire family assembled in the kitchen, hovering over Mom, impatiently waiting for the first batch to be done, hardly allowing them to cool before we gobbled one. With little or no prompting, Mom also served them on special occasions. Most of us preferred them with anchovies. But even if you aren't an anchovy lover, try one, they are delicious. They also can be filled with raisins or served plain. What a versatile, exotic creation! Recently, my granddaughter Jennifer called to tell me she wanted to make *Zeppole.* Her Mom was away. She asked the equivalent of 1 envelope active dry yeast since her Mom buys it in bulk and keeps it frozen. She suggested I include it in my cookbook. Good idea, Jennifer! Various versions are served as street food at feasts and festivals, such as the Feast of St. Anthony. They are filling, so if serving them as an antipasto, I suggest you serve them about an hour prior to dinner.

> 1 package active dry yeast, or 2½ teaspoons loose
> 1¼ cups lukewarm water
> 3 cups all-purpose flour
> ¼ teaspoon salt
> 1 2-ounce can of flat anchovies
> ½ cup vegetable oil for frying

In a large measuring cup, dissolve yeast with ¼ cup lukewarm water. Measure flour and salt onto a wooden pastry board. Make a well in the center of the flour. Gradually add the dissolved yeast and the remaining water, pulling flour into the liquid. Knead for 6 to 8 minutes or until smooth and elastic. Put dough into an oiled bowl, turn to coat, and cover with a thick towel. Let rise in a warm place, free from draft, until doubled in size, about 2 to 2½ hours.

Empty anchovies into a small dish and cut each fillet in two. Drain oil. In a large, heavy skillet add oil over medium-high heat.

Pinch off a piece of risen dough about the size of a golf ball. With fingers, stretch into a rectangle, about 2-by-5-inches in size and put on wax paper. Repeat the process until all of the dough is used up. Put one or two pieces of anchovy in the center of a *zeppole*, fold over, twist, and pinch all edges tightly.

Fry briskly, a few at a time without crowding. Turn until all sides are golden and crisp, about 3 or 4 minutes. Remove with slotted spoon and drain on paper towels. Keep warm in low oven until all are cooked.

Makes 20 to 25 zeppole

VARIATIONS:
- Zeppole with raisins and confectioner's sugar: Insert 8 to 10 raisins in center of each *zeppole* and proceed as above. Drain on paper towels and sprinkle with sifted confectioner's sugar while still hot.
- Plain zeppole: Follow preceding recipe, except omit anchovies.

Fiori di Zucchini Fritti
Fried Zucchini Flowers

I recently heard the expression "fear of frying." While true that few of us fry many things these days, don't let that fear keep you from trying this highly delectable treat. Little oil is absorbed if they are fried in hot fat and drained on paper towels. Also called *frittelle,* this century-old recipe is a family favorite. My father had a large vegetable garden. He picked the male yellow-orange zucchini flowers early in the morning while they were open (the female flowers have a bulge near the stem and continue to produce fruit) and refrigerated them unwashed until Mom was ready to cook them. After cleaning them, she dipped them in a batter and fried them into a crisp, tasty delicacy. The amount of batter depends on the size of the flowers but this recipe is sufficient for about 20 to 24 medium flowers. If you don't grow zucchini, look for the flowers in a farmer's market or in an Italian specialty store. This is one of my favorite dishes, so I was especially excited while in Reggio Calabria when I came upon a vendor unloading many crates of the brightly colored zucchini blossoms at an outdoor market. I had never seen so many in one place at one time! I asked if I could take a picture of the flowers. He readily consented but only if he could be in the picture too, all the while explaining in Italian how they should be cooked!

2	eggs
1	tablespoon olive oil
¼	cup warm water
½	teaspoon salt
¼	teaspoon freshly ground black pepper
½	cup all-purpose flour
20 to 24	zucchini flowers
6	tablespoons vegetable oil, divided

In a medium bowl, beat eggs lightly. Add olive oil, warm water, salt, and pepper. Mix thoroughly. Gradually add flour and mix until the consistency of a smooth pancake batter. Let stand for at least 30 minutes.

Meanwhile, open the zucchini flowers, carefully remove pistils and stigmas and discard. Remove green leaves, any wilted parts, and the stem. Gently wash in cold water, and put on paper towels to air dry.

In a large, heavy skillet, add 3 tablespoons of the vegetable oil over medium-high heat. When the oil is very hot, use tongs to dip flowers in the batter, one at a time, turning slowly until all sides are coated. Carefully place in the skillet; do not crowd. Fry for 3 to 5 minutes, turning frequently, until crisp. Add more oil as needed. Drain on paper towels and keep warm.
Serve immediately.

Makes 20 to 24 fried zucchini flowers.

Zucchini Frittelli
Zucchini Fritters

Known as *cucuzze* in Calabrian dialect, zucchini has been popular in Italy since the sixteenth century. These glistening, scrumptious fritters are an ideal choice for an antipasto. Cook them just ahead of serving time, and serve them immediately. If you plan to serve a selection of antipasti, these fritters pair especially well with *Peperoni Arrostiti* (Roasted Peppers, page 52) and *Funghi Marinati con Olio e Limone* (Mushrooms Marinated with Oil and Lemon, page 49), providing contrast in texture, flavor, and color.

> 2 eggs
> ½ cup fine dried bread crumbs
> ½ cup all-purpose flour
> 2 tablespoons freshly grated Parmesan or pecorino cheese
> 1 tablespoon fresh Italian parsley, finely chopped
> 2 medium zucchini, coarsely grated (about 2 cups)
> ½ teaspoon salt
> ¼ teaspoon freshly ground black pepper
> 4 tablespoons olive oil, divided

In a large bowl, with a whisk, beat eggs thoroughly. Add bread crumbs, flour, cheese, and parsley. Mix well. Add zucchini, salt, and pepper. Mix again. Let mixture stand for 10 to 12 minutes.

In a medium skillet, heat 2 tablespoons olive oil over medium-high heat. With a tablespoon, drop batter into the oil. Sauté for 4 to 6 minutes until cooked through and a medium golden brown, turning once. Put on paper towels to drain. Keep warm in a low oven. Add more oil as needed. When all of the batter is cooked, place fritters on a serving platter and serve.

Serves 8 as an antipasto, or 4 as a side dish

ZUPPE

SOUPS

Sette cose fa la zuppa: Cura fame, e sete attuta, empie il ventre, netta il dente, fa' dormire, fa' smaltire, e la quancia colorire.

Soup does seven things: It appeases your hunger, quenches your thirst, fills your stomach, cleans your teeth, makes you sleep, helps you digest, and puts color in your cheeks.

CALABRIAN PROVERB

Soups were born of poverty, created by peasants and oftentimes servants, who used leftover scraps of food from their masters combined with what they could grow or forage. Soups had to be versatile—they were a major food staple. And they had to be substantial in order to appease hunger and fill the stomach. Sometimes an egg or two or a generous amount of grated cheese was added to enrich the soup. Various fresh herbs were added to enhance them, especially if they were meatless. But all of the ingredients had to blend and be compatible with the other flavors, requiring skill to achieve that often comes only with experience.

Soups are very much in vogue now both in Italy and in the United States. They are gaining popularity as a hearty, often meatless, meal-in-one-bowl, especially those laden with vegetables and legumes. And they are easy to make. They can be made a day ahead and, in fact, taste better the second day, after their flavors have had a chance to mingle. Plus, most soups freeze well.

One rule applies to soups made with meat: Begin with cold broth or water and bring to a boil slowly. This extracts juices from the meat and bones, adding flavor to the soup. Using hot liquid or quickly boiled liquid results in a cloudy broth and stringy meat.

An easy way to remove fat from broth or soup is to refrigerate until the fat congeals and can easily be spooned out. Otherwise, buy an inexpensive, large cup especially designed with a long spout. Pour the soup into the cup and let stand for a minute until the fat comes to the top. Then slowly pour the soup back into the pot—the fat remains in the cup and can be thrown away. In a pinch, run a paper towel over the top surface.

Once you get in the habit of making soups, you can enhance them by making your own broth to use in place of water. Making broth is also a thrifty way to use leftovers and may even dictate the choice of soup you make. Get into the habit by marking freezer containers of various sizes "Chicken Broth" or "Vegetable Broth." Freeze leftover vegetable cooking water with its important nutrients. To that add leftover bones, bits of meat, leftover vegetables, and washed onion and potato skins. Bouillon cubes are a poor substitute for homemade broth. If a recipe calls for broth and no homemade broth is available, it is better to use canned broth.

Soups are perfect for adding more vegetables to your diet, not only the old standards of carrots, celery, and onions, but also fennel, escarole, and zucchini, for example. Of special importance to many soups are dried beans. One of the oldest cultivated foods, dating back to 7000 B.C., dried beans are nutritious and delicious. High in protein and fiber, virtually fat free, they produce rustic, thick, creamy, and hearty soups.

The pastas added to soups are as varied as the soups themselves but are usually small in size. If you find yourself without the traditional pastina or other tiny pasta, fine egg noodles, or tortellini, here is a good tip I learned from my mother. Wrap 8 ounces of spaghetti in a clean dishtowel and crush them with a rolling pin for instant pastina!

Soups are very much a part of Italian cuisine. Each province has its favorites, and Calabria is no exception. There are soups of all kind in the Calabrian repertoire, clearly defined. They are: *brodo, brodetto, minestra, minestrone, zuppa,* and *stufato.*

Brodo, broth or stock, serves as a basis for hearty, full-bodied soups. It also can be served as a light, thin soup. Light soups are usually the choice if pasta is to be served. Beef, chicken, and vegetable broths are included in soups, sauces, and vegetable dishes. Beef broth can include leftover vegetables, beef and veal bones, and any leftover bits of meat, but not lamb or pork bones since they produce too strong a taste. Chicken broth can include leftover chicken, turkey, capon bones, and carcasses, and any leftover bits of meat. Vegetable broth can include leftover bits of vegetables, washed onion skins, and potato peelings. Many of the soup recipes in this book are meatless and will therefore especially appeal to vegetarians.

Brodetto is a fish broth made with fish bones, heads, and trimmings. It serves as a base for fish soups to be used in place of water, providing added flavor.

Minestra is a medium- or full-bodied soup made with a wide variety of vegetables and pasta, and no bread. Some *minestre*, called *minestrine*, are thin soups made for children and people who are sick. Probably the best known *minestra* not only in Calabria, but with variations in all of Italy (and the world) is *Minestra di Pollo con Scarola e Polpettine* (Chicken Soup with Escarole and Little Meatballs, page 76).

Some *minestra* soups are called *minestrone*. Italians often serve *minestrone*, a big soup, laden with vegetables and thickened with pasta. It is so hearty that it can star as the main dish rather than just the first course. Served with a fresh, crusty bread and salad, it is especially lusty and bountiful. An outstanding *minestrone* served in Calabria is the well-known *Pasta e Fagioli* (Pasta and Beans, page 79). Often called soul food or comfort food, immigrants brought the humble soup to this country. In time, however, such dishes were abandoned in favor of more sophisticated ones. But beans are back, appearing on many restaurant menus not only in soups, but also in appetizers, salads, and many side dishes.

Zuppa is a soup that contains bread or is served over bread (*zuppa* stems from the word *zuppo,* which means to soak or sop up). The bread should be old or dried, but not toasted. *Zuppe* do not contain pasta, rice, or cream.

Stufato, called *Bollito Misto* in some areas, is traditionally a meat stew.

Mom served us hearty soups often. A favorite was *Minestrone di Verdura alla Bova Superiore* (Vegetable Soup, Bova Superiore Style, page 82). "Soup for the soul" she used to say as she stirred away, practicing her craft. But I also remember a favorite soup my mother served my sister and me when we were little, *Pastina al Latte* (Pastina and Milk, page 74). She then served it to her three grandsons and it became their favorite as well. See the recipe to find out how this simple soup has (at least) three other versions in addition to Mom's.

Brodo
Broth

Broths are the basis for hearty, fullbodied soups. Below are four recipes for broths or stock, as broth is sometimes called: beef, chicken, fish, and vegetable. Beef, chicken, and vegetable broths can be served as is; portions can be frozen; or they can be strained and frozen as clear broth to be added to soups and stews for added impact and flavor. Fish broth is used in lieu of water for flavorful fish soups. It is important to use cold water when making broths in order to extract the most flavor from the meat or fish. Broths should be simmered slowly in a covered saucepan, as cooking it quickly toughens the meat. Leftover cooking liquids, vegetables, bones, and bits of meat can be frozen and later added to broths. You can also add a rinsed onion skin to any broth for extra color and flavor.

Brodo di Manzo: *Beef Broth*

For beef broth, use the least expensive, well-flavored cuts of meat. They need to cook for a long time, perfect for broth. Bones from beef and veal can be added for extra flavor and nutrients, but not from lamb or pork because they produce too strong a flavor. For an even lighter broth, use bones only.

    4 quarts cold water
    1 pound beef or veal bones (in any combination)
    ½ pound of an inexpensive cut of beef, cut into 1-inch cubes
    1 medium onion, coarsely chopped
    1 carrot, diced
    1 potato, peeled and diced
    1 stalk celery and leaves, coarsely sliced
    1 small fresh tomato, coarsely chopped
    6 peppercorns
    1 bay leaf
    1 tablespoon fresh Italian parsley, coarsely chopped

In a large soup pot, add all ingredients over high heat. Cover and bring to a boil. Take soup pot off burner and lower heat immediately. Return to burner and simmer slowly for 2 hours. Skim fat off top as required. Serve as is. To freeze broth only, strain through a colander or sieve, cool, and freeze in 8- or 16-ounce containers for convenient use in soup or stew recipes.

Makes about 4 quarts

Brodo di Pollo: *Chicken Broth*

If you can find chickens with their heads and feet attached, snap them up. You will be rewarded with a broth rich in flavor. You can add any leftover chicken, capon, or turkey bones or carcasses for added flavor.

    1 roasting chicken (3 to 4 pounds)
    4 quarts water
    3 stalks celery and leaves, coarsely sliced
    2 large carrots, diced
    1 large onion, coarsely chopped
    1 small fresh tomato, coarsely chopped
    6 whole peppercorns
    1 tablespoon fresh Italian parsley, coarsely chopped

Cut chicken into 8 pieces, removing skin and fat. Rinse thoroughly but quickly under cold running water. In a large soup pot, add all ingredients over high heat. Cover and bring to a boil. Take soup pot off burner and lower heat immediately. Return to burner and simmer slowly for 2 hours. Skim fat off top as required. Serve as is. To freeze broth only, strain through a colander or sieve, cool, and freeze in 8- or 16-ounce containers for convenient use in soup or stew recipes.

Makes about 4 quarts

Brodo di Pesce: *Fish Broth*

If you have friends who go fishing, ask them to save you fish trimmings; otherwise you can purchase them at fish markets anywhere. Also called *brodetto*, this broth is used in place of water to produce the most flavorful fish soups.

4 quarts cold water
2 pound of bones, heads, and trimmings from fish
1 small onion, coarsely chopped
1 stalk celery and leaves, coarsely sliced
1 carrot, diced
1 small fresh tomato, coarsely chopped
6 peppercorns
1 slice lemon with skin
1 bay leaf

In a large soup pot, add all ingredients over high heat. Cover and bring to a boil. Take soup pot off burner and lower heat immediately. Return to burner and simmer slowly for 2 hours. To freeze broth, strain through a colander, sieve, or cheesecloth. Cool and freeze in 8- or 16-ounce containers for convenient use in soup or stew recipes.

Makes about 4 quarts

Brodo di Verdura: *Vegetable Broth*

When meat was not available to the poor, vegetable broth was in great use. Because vegetable broth does not have the impact of a meat broth, oil is added to enhance the flavor.

6 quarts cold water
2 tablespoons extra-virgin olive oil
2 large onions, coarsely chopped

2 large carrots, diced
3 stalks of celery with leaves, coarsely sliced
2 potatoes, peeled and diced
2 fresh tomatoes, coarsely chopped
6 peppercorns
2 tablespoons fresh Italian parsley, coarsely chopped
1 tablespoon fresh basil, coarsely chopped
1 bay leaf

In a large soup pot, add all ingredients over high heat. Cover and bring to a boil. Take soup pot off burner and lower heat immediately. Return to burner and simmer slowly for 1 hour. Serve as is. To freeze broth only, strain through a colander or sieve, cool and freeze in 8- or 16-ounce containers for convenient use in soup or stew recipes.

Makes about 6 quarts

Brodo Pieno
Broth with Eggs, Bread Crumbs, and Cheese

This well-flavored soup comes to us with an ancient tradition. It was once a favorite of Roman legionnaires. Some versions call for greater amounts of bread crumbs and cheese, but I prefer this lighter version.

8 cups homemade *Brodo di Pollo* (Chicken Broth, page 68)
4 eggs
¼ cups dry bread crumbs, finely grated
¼ cup freshly grated pecorino or Parmesan cheese
2 tablespoons fresh Italian parsley, finely chopped
½ teaspoon salt

In a large soup pot, add broth over medium-high heat, reserving ½ cup.

Add eggs to a small mixing bowl and beat until frothy. Slowly stir in bread crumbs, cheese, parsley, and salt. Add reserved broth and mix well.

When the broth comes to a soft boil, gradually stir in the egg mixture. Cook for 2 to 3 minutes. Remove from heat and serve immediately.

Serves 6 to 8

TIP: If using canned broth, omit the salt.

Mariola, Uno e Due
Broth I with Omelet Ribbons, and
Broth II with Omelet Squares

Just as music has variations on a theme, so does food. The first omelet has more bread crumbs and less eggs than the second and is cut into ribbons. The second omelet is thin and is cut into small squares. The word *mariola,* which refers to the omelets, appears to have two meanings. One is said to have an ancient religious connection to Mary, the mother of Jesus. The other refers to a paste made of bread crumbs, eggs, grated cheese, fresh parsley, and black pepper mixed and added to a broth. These interesting Calabrian concoctions were new to me. What a find! Next time you plan to serve chicken soup, serve up something new.

Mariola Uno: *Broth I with Omelet Ribbons*

- 2 eggs
- ½ cup finely grated dry Italian bread crumbs
- 4 tablespoons freshly grated pecorino or Parmesan cheese, divided
- 2 tablespoons fresh Italian parsley, finely chopped
- 2 cloves garlic, finely minced
- ¼ teaspoon salt
  freshly ground black pepper to taste
- 4 teaspoons olive oil, divided
- 5 cups homemade *Brodo di Pollo* (Chicken Broth, page 68)
  or *Brodo di Verdura* (Vegetable Broth, page 69)

Add eggs to a large mixing bowl and beat until frothy. Add the bread crumbs, 1½ tablespoons cheese, parsley, garlic, salt, and pepper. Mix well. If the mixture seems too moist, add a sprinkling more of bread crumbs. The exact amount will depend on the size of the eggs and how dry the bread crumbs are. When thoroughly mixed, form into 2 round, flattened cakes.

In a 6-inch skillet, add 2 teaspoons of the olive oil over medium heat. Put an omelet into the skillet, lower heat and cook for 5 to 6 minutes, turning once with a wide spatula, until both sides are golden and the egg is cooked through. Remove and set aside. Add remaining olive oil to skillet and cook the second omelet. Remove and cut omelets in half and into ½-inch-wide ribbon-like strips.

In a medium size pot, add broth and bring to a soft boil over medium heat. Add egg strips and remaining cheese. Stir for 1 minute to heat through. Serve immediately. Pass freshly ground black pepper at the table.

Serves 4

Mariola Due: *Broth II with Omelet Squares*

  4 eggs
  4 tablespoons freshly grated pecorino or Parmesan cheese
  3 tablespoons fresh Italian parsley, finely chopped
  2 tablespoons bread crumbs
  2 cloves garlic, finely minced
  ¼ teaspoon salt
  ⅛ teaspoon freshly ground black pepper
  4 teaspoons olive oil, divided
  5 cups homemade *Brodo di Pollo* (Chicken Broth, page 68)
     freshly ground black pepper to taste

Add eggs to a large mixing bowl and beat until frothy. Add cheese, parsley, bread crumbs, garlic, salt, and pepper.

In a 6-inch skillet, add 1 teaspoon of the olive oil over medium heat. Ladle ¼ of the mixture into the skillet. (There will be 4 thin omelets.) Spread the mixture to the edges of the skillet with the back of a tablespoon. Cook for 2 to 3 minutes or until bottom is golden brown and little liquid remains on top. Turn omelet and cook for 2 or 3 minutes or until golden brown. Slip omelet onto a platter and reserve. Add 1 teaspoon olive oil before cooking each of the other 3 omelets. When all are done, cut into ¾-inch squares.

Add broth to a medium pot and bring to a soft boil over medium-high heat. Add omelet squares and stir for 1 minute to heat through. Serve immediately. Pass freshly ground black pepper at the table.

Serves 4

TIP: If using canned broth, omit the salt.

Pastina in Brodo con Uova
Pastina and Broth with Eggs

When my search for this recipe was successful, I was delighted. My mother served it for lunch when I was a little girl but we had all forgotten the proportions. Though a simple dish, I loved it. It spelled warmth and caring.

    4   cups homemade *Brodo di Verdura* (Vegetable Broth, page 69)
        or *Brodo di Pollo* (Chicken Broth, page 68)
    2   eggs
    3   tablespoons freshly grated pecorino or Parmesan cheese
    1   teaspoon fresh Italian parsley, finely chopped
    ¼   teaspoon salt
    ½   cup pastina or other very small pasta
        freshly ground black pepper to taste

Add the broth to a large saucepan over medium heat. Cover and simmer until hot.

Add eggs to a small bowl and beat lightly. Add the cheese, parsley, and salt. Mix thoroughly.

Bring a medium pot of water to a boil over high heat. Add salt to taste. Stir in the pastina and cook al dente. Drain and add pastina to the broth.

Raise heat and bring broth to a soft boil. Stirring constantly, slowly dribble the egg mixture into the broth. Swirl it with a fork for 1 to 2 minutes or until eggs begin to set. Remove from heat and let stand for 1 minute or until the eggs are cooked through. Ladle into bowls. Pass freshly ground black pepper at the table.

Serves 4 to 8

Pastina al Latte
Pastina and Milk

I recall my mother serving this soup to my sister and me when we were children, and we loved it. I had all but forgotten it until I came upon it while researching recipes. It originated in the Near East, and there are several versions of it. One version, called *lagane al latte,* is made with tiny, hand-cut fettuccine cooked in milk and sprinkled with pecorino cheese. Another version, *tagliarine al latte,* also includes hand-cut fettuccine with milk but is not made with cheese. Instead, a touch of saffron is added to the milk. Mom's version is made with pastina, a tiny soup pasta, and is without cheese. I tried the first two versions but prefer the one I was raised with. Amazingly, while I was in Egypt on a cruise of the Nile, a fourth version appeared on a luncheon buffet table! Called "Noodles and Milk," the noodles were small broken pieces of spaghetti, and the milk was a soft, cocoa brown color, so I guessed it contained brown sugar. My guess proved correct. When I asked my sons, John and David, and my nephew, Arnold De Marco, what their favorite Grandma Jennie soup was, all three said pastina and milk. Now that the recipe has been rediscovered, my sons can serve it to their children, and I to my grandchildren.

¼   cup pastina, or any other tiny or hand-cut macaroni
1½ cups milk
⅛   teaspoon of salt (or less)

Bring a medium pot of water to boil over high heat. Add salt to taste. Stir in the pasta and cook until almost tender. Drain pasta and return to saucepan. Add milk, lower heat to medium, and allow the milk to heat slowly. Do not boil. Cool slightly and serve.

Serves 2

Millicuselle
Multi-bean Soup with Savoy Cabbage and Macaroni

This soup is full of beans! Whether called *Millicuselle* or *Millecosedde*, the name of this wonderfully satisfying soup translates literally as "1,000 little things." There are indeed many ingredients in it, but not quite 1,000. Even so, you can taste each ingredient. Easy to make, it is wholesome, hearty, and ready to warm you on a blustery night. And it freezes well, as long as you do not add pasta before freezing.

½ cup dried cannellini beans
¼ cup dried chickpeas
¼ cup dried cranberry beans
1 teaspoon plus 1 tablespoon olive oil
2 ounces pancetta or lean bacon (optional)
2 stalks celery with leaves, coarsely chopped
1 carrot, thinly sliced
1 medium onion, coarsely chopped
2 cloves garlic, finely minced
½ pound fresh button mushrooms, thickly sliced
1 16-ounce can Italian plum tomatoes, coarsely chopped
½ small head Savoy cabbage, shredded (about 4 cups)
½ teaspoon salt
¼ crushed red pepper
8 ounces tubettini or other small macaroni
6 cups water
¼ cup dried lentils, rinsed

Using the quick soak method, put the cannellini beans, chickpeas and cranberry beans in a large pot with enough cold water to cover by 1½ inches over high heat. Bring to a rolling boil and boil rapidly for 2 minutes. Remove from heat, cover, and let stand for 1 hour.

In a large, heavy skillet add 1 teaspoon oil over medium heat. Add pancetta or bacon and sauté for 4 to 6 minutes or until a light golden brown. Remove and reserve. Drain fat and wipe clean with paper towel, but do not wash skillet. Add 1 tablespoon oil. Add celery, carrot, onion, and garlic. Sauté for 10 minutes, stirring often, or until vegetables are soft but not brown.

Add mushrooms to the skillet and sauté for 2 to 3 minutes or until they just begin to brown. Add the tomatoes, cabbage, salt, and pepper. Stir and simmer for 5 minutes.

Drain beans and rinse in cool water. In a large soup pot over high heat, add reserved pancetta or bacon, beans, water, lentils, and sautéed vegetables. Bring to a boil. Reduce heat quickly and simmer for 40 to 45 minutes, or until all the beans are tender but still retain their individual shapes. If the soup seems too thick, add a little hot water.

When the beans are almost tender, bring a medium pot of water to a boil over high heat. Add salt to water. Stir in the pasta and cook al dente. Drain, add pasta to the soup, stir well, and serve immediately.

Serves 10 to 12

TIP: 1 cup dried beans (½ pound) makes 2½ cups cooked beans.

Minestra di Pollo con Scarola e Polpettine
Chicken Soup with Escarole and Little Meatballs

This soup serves a dual purpose. As the traditional Easter soup in Calabria and southern Italy, it is referred to as *minestra di Pasqua*. When served at weddings it is known as *minestra di sposalizio,* or wedding soup. To describe this soup as spectacular is not an exaggeration. Too delicious to reserve for only those two occasions, it is served on other special occasions as well. Hearty and nutritious, it can be prepared a day ahead or frozen. If you plan to freeze it, do not add pasta until just before serving. For a lighter version of this universally loved soup, simply eliminate the escarole and little meatballs.

SOUP:
1 roasting chicken (3 to 4 pounds)
4 quarts cold water, enough to cover chicken
1 pound escarole, coarsely chopped
2 stalks celery with leaves, coarsely chopped
2 carrots, coarsely chopped
1 large, fresh tomato, coarsely chopped
1 medium to large onion, coarsely chopped
1 teaspoon salt
8 ounces small soup pasta such as pastina
freshly grated pecorino or Parmesan cheese to taste
freshly ground black pepper to taste

    2 slices dry bread, crusts removed

3 to 4 tablespoons water

    ¾ pounds very lean, finely ground beef

    1 egg, lightly beaten

    2 tablespoons freshly grated pecorino or Parmesan cheese

    1 tablespoon fresh Italian parsley, finely chopped

    1 clove garlic, finely minced

    1 teaspoon salt

    ¼ teaspoon freshly ground black pepper

Cut chicken into 8 pieces and remove skin and fat. Rinse thoroughly but quickly under cold running water. To a large soup pot over medium-high heat, add cold water and chicken. Bring to a boil slowly, skimming the surface periodically. Immediately lower heat, cover, and simmer for 1½ hours.

While the broth is simmering, prepare the meatballs. In a medium mixing bowl, soak bread in water for several minutes until softened. Squeeze until almost dry and discard liquid. Shred bread and add the beef, egg, cheese, parsley, garlic, salt, and pepper. Mix thoroughly. Shape into uniform ½-inch meatballs and set aside.

After 1½ hours, remove the chicken from the pot and let cool. Add escarole, celery, carrots, tomato, and onion to the pot. Cover and simmer over low heat for 15 minutes. Add meatballs and simmer for 15 minutes until no pink remains in center. Remove chicken meat from bones, break up into bite size pieces, and return to pot.

About 15 minutes before serving time, bring a medium pot of water to a boil over high heat. Add salt to taste. Stir in the pasta and cook al dente. Drain and add to soup. Stir well and serve. Pass cheese and pepper at the table.

Serves 8 to 10

TIP: Mom showed me a neat little trick when she was out of tiny soup pasta. She wrapped 8 ounces of spaghetti in a clean dishtowel and crushed them with a rolling pin for instant pastina!

Minestra di Lentìcchie con Pomodori e Scarola

Lentil Soup with Tomatoes and Escarole

Lentils are one of the first foods cultivated by man, said to have spread from Asia to Europe. They combine well with tomatoes and greens in this recipe to produce a hearty soup. My cousin, Mimma Dieni Favasuli of Bova Marina, made this soup for me during my most recent visit. It was excellent. She told me that originally the greens used were called *segara*, a wild green. However, escarole or spinach has since replaced it.

1	pound dried lentils, rinsed
6	cups cold *Brodo di Verdura* (Vegetable Broth, page 69) or water
1	bay leaf
1	tablespoon olive oil
1	large onion, coarsely chopped
2	celery stalks and leaves, coarsely chopped
2	cloves garlic, finely minced
1	carrot, thinly sliced
1	16-ounce can Italian plum tomatoes, coarsely chopped
2 to 2½	cups escarole or 4 cups spinach, washed and coarsely chopped
1	tablespoon fresh Italian parsley, finely chopped
1	teaspoon salt
½	teaspoon freshly ground black pepper
1	cup small pasta such as ditalini

In a large soup pot, add the lentils, broth or water, and bay leaf over high heat. Cover and bring to a boil. Lower heat and simmer slowly for 45 minutes, stirring occasionally. Remove bay leaf and discard.

In a small skillet, add the olive oil over medium heat. Sauté the onion, celery, garlic, and carrot for 8 to 10 minutes, stirring often, until the vegetables are soft but not brown. Add to soup pot along with the tomatoes, escarole or spinach, parsley, salt, and pepper. Stir and simmer for 10 to 12 minutes or until lentils are soft.

Bring a medium pot of water to a boil over high heat. Add salt to taste. Stir in the pasta and cook al dente. Drain pasta and add to soup. Stir thoroughly and serve hot.

Serves 6 to 8

Pasta e Fagioli
Pasta and Beans

Italian soul food, some call it. Others call it comfort food. The combination of grains and legumes produces a rustic, thick, and hearty soup that was served often in Calabria and southern Italy. Immigrants brought the humble soup to America, but in time it was abandoned in favor of more sophisticated dishes. Now it is back, appearing on more and more restaurant menus and appreciated by vegetarians and others who want to cut down on meat. Affectionately called *pasta fazool* by Italian-Americans, the dish received national (if not international) recognition when those words appeared in the 1953 song "That's Amore" sung by the late, silky voiced Dean Martin in the film *The Caddy*. It was later the theme song in the 1987 movie *Moonstruck*, giving *pasta fazool* a second surge of popularity.

1	cup dried cannellini beans
2	tablespoons olive oil
1	large onion, coarsely chopped
1	stalk celery with leaves, coarsely chopped
3	large cloves garlic, finely minced
1	pound Italian plum tomatoes, coarsely chopped, or 1 16-ounce can Italian plum tomatoes
4	cups homemade *Brodo di Verdura* (Vegetable Broth, page 69), *Brodo di Pollo* (Chicken Broth, page 68), or water
3	tablespoons fresh Italian parsley, coarsely chopped
1 ½	teaspoon salt
¼	teaspoon crushed red pepper
6 to 8	ounces small pasta such as ditalini or shells

Using the quick soak method, put the rinsed and picked-over cannellini beans in a large pot with twice their quantity of cold water. Bring to a rolling boil and boil rapidly for 2 minutes. Remove from heat, cover, and let stand for 1 hour or more. Drain and rinse in cool water.

In a large soup pot, add the olive oil over medium heat. Sauté the onion, celery, and garlic for 4 to 5 minutes or until vegetables begin to soften. Raise heat and add the beans, tomatoes, water or broth, parsley, salt, and crushed red pepper. Bring to a boil, reduce heat, and simmer covered for up to 60 minutes or until beans are tender.

Bring a large pot of water to a boil over high heat. Add salt to taste. Stir in the pasta and cook al dente. Drain pasta and add to the soup. Stir thoroughly and serve hot.

Serves 6 to 8

Pasta (Lagane) e Ceci
Pasta (or Noodles) with Chickpeas

A meal in one bowl, chickpeas and pasta combine in this old Calabrian dish that exemplifies simple but savory home cooking. This dish is traditionally served on All Souls Day, November 2, but is also enjoyed throughout the year. The diverse texture of the two pasta choices give this dish a dual personality. Try it with the tiny ditalini or the 1-inch-wide lagane, another name for tagliatelle, and taste the difference for yourself.

> 2 16-ounce cans chickpeas
> 1 tablespoon olive oil
> 1 medium onion, coarsely chopped
> 1 stalk celery with leaves, coarsely sliced
> 2 cloves garlic, finely minced
> 4 cups cold water
> 1 16-ounce can Italian plum tomatoes, coarsely chopped
> 2 tablespoons parsley, finely chopped
> 1 bay leaf
> ½ teaspoon salt
> ¼ teaspoon crushed red pepper
> 8 ounces small soup pasta such as ditalini or lagane

Rinse and drain chickpeas and set aside.

In a large saucepan, add olive oil over medium heat. Add onion and celery and sauté for 4 to 6 minutes, or until vegetables are soft but not brown. Add garlic and sauté for 1 to 2 minutes or until a light golden brown. Add chickpeas, water, tomatoes, parsley, bay leaf, salt, and crushed red pepper. Lower heat and simmer for 10 minutes.

Bring a large pot of water to a boil over high heat. Add salt to taste. Stir in pasta of choice and cook al dente. Drain pasta and add to soup. Stir thoroughly, remove bay leaf, and serve hot.

Serves 4 to 6

Pancotto
Tomato and Bread Soup

This flavorful old peasant soup still has wide appeal. Home cooking at its best, *pancotto* translates as cooked bread. All of Italy appears to serve it, even though Calabrians and southern Italians claim it as their own. In northern Italy, it is called *pappa al pomodoro*. It is a testimonial to its great taste that this simple soup from the *povera cucina,* kitchen of the poor, endures. I enjoyed it while in Calabria and serve it at home, especially when fresh tomatoes are in season.

2	tablespoons extra-virgin olive oil
1	medium white or red onion, coarsely chopped
3	cloves garlic, finely minced
2	pounds very ripe tomatoes or 1 28-ounce can Italian plum tomatoes
4	cups homemade *Brodo di Verdura* (Vegetable Broth, page 69), *Brodo di Pollo* (Chicken Broth, page 68), or water
½	teaspoon salt
¼	teaspoon crushed red pepper
⅓	loaf of Italian bread, several days old, cut into 1-inch chunks
3	tablespoons fresh basil, thinly slivered
2	tablespoons fresh Italian parsley, finely chopped

In a large, heavy saucepan, add olive oil over medium heat. Add onion and sauté for 3 to 4 minutes or until onion is translucent. Add garlic and sauté for 1 to 2 minutes or until light golden brown.

Plunge tomatoes into boiling water for 10 to 15 seconds. Remove, peel, and chop coarsely. Add tomatoes, broth, salt, and crushed red pepper to saucepan. Lower heat, cover, and simmer for 15 minutes.

Add bread chunks to broth. Simmer for 15 minutes. Remove saucepan from heat. Add basil and parsley. Stir well. Let stand for at least 5 minutes to allow the bread to absorb most of the liquid. The soup will be thick. Ladle into individual soup bowls and drizzle with a tiny circle of extra-virgin oil, if desired. Serve hot or warm.

Serves 4 to 6

Minestrone di Verdura alla Bova Superiore
Vegetable Soup, Bova Superiore Style

My aunt, Catherine Marino Dieni (Zia Teta) of Bova Marina, originally from Bova Superiore, gave me this recipe. It is almost identical to the one my mother made! An easy-to-prepare and wholesome soup, this minestrone is thick, hearty, and bursting with vegetables. At one time in Calabria, this functioned as a one-dish meal. It still can. There are many variations, depending on whatever vegetables are in season.

1	cup dried cannellini beans
2	tablespoons olive oil
1	large onion, coarsely chopped
3	cloves garlic, finely minced
6	cups cold broth or water
2 to 2½	cups escarole, coarsely chopped
1	16-ounce can Italian plum tomatoes, coarsely chopped
1	medium potato, peeled and cut into ½-inch pieces
1	stalk celery with leaves, coarsely chopped
1	carrot, coarsely chopped
2	tablespoons fresh Italian parsley, coarsely chopped
1½	teaspoons salt
½	teaspoon freshly ground black pepper
8	ounces small soup pasta

Using the quick soak method, put the rinsed and picked-over cannellini beans in a large pot with twice their quantity of cold water. Bring to a rolling boil and boil rapidly for 2 minutes. Remove from heat, cover, and let stand for 1 hour or more. Drain and rinse in cool water

In a large soup pot, add olive oil over medium heat. Sauté onion for 3 to 4 minutes or until translucent. Add garlic and sauté for 1 to 2 minutes or until light golden brown. Add beans and broth or water. Lower heat, cover, and simmer for 20 minutes. Add escarole, tomatoes, potato, celery, carrot, parsley, salt, and pepper. Cover and simmer for 15 minutes or until beans are thoroughly cooked.

Bring a large pot of water to a boil over high heat. Add salt to taste. Stir in the pasta and cook al dente. Drain pasta and add to soup. Stir thoroughly and serve hot.

Serves 8

- 1 yellow or red pepper, seeded and cut into ½-inch pieces, can be sautéed with the onion.
- ½ small eggplant, cut into ½-inch pieces, can be sautéed with the onion.
- 4 cups spinach, coarsely chopped, can be substituted for the escarole.

Zuppa di Asparagi con Uova e Formaggio
Asparagus Soup with Eggs and Cheese

Quick, nutritious, and delicious, this soup tastes best when homemade chicken broth is used. Serve it chunky as is, or pureed in a food processor or blender. If you puree it, do so before you add the egg mixture. If you plan to freeze it, do not add the egg mixture until just before serving.

1½	pounds fresh asparagus
2	tablespoons olive oil
2	cloves garlic, finely minced
1	quart homemade *Brodo di Pollo* (Chicken Broth, page 68) or water
½	teaspoon salt
¼	teaspoon freshly ground black pepper
2	large eggs
4	tablespoons freshly grated pecorino or Parmesan cheese
1	tablespoon fresh Italian parsley, finely chopped
4 to 6	half-inch slices day-old Italian bread

Wash and trim tough ends of asparagus. Pat dry with paper towels. Cut into 1-inch pieces.

In a large soup pot, heat olive oil over medium heat. Add garlic and sauté for 1 to 2 minutes or until light golden brown. Remove garlic and reserve.

Add asparagus to the pot and sauté for 3 to 4 minutes, turning frequently or until lightly browned. Return reserved garlic to the pot and add broth or water, salt, and pepper. Lower heat and simmer for 10 to 12 minutes or until asparagus is tender.

In a small bowl, beat the eggs. Add cheese and parsley. Mix ½ cup of the soup slowly into the eggs. Remove pot from stove and dribble the egg mixture into the soup in a thin stream, stirring constantly. Return pot to the burner and raise heat. Heat just until soup is thickened.

Put bread in individual soup bowls. Ladle hot soup over the bread. If desired, additional cheese can be passed at the table.

Serves 4 to 6

Zuppa di Finocchio
Fennel Soup

Calabrians enjoy the sweet licorice flavor of this Mediterranean vegetable and serve it in a variety of ways. It always appears on antipasti tables on Christmas Eve and Christmas Day. It is also added to pasta sauces. Here fennel stars as the main ingredient in a quick-to-fix soup. Serve it over chunks of stale Italian bread. The bread retains its crunch while soaking up the flavor.

> 3 large heads of fennel (about 2 to 2¼ pounds)
> 2 tablespoons extra-virgin olive oil
> 2 cloves garlic, finely minced
> 4 cups homemade *Brodo di Manzo* (Beef Broth, page 68),
> *Brodo di Verdura* (Vegetable Broth, page 69), or water
> 1 tablespoon fresh Italian parsley, finely chopped
> ½ teaspoon salt
> ¼ teaspoon freshly ground black pepper
> 4 to 6 half-inch slices day-old Italian bread
> 4 to 6 tablespoons freshly grated pecorino cheese

Cut off the feathery stems of the fennel. Strip off the stringy outer layer. Wash, rinse, and pat dry with paper towels. Chop coarsely and set aside.

In a large saucepan, heat olive oil over medium heat. Sauté garlic for 1 to 2 minutes or until light golden brown. Add the fennel and sauté for 5 to 8 minutes or until fennel is lightly browned. Add broth or water, parsley, salt, and pepper. Bring to a boil. Lower heat and let simmer for 30 to 35 minutes or until fennel is tender.

The soup can be served as is or pureed in a food processor or blender for a smoother texture. Put bread in individual soup bowls and sprinkle 1 tablespoon cheese over each slice of bread. Ladle hot soup over the bread and serve immediately.

Serves 4 to 6

Zuppa di Pesce
Fish Soup with Tomatoes, Shrimp, and Cod

This tasty, tangy, and tantalizing soup qualifies as a one-dish meal, is easy to prepare, and is ready to eat in 30 minutes. Plan in advance to have some day-old Italian bread; otherwise, toast fresh Italian bread or other solid country-style bread.

- 1 pound cod or haddock
- 1 pound medium shrimp
- 1 tablespoon olive oil
- 1 medium onion, coarsely chopped
- 2 celery stalks with leaves, finely sliced
- 1 28-ounce can Italian plum tomatoes, coarsely chopped
- 3 cups homemade *Brodo di Pesce* (Fish Broth, page 69), *Brodo di Verdura* (Vegetable Broth, page 69), or water
- 3 tablespoons fresh Italian parsley, finely chopped, divided
- 1 bay leaf
- ½ teaspoon oregano
- ¼ teaspoon freshly ground black pepper or crushed red pepper
- 4 half-inch slices day old crusty bread

Thoroughly but quickly rinse cod or haddock under cold running water, cut into 1-inch pieces, and set aside. Rinse shrimp and set aside. Do not shell shrimp yet.

In a large saucepan, add olive oil over medium heat. Stir in onion and celery and sauté for 8 to 10 minutes or until celery is tender. Add tomatoes, broth or water, 2 tablespoons parsley, bay leaf, oregano, and pepper. Simmer for 10 minutes. Lower heat, then add shrimp and cod. Cover and cook for 1 minute. Remove shrimp, shell, and devein. Meanwhile, let soup simmer for 4 or 5 minutes or until cod is almost cooked through. Return shrimp to pot and let simmer for 1 minute or until shrimp is heated through. Remove bay leaf.

Put bread in individual soup bowls and ladle hot soup over bread. Sprinkle with remaining parsley and serve immediately.

Serves 6 to 8

Zuppa di Pesce con Olive e Vino
Fish Soup with Olives and Wine

Calabrian fish soups contain more fish than those of northern Italy. This soup contains a mound of flat fish and shellfish. The recipe originated in the ancient town of Crotone. There is leeway in the choice and proportion of each fish. However, the gross amount should be about 5 pounds, and the net cleaned amount should be about 3½ to 4 pounds. These days you can often buy squid already cleaned. If not, to clean squid, refer to *Frutti di Mare* (Marinated Seafood Salad, page 199).

¾	pound each of squid, mussels, whiting, flounder, red mullet, cod, and shrimp
2	tablespoons olive oil
1	onion, coarsely chopped
2	cloves garlic, finely minced
8	cups *Brodo di Pesce* (Fish Broth, page 69)
1	cup dry white wine
½	cup black olives, brine-cured, pitted and halved
2	celery stalks with leaves, finely sliced
4	tablespoons fresh Italian parsley, coarsely chopped, divided
1	bay leaf
1½	teaspoons salt
½	teaspoon crushed red pepper
6 to 8	half-inch slices day-old Italian bread

Wash and clean or rinse fish thoroughly. Cut larger fish into large chunks and set aside. Because you will add the shellfish to the liquid in their shells, it is important to rid them of all sand. Do not shell shrimp yet.

In a very large soup pot, heat olive oil over medium heat. Sauté onion for 3 to 4 minutes or until translucent. Add garlic and sauté 1 to 2 minutes or until a light golden brown. Add the squid and wine and cook for 5 minutes.

Meanwhile, in another large pot, add scrubbed mussels to 2 cups cold water over medium-high heat. Cover and steam until they open. Remove with slotted spoon and set aside. Discard any that do not open. Strain liquid with cheesecloth and add liquid to soup pot. Add the whiting, flounder, red mullet, olives, celery, 3 tablespoons parsley, bay leaf, salt, and crushed red pepper. Simmer slowly for 10 minutes.

Add the cod, mussels, and shrimp. Simmer for 1 minute. Remove shrimp, shell, devein, and rinse. Lower heat and simmer soup for another 5 to 7 minutes or until all other fish is cooked through. Return shrimp to pot and simmer for 1 to 2 minutes or until shrimp are heated through. Remove bay leaf.

Put bread in individual soup bowls and ladle hot soup over bread. Sprinkle with the remaining parsley and serve immediately.

Serves 8 to 10

VARIATION: For an altogether different presentation, add one 16-ounce can of Italian plum tomatoes, coarsely chopped, along with the squid and wine.

Zuppa di Cipolle, Licurdia
Onion Soup

The Calabrian version of onion soup is sweet yet assertive and is ready in less than an hour. If you are unaccustomed to hot spices, begin with less crushed red pepper. Native to the town of Cosenza, onion soup gained importance throughout southern Italy. Vegetarians can substitute vegetable broth or water for the chicken broth. Soup served over stale Italian bread has a texture not to be missed—quite different from soft non-Italian bread.

>   2   tablespoons olive oil
>   2   pounds sweet onions, thinly sliced
>   1   teaspoon crushed red pepper
>   2   quarts homemade *Brodo di Pollo* (Chicken Broth, page 68),
>   *Brodo di Manzo* (Beef Broth, page 68), or water
> 1½   teaspoons salt
>   8   half-inch slices day-old Italian bread
>   8   tablespoons freshly grated pecorino cheese

In a large saucepan, add the olive oil over medium heat. Sauté the onions and crushed red pepper for 4 to 5 minutes, or until a pale gold.

Add the broth or water and salt, cover, and bring to a boil. Lower heat and simmer for 40 minutes. Uncover and let simmer for an additional 10 minutes or until the onions are fully cooked.

Put bread in individual serving dishes, ladle soup over the bread, sprinkle with cheese, and serve immediately.

Serves 6 to 8

TIP: If using canned broth, omit the salt.

Zuppa di Piselli
Pea Soup

A hearty, steaming dish of pea soup is a treat from fall through spring. The savory dish is easy to make and, like most soups, freezes well. Vegetarians can enjoy it by omitting the bone.

1	ham, pork, or veal bone
8	cups cold water
1	large onion, coarsely chopped
1	stalks celery with leaves, coarsely sliced
1	carrot, coarsely chopped
1	large ripe tomato, coarsely chopped
1	bay leaf
½	teaspoon salt
¼	teaspoon freshly ground black pepper
1	pound split green peas
6 to 8	half-inch slices day-old Italian bread
	freshly grated pecorino or Parmesan cheese

In a large pot over high heat, add all ingredients except peas and bring to a boil. Immediately lower heat, cover, and simmer for 1 hour.

Remove bone and discard. Add peas and simmer for 50 to 55 minutes or until peas are tender. Remove bay leaf.

Put bread in individual soup bowls. Ladle soup over the bread and serve hot. Pass grated cheese at the table.

Serves 6 to 8

PASTA, SALSE, E POLENTA

PASTA, SAUCES, AND POLENTA

*La differenza fra 'u Re e me e ca 'u Re manga quanto pasta vuole,
ma io mango quanto pasta tenio.*

The difference between the King and me is that the King eats as much pasta
as he likes, while I eat as much pasta as I've got.

C ALABRIAN PROVERB

Pasta is the jewel of Italian cuisine. It is, in fact, a cultural trademark. The serving of pasta is still a rite in Calabria, and Calabrians treat it with utmost reverence. If they have a relative or friend down on his luck, they will say, "There will always be a plate of macaroni for you in our house," with deeper and more caring meaning than might first be thought.

Pasta is so central to the cuisine and such serious business that in times past, a girl was expected to be skilled at making 15 different shapes of homemade *maccarruni*, as it is called in Calabrian dialect, in order to be considered marriageable. In today's world, that is no longer the case, but most young Italian girls are still taught to make some homemade pastas for use at least on holidays and special occasions.

So revered is pasta in Italy that there is an entire museum in Rome dedicated to it. The *Museo Nazionale delle Paste Alimentari* (Italian National Pasta Museum) contains colorful displays devoted to pasta and its preparation throughout the ages. Housed in an elegant 11-room Renaissance palace, the museum, which opened in 1993, is located near the Trevi Fountain. Its predecessor, the *Museo Storico degli Spaghetti* (Historical Spaghetti Museum), was located in Pontedassio, near Genoa, having closed in the late 1980s.

The museum's ancient documents reveal that pasta is one of the oldest foods, dating as far back as 5000 B.C. Displays include historical maps illustrating the spread of pasta throughout the Mediterranean, exhibits explaining the development of its various shapes, and ancient kitchen utensils. Lithographs, graphics, and etchings depict scenes of the Italian's love of pasta. Etruscans made reference to it in 600 B.C.; forests in Sicily were cut down to grow wheat and maintain a granary for the Roman Empire. The Romans made some form of noodles and gnocchi from excess wheat and dried them in the sun.

Reference to pasta is made in the most ancient of European cooking books written by first-century Roman gastronome Marcus Apicius, entitled *De re Coquinaria* (*Concerning Cooking*). He described lasagne, gnocchi, vermicelli, and a chopped meat sauce. According to Joseph Dommers Vehling, who translated Apicius' book into English in 1936, one need look only to southern Mediterranean cooking to find Apician traditions still alive!

A bas-relief carving found in Etton Cerviteri, 30 miles north of Rome, depicted tools that are still used today to make pasta; a reference to pasta was found in eighth-century Greek writings; and in the mid-1300s pasta was mentioned in Boccaccio's classic *Decameron*. All this occurred long before the birth of Marco Polo. The myth that Marco introduced pasta from China is just that, a myth.

Southern Italians have even fought for their pasta. In the mid 1600s, the people of Bari, Apulia, revolted against the Spaniards who, after taxing just about everything else in sight, tried to tax flour. Legend has it that an added indignity simultaneously imposed on them was that soldiers were allowed to monitor the amount of flour used in the kitchen. Protecting their women and protesting the taxes brought on a week of determined fighting. The Spaniards relented and abolished the tax.

Pasta certainly caught on quickly in America. Thomas Jefferson was among the first to bring a pasta machine here from Italy. Here and in the rest of the world, Italian restaurants abound where a variety of pasta dishes are served. Pasta is an international favorite. Even in France, where once only French cuisine appeared on menus, many restaurants now include at least one pasta dish.

Pasta is versatile and exciting. You can stuff it with ricotta cheese, meat, spinach, vegetables, or fish; you can bake it with meat, cheese, vegetables, or a combination thereof. You can boil and dress it with sauces that are spicy and tangy or mellow and sweet, red or white, to which you can add vegetables, meat, fish, or other tantalizing ingredients. And you can add various sizes and shapes of pasta to soups and stews.

Pasta comes in a rainbow of colors. You can color it green by adding spinach, red by adding a pureed red pepper or tomato concentrate, yellow by adding eggs, a soft, light brown by adding whole wheat flour. Designer pasta, as I call it, comes flavored with lemon or garlic, or artichoke or asparagus. And you can serve pasta hot or cold, though cold pasta salads are an American concoction frowned upon by Italians. *Pasta* is the generic term for the many different products on the market today, but when I was a little girl, we used the term *macaroni*.

Each city and village in southern Italy and Calabria has its own homemade pasta specialty. Names and shapes vary from town to town depending on the local lore. Calabrians are known for several but foremost for their wonderfully chewy fusilli, which they lovingly refer to as *maccarruni*. It is said that they learned how to make fusilli from the Arabs. They fashioned bits of dough around a piece of metal similar to a knitting needle to create hollow shapes that dried faster. For those wishing to try their hand at making fusilli, included is *Fusilli Fatti col Ferro* (Fusilli Made with an Iron Tool, page 100).

I ate fusilli three times in my most recent visit to Calabria while researching this book. First, at my aunt Katherine Dieni's home where she and my cousins Mimma Favasuli and Mary Cuppari made them especially for me. I was thrilled to observe how adept they were at magically transforming the dough into such a delightful treat! Aunt Teta and I helped, and before very long, we had made enough fusilli to feed 15. Topped with Mimma's chunky tomato-based herb sauce, the dish and the rest of the meal were sensational.

Later in the week, Ellenia and her husband (my cousin) Rocco Minniti, invited us to a gathering in their gracious home to celebrate their daughter Manella's eighteenth birthday. In addition to other visually appealing and delicious treats—home cooking at its best—we were served fusilli with a savory *sugo*.

Finally, I ate fusilli in Antica Trattoria La Locanda di Alia, a handsome restaurant in Castrovillari, in northern Calabria, considered one of the best in the province. The chefs and owners, Gaetano and Pinuccio Alia, told me their fusilli were eggless. I was charmed by the quote on the menu by Virginia Woolf: "You cannot think well, you cannot love well, if you do not eat well." Especially fitting, I thought, for that part of the world.

Calabrians are also generally credited with perfecting lasagne, which has become an international favorite. Derived from the Latin word *lasanum*, meaning pots, the ancient Romans served a form of lasagne. I have included two very different but equally luscious lasagne recipes. The famed multi-layered *Sagne Chjine* (Calabrian Lasagne with Vegetables and Tiny Meatballs, page 104), is Calabria's finest version, worthy of the most elegant occasion. A less intricate but no less delicious lasagne is *Lasagne al Forno* (Baked Lasagne, page 103).

Homemade pasta is easier to make than you can imagine. Prior to pasta machines, pasta was kneaded, rolled to the desired thickness with a long rolling pin, and cut by hand. My dad, and many other Italian-Americans, fashioned a three-foot rolling pin out of a broom handle for Mom to use. She made homemade pasta quite often.

Today, there are literally hundreds of delicious sauces to complement various types of pasta, of which tomato-based sauces are king, especially in sun-drenched southern Italy where the tomato is revered. Tomato sauces vary from one region to another, one village to another, and even one family to another.

Some are lusty and tangy, some are light or hearty; some are ready in 20 to 30 minutes, others must simmer longer.

Since tomatoes are so basic to Italian cooking, it surprises many to learn that the tomato did not reach Europe until the sixteenth century. Europeans were slow to discover its use; southern Italians were the first to recognize its culinary potential. They began experimenting with it and soon cooks and chefs were crafting delectable tomato sauces, which exalted pasta into a national treasure, opening up a new world of flavors. The latest good news for tomato sauce lovers is that a six-year study conducted by Dr. Edward Giovanucci of the Harvard School of Public Health found cooked tomatoes to be rich in lycopene, an antioxidant that may protect men against prostate cancer.

To their beloved tomato sauces, Calabrians began adding other ingredients, creating pasta toppings that demonstrated their vast imagination and inventiveness. Some sauces contain vegetables such as eggplant, mushrooms, broccoli, peppers, artichokes, cauliflower, and zucchini, while others contain fish, chicken or meat, broth, wine, cheese, olives, capers, anchovies, bread crumbs, and, of course, a wide variety of herbs. The combinations are endless. Is it any wonder that Calabrians proudly state that their creativity begins in the kitchen?

Yet not all sauces contain tomatoes, even in the south. Calabrians also produce other terrific sauces *senza pomodori*, as they proudly point out. Seafood and pasta have long been natural partners. Combining them in a sauce called *Pasta alle Vongole in Bianco* (Pasta with White Clam Sauce, page 109) was so successful, it became referred to as the queen of pasta and seafood sauces. Another is the unusual and appetizing *Pasta con le Sarde e Finocchio* (Pasta with Sardines and Fresh Fennel, page 114). Another simple but sassy sauce is made with olive oil, anchovies, garlic, herbs, and sprinkled with toasted bread crumbs, *Pasta con Alici e Mollica* (Pasta with Anchovies and Toasted Bread Crumbs, page 106). Calabrians also create pasta toppings with vegetables, as in the tangy *Pasta con Broccoli* (Pasta with Broccoli, Anchovies, Pine Nuts, and Pecorino Cheese, page 108). These are a few examples of imaginative and satisfying sauces, without tomatoes, born of simplicity but elevated to an enticing level.

With all of these options, Calabrians have a knack for knowing which ingredient in what proportion to add to a sauce. A simple tomato sauce with onion, garlic, and basil is refreshing—add capers and it takes on a tangy flavor; add mashed anchovies or olives with a pinch of crushed red pepper and it yields a piquant taste; add prosciutto and it becomes a triumph, a creation fit for royalty!

Calabrians (and all Italians) seem to know instinctively how to match the right sauces to the right pastas. Thin sauces such as anchovy or clam sauces go well with thin pasta like angel hair, thin spaghetti, or linguine. Most regular tomato sauces go well with regular spaghetti or short macaroni such as ziti. Hearty meat sauces pair well with large pastas, and light sauces such as marinara sauce work best with fresh pasta. A sauce that contains pine nuts is best served with a pasta that will entrap them, such as farfalle or shells.

Calabrians also understand that a sauce is only as good as its ingredients. They, and all southern Italians, stress the importance of using the freshest tomatoes, the fleshy plum variety—sweet and soft. For Americans, depending on the season and one's region, top-quality canned tomatoes may be better than fresh. Even though Calabria has a long growing season, one can see tomatoes set out to dry in the sun for use when fresh tomatoes are not available (cherry tomatoes are the favorites—small but with big taste). Sun-dried tomatoes provide intense flavor and chewy texture when added to sauces, soups, or vegetable dishes.

Italians also insist on fresh herbs and good-quality olive oil. The difference between fresh and dried herbs is enormous. Fortunately, these days, fresh herbs are available in most markets year-round. The two Calabrians use most frequently are basil and parsley. It has been said that basil and tomatoes are lovers, and so they are. Basil is included in many dishes, especially those that contain tomatoes. Flat Italian parsley is much more flavorful and aromatic than the curly type. Basil and parsley should be added near the end of the cooking period for maximum flavor. Alternately, half can be added at the beginning and half at the end.

The aromas that float out of Italian kitchens when any of these sauces are cooking are not only tempting to the family but also the envy of the neighborhood. Over the years, our non-Italian neighbors had a way of coming over to chat, peek into the pot, and get a taste. Often the taste was accompanied by a sip of Dad's homemade wine. My sister and I swooned over those aromas. As little girls, we rushed home from church hungry from fasting since the previous night in order to receive Holy Communion. We inhaled the wonderful aromas that permeated the house as we dashed into the kitchen, quickly broke the fast, and devoured a slice of homemade bread covered with sauce and sometimes a meatball or a sausage.

I remember hearing sauces called by different names: *salsa, ragu, sugo,* and even gravy. *Salsa* is the name most often used to describe a meatless tomato sauce, *ragu* to describe a tomato sauce that contains one or more meats—a sort of stew as in *Ragu con Carne Varie* (Tomato Sauce with a Variety of Meats, page 132). *Sugo* describes a sauce with or without meat, meat stock, or vegetables but generally cooked longer than *salsas*. However, I am told that over the years the terms *ragu* and *sugo* became interchangeable, and today only *ragu* is used. Tomato paste is sometimes added to a *ragu* to give it a darker, deeper texture and taste, but less often, if ever, to a *salsa*.

In Italy, pasta, listed under *primi piatti* on menus, is served after antipasto and before the fish or meat dish, called the *secondo piatto*. However, both in Italy and in the United States, pasta is often the main course served with or without a small portion of fish or meat. Pasta dishes are referred to as *pasta asciutta* (dry pasta), meaning pasta served with little or no liquid, as opposed to *pasta in brodo*, meaning pasta served in broth or soups.

When cooking pasta, use at least 5 quarts of water per pound of pasta but do not add salt if you want it to boil faster. After the water boils, add up to 1½ tablespoons of salt to taste when you add the pasta. Do not add oil to the water to prevent pasta from sticking. Adding oil only causes the sauce to slide off the pasta when you want it to cling. Instead, stir pasta frequently with a wooden fork to separate it and to prevent sticking. Never rinse pasta; it should be served hot! Rather than rinsing in cold water to stop the cooking process, remove when it is still al dente (literally translated as "to the tooth" but meaning "just until firm and chewy"). And rather than drain every last drop of water, let a tiny amount remain to keep it from sticking.

Above all, ignore instructions on most packages on how long to cook pasta. If you don't you may end up with mush. Many instructions call for too much cooking time. Pastas made with different wheat, in different sizes and shapes, take different amounts of time to cook; therefore, it is difficult to give exact cooking times. Recipes in this book call for cooking pasta al dente. When cooking pasta, it is important to stay on top of it, tasting it often. One minute it is too hard, yet in another minute it will be *stracatto*—overcooked. One must also realize that pasta continues to cook after it is strained and a hot sauce added. To retain its heat, pasta should be served in soup plates.

Happily for pasta lovers, pasta is perhaps the original fast food. Many sauces take no longer to prepare than for the pasta to cook. Furthermore, pasta is one of the world's most perfect foods. Ranking low on the food pyramid released by the U.S. Department of Agriculture, it is high in energy and low in fat. One cup of cooked pasta contains about 200 calories, one gram of fat, lots of iron and B-vitamins, and if you make or buy eggless pasta, there is no cholesterol. Pasta is a great source of energy, better than potatoes, and with more protein as well. International marathon runners eat heaping dishes of pasta the night before a race, a blissfully indulged custom in the North End, the Italian section of Boston, with its charming Old World atmosphere.

Busy Italians can buy a wide variety of homemade macaroni at the local *pastificio*, where it is made fresh daily, or in the supermarket. It is a treat to walk the aisles of an Italian supermarket to view the hundreds of intriguing sizes and shapes of first-rate dried pastas available—round, square, curved, coiled, ridged, tiny, mid-sized, huge; shaped like bows, ears, animals, rice, and so on.

Their American counterparts can also buy several varieties of homemade fresh pasta at most supermarkets including fettuccine, linguine, angel hair, tortellini, ravioli, and gnocchi. Almost 150 different pasta shapes are produced in the United States. Italian specialty stores have a wide selection of homemade fresh pastas and usually carry a greater variety of imported dried pastas than do supermarkets. Pasta imported from Italy, also available in most supermarkets and all Italian specialty stores, is made from durum wheat and is far superior to other kinds.

Governments may come and go, but one thing in Italy never changes: Italians love pasta. It is part of the heart and soul of Italy. It is the very essence of being Italian. For pasta is the jewel of Italian cuisine!

Some large pastas are:

Bocconcini	Grooved tube, 1½-inches long
Bucatini	Long, thick hollow tubes
Canellini	Tiny reeds
Cannelloni	Large reeds, for stuffing
Capelli d'angelo	Angel hair
Capellini	Very fine strands, slightly thicker than capelli d'angelo
Cavatelli	Small hollow shells
Conchiglie	Medium shells
Conchiglioni	Large shells, for stuffing
Ditali	Medium tubular shapes, ½-inch long
Farfalle	Large butterflies, shaped like bow ties
Fettuccine	Small ribbons, ¼-inch-wide homemade noodles (also called tagliarini, tagliolini)
Fusilli	Short spiral, curly strands
Fusilli bucati	Long curly strands with a hole
Gemelli	Twins—short spaghetti lengths, twisted like a rope
Gnocchi	Medium oblong shells made with potatoes or ricotta
Lasagne	Large, egg or plain, wide flat sheets of pasta for baking
Linguine	Narrow, flat noodles about ⅛-inch wide
Macceroncelli	Tube shaped pasta
Manicotti	Very large tubular pasta, usually for filling with ricotta
Mezzani	Medium-sized macaroni, narrower than ziti, 2½-inches long, plain or grooved
Mostaccioli	Smooth or grooved, hollow tubular pasta cut diagonally into 2½-inch lengths

Pappardelle	Wide ribbons about 1-inch wide
Penne	Pens, tubular pasta with ends cut on the diagonal, 2½-inches long, plain or ridged
Perciatelli	Small pierced pasta, slightly larger than spaghetti
Ravioli	Square pasta, about 2 inches, filled with cheese, meat, vegetables, or spinach
Rigatoni	Large, grooved, tubular pasta cut into 3-inch lengths
Rotelle	Medium spirals
Rotini	Small spirals
Shells	Seashells, various sizes
Spaghetti	Long, thin tubular lengths
Spaghettini	Long, very thin tubular lengths
Tagliarini	Homemade noodles, ¼-inch wide
Tagliatelle	Homemade noodles, ¾-inch wide
Vermicelli	Long, very thin tubular lengths, thicker than capellini but thinner than spaghettini
Ziti	tubular macaroni, cut into 2½-inch lengths, plain or grooved

Some small pastas added to soups are:

Acini di pepe	Tiny round or square pasta dots called peppercorns because they resemble them
Cappelletti	Small pasta shaped like little hats
Cappelli di prete	Small pasta shaped like priests' hats
Conchigliette	Tiny shells
Ditalini	Small tubular shapes, ¼-inch long
Farfallette	Small bows or butterflies
Farfalline	Tiny bows
Orzo	Small pasta that resembles rice
Pasta grattata	Homemade pasta, rolled into a ball, and grated on a flat grater
Pastina	Tiny flat pasta, sometimes in the shape of stars, ⅛-inch in diameter
Pastina al uova	Shaped like pastina but made with eggs
Stelle	Star-shaped pasta
Stelline	Small stars
Tortellini	Small ring-shaped macaroni, stuffed with cheese or meat
Tubettini	Tiny tubular shapes, ⅛-inch long

POLENTA
CORNMEAL

Polenta cannot be ignored when discussing pasta because polenta, more than pasta or bread, was one of the few staples of *la cucina povera* (the poor kitchen) or *la cucina invernale* (the winter kitchen). In ancient times, it supplanted pasta and bread of necessity since wheat was far more expensive. It thus became known as "the meat of the poor." The name *polenta* derives from the Roman word *pulmentum*, originally describing a cereal, coarse gruel, millet, or even ground chestnuts, not corn. A semi-coarse ground corn, today's polenta is either yellow or white, although yellow is more typical. It serves as a basis for many dishes and is quite versatile. The leftover mush can be cooled and sliced, then toasted, baked, fried, sautéed, or grilled.

The cultivation of corn began in Spain and Portugal in the early 1500s from the seeds brought by Columbus after his 1492 voyage. By the early 1500s, it was introduced to various regions in Italy. It took several decades before it spread throughout Europe, England, and eventually Asia. In southern France, it was first grown for ornamental purposes only. During the famine of the early 1600s, peasants everywhere were grateful for affordable cornmeal. Unfortunately, although polenta was filling, it lacked wheat's nutrients, and for those whose diet included little else, vitamin deficiency resulted. It wasn't until after World War II that extensive polenta usage began to diminish, but by no means did it disappear. Today very popular, it is served by choice. In some parts of Italy, polenta continues to be served at Carnivale and other festivals.

Although Naples, Lombardy, and Veneto were the front-runners of various polenta dishes, it has traditionally been a staple and mainstay more of northern Italy, appearing first as a main dish and then as a side dish. Southern Italians have always preferred pasta to polenta; however, occasionally they too prepare it for their table.

Calabrians often serve soft polenta as a cereal with milk. It is one of the first solid foods given to children after they are weaned. However, they too cook it firm and add toppings such as cheese, sauce, vegetables, and meats. I have included a favorite Calabrian recipe of polenta and sausage as well as a simpler recipe.

Pasta Fresca all' Uova
Homemade Pasta with Eggs

Every little girl in Calabria and southern Italy is lovingly taken by the hand by her mother or grandmother (as my mother did with me) and taught to make several varieties of fresh pasta. When my mother made "homemade macaroni," she would place a white bed sheet, reserved for this purpose only, on the bed. The strips, and later the cut pasta, were placed on the bed sheet to dry until ready to use. Mom's rolling pin, made by Dad, was fashioned from a broom handle, 3 feet long with smooth, rounded edges. Homemade pasta is not difficult to make with or without a pasta machine. Get the children to help; they love making it. Make it a leisurely Sunday family project.

Use this dough to make tagliarini, tagliatelle, thin soup noodles, lasagne, and fusilli, but not ravioli. You can substitute all fancy durum flour for the unbleached or all-purpose flour, or you can use part fancy durum, from ½ cup to 1½ cups. If using all durum flour, add 1 tablespoon olive oil; if using half or part durum only, reduce the amount of oil accordingly.

> 3½ **cups plus 2 tablespoons unbleached or all-purpose flour**
> 4 **eggs**
> 1 **teaspoon salt**

Mound 3½ cups flour and salt on a floured surface. Make a well in the center, gradually add eggs, and with a fork beat eggs lightly. Gradually pull in flour until it is absorbed. If dough seems too sticky, add a bit more flour; if it is too hard and doesn't mix easily, add a few drops of water. Mix dough well and form into a ball. Proceed with instructions for using pasta machine or for rolling by hand.

Using pasta machine: Pasta machines have two parts: one for rolling and one for cutting. Set machine at its widest setting for rolling. Break off dough the size of a golf ball. Turn the machine handle to pass the dough through the machine 8 times to knead, folding the dough in half and lowering the setting 1 notch each time until you reach the next-to-last notch. Place flat, unfolded strips on a lightly floured surface or bed sheet. Let rest for 10 minutes to make cutting easier. Repeat process until all dough is rolled out.

Remove the rolling part of the pasta machine and add the cutting attachment. Pass strips of pasta through the desired cutting slot, wide for fettuccine or thin for soup noodles. Place on floured surface or bed sheet and sprinkle lightly with flour until ready to cook.

Rolling by hand: Put dough on floured surface; knead for 7 minutes or until dough is smooth, evenly golden colored, and elastic. Scrape away loose or caked dough; place dough on lightly floured surface; cover with large bowl; and let rest for at least 10 minutes to make cutting easier.

Break off dough the size of a golf ball and, with a rolling pin, roll each into a thin strip, about 1/16-inch thick. Place on a floured surface or bed sheet and sprinkle lightly with flour. Repeat process until all dough is rolled out.

When all strips are rolled, flour both sides so dough will not stick. Roll up each strip in jelly-roll fashion. With a sharp knife and without applying too much pressure on the dough, cut crosswise into the desired width. You also can cut individual strips with a pastry wheel. Gently unfold strips, shake to separate, and put on a floured surface or bed sheet until ready to cook.

Serves 4

TIP: Homemade, fresh pasta takes less time to cook than dried pasta and does not get al dente. It cooks in 1 to 2 minutes, so do not leave unattended.

Pasta Fresca senza Uova
Homemade Pasta without Eggs

Eggless homemade pasta is close to commercial dry pasta. This dough was (and is) used by Calabrians and southern Italians, possibly when they could not afford eggs. Very few American cookbooks carry an eggless fresh pasta recipe. This dough, like dough with eggs, makes the following homemade pastas: tagliarini, tagliatelle, thin soup noodles, lasagne, or fusilli, but not ravioli.

3¼   cups plus 2 tablespoons semolina flour
       (or all-purpose or unbleached flour)
   1   teaspoon salt
   1   tablespoon olive oil
   1   cup warm water

Mound 3¼ cups flour and salt on a floured surface. Make a well in the center, gradually add oil and water, and with a fork gradually pull in flour until it is absorbed. If dough is too sticky, add a bit more flour; if it is too hard and doesn't mix easily, add a few drops of water. Mix dough well and form into a ball. Proceed with instructions for using pasta machine or rolling by hand.

Using pasta machine: Follow directions for *Pasta Fresca all' Uova* (Homemade Pasta with Eggs, page 98).

Rolling by hand: Follow directions for *Pasta Fresca all' Uova* (Homemade Pasta with Eggs, page 98), except allow dough to rest 15 minutes instead of 10.

TIP: Homemade, fresh pasta takes less time to cook than dried pasta and does not get al dente. It cooks in 1 to 2 minutes, so do not leave unattended.

Fusilli Fatti col Ferro
Fusilli Made with an Iron Tool

Fusilli are the favorite homemade Calabrian macaroni. They are also called *fusilli alla Silana* after the Sila mountain region. In dialect, they are called *maccarruni a ru ferru.* Shaped like a loose coil or corkscrew, each fusilli hold lots of sauce in its twists. During my last trip to Calabria, my Aunt Teta and cousins Mimma Favasuli and Maria Cuppari of Bova Marina made them as part of the midday meal. I was thrilled to see how adept they were at magically transforming the dough into such a treat! Another night, cousins Ellenia and Rocco Minniti of Reggio Calabria invited us to their gracious home to celebrate their daughter Manella's eighteenth birthday. They too served fusilli along with a multi-course meal.

1   Recipe *Pasta Fresca senza Uova* (Homemade Pasta without Eggs, page 99)

Follow directions in first paragraph of instructions, then continue as follows.
Whether using a pasta machine or rolling by hand, cut rolled strips into ¼-inch-by-6-inch pieces. Wrap one end of cut piece securely around the tip of a medium-sized knitting needle, about size 7, which is flat at both ends. Twist the dough around the needle and press to secure end. Roll to flatten slightly and to secure the coil. Slide dough off needle and put fusilli onto a lightly floured surface or bed sheet until ready to cook.

Serves 4

TIP: If you don't have knitting needles, substitute wooden skewers used to pierce foods to be cooked on a grill.

VARIATION: For a slightly softer dough, an egg may be added. In a measuring cup, add 1 egg and beat lightly. Add water to make 1 cup of liquid. Use this mixture in place of the warm water called for.

Truccette con Salsa Ortolana
Homemade Pasta Squares with a Garden Sauce

This dish, a winner and a vegetarian delight, was contributed by Chef Antonio Bonaccorso of the Ristorante Bonaccorso in Reggio Calabria. *Truccette*, from the verb *truccare*, means to make up; *ortolana* means from the garden. A review of the ingredients quickly reveals how the dish earned its name. The combination of tomatoes, peppers, zucchini, and eggplant create a sauce made up from the garden. Although the sauce may be traditional Calabrian, Signor Bonaccorso told me the pasta squares are his creation. The clever turnovers have a delightfully chewy texture. I totally enjoyed this dish and hope you will too!

1 recipe *Pasta Fresca all' Uova* (Homemade Pasta with Eggs, page 98)
3 tablespoons extra-virgin olive oil, divided
1 medium onion, coarsely chopped
2 cloves garlic, finely minced
1 small zucchini, ½ to ¾ pound, unpeeled and sliced
1 small eggplant, ½ to ¾ pound, unpeeled and diced
1 28-ounce can Italian plum tomatoes, coarsely chopped
2 tablespoons fresh Italian parsley, finely chopped, divided
2 tablespoon fresh basil, coarsely chopped, divided
½ teaspoon salt
¼ teaspoon freshly ground black pepper
1 medium red pepper, roasted and sliced
1 medium yellow pepper, roasted and sliced

Follow directions for making and rolling pasta dough. Directions and illustrations for cutting and folding the pasta squares follow at end of this recipe.

In a large, heavy skillet, heat 2 tablespoons olive oil over medium heat. Sauté onion for 3 to 4 minutes or until translucent. Add garlic and sauté for 1 to 2 minutes or until light golden brown. Remove onions and garlic, reserve, and set aside. Add zucchini and eggplant and sauté for 4 to 5 minutes, or until golden brown, stirring frequently. Remove with slotted spoon and add to reserved onions and garlic.

Add remaining tablespoon olive oil. Add tomatoes, 1 tablespoon each of parsley and basil, and salt and pepper. Simmer uncovered for 20 minutes.

Meanwhile, roast peppers as directed for *Peperoni Arrostiti* (Roasted Peppers, page 52). To the tomatoes, add cooked onion, garlic, zucchini, eggplant, roasted pepper strips, and the remaining parsley and basil. Mix thoroughly and simmer for 2 minutes to allow ingredients to blend.

Bring a large pot of water to a boil over high heat. Add salt to taste. Stir in the cut and folded pasta and cook for only 2 to 3 minutes. Do not leave unattended. Drain pasta and put on serving platter. Ladle some sauce over top of pasta and serve immediately. Pass extra sauce at the table.

Serves 4 to 6

Directions for Cutting and Folding Pasta Squares:

Using the drawings below as a guide, cut the rolled strips into 2½-inch squares. Starting at the top right corner, fold over ¼ of the square as shown in illustration 1. Fold over the second ¼ and the third ¼ as shown in Illustration 2 and 3. Once you have folded the fourth and final portion of the square as in Illustration 4, your turnover will be complete. Gently press after the last fold to secure. Roll scrap cuttings into a strip to use all of the dough. Although making these squares is easy, practice making the first one with a piece of paper cut to size, since the dough does not separate easily once folded. Don't worry if any are slightly askew—it won't affect the taste whatsoever.

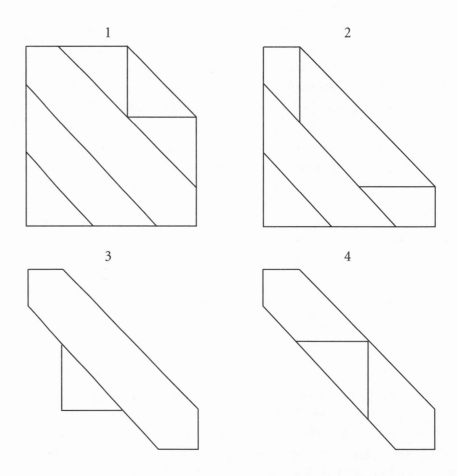

Lasagne al Forno
Baked Lasagne

Lasagne, popular with the ancient Romans, is still a top choice in Calabria and in America. There are many variations, but this meatless version is perhaps the most traditional. I like to use *Salsa Marinara, Pronto!* (Mariner's Style Tomato Sauce—Quick, Easy, and Perky, page 130) with it; however, *Ragu con Carne Tritata* (Tomato Sauce with Ground Meat, page 131) is often used. Lasagne is served on Christmas day in Calabria and in the United States, often accompanied by *Braciole di Manzo alla Calabrese* (Rolled Stuffed Beef, Calabrian Style, page 148). It is so favored that it is served year-round on special occasions. This can be assembled early in the day and refrigerated. Remove 1 hour prior to baking. Final tasting honors go to my son David, his wife, Diane, and my granddaughters, Katherine and Jennifer.

  1 pound fresh or dried lasagne
  2 tablespoons olive oil
  2 pounds fresh ricotta
  4 ounces freshly grated pecorino or Parmesan cheese
  1 large egg, lightly beaten
  2 tablespoons fresh Italian parsley, finely chopped
  ½ teaspoon salt
  ¼ teaspoon freshly ground black pepper
  1 recipe *Salsa Marinara, Pronto!* (Mariner's Style Tomato Sauce—Quick, Easy, and Perky, page 130) or *Ragu con Carne Tritata* (Tomato Sauce with Ground Meat, page 131)
  8 ounces mozzarella cheese, thinly sliced or shredded, divided

If making your own lasagne, follow directions in either *Pasta Fresca all' Uova* (Homemade Pasta with Eggs, page 98) or *Pasta Fresca senza Uova* (Homemade Pasta without Eggs, page 99), except for the last paragraph. Then continue as follows.

Whether using a pasta machine or rolling by hand, cut rolled strips into pieces about 3-inches wide by 14-inches long. Put cut strips onto a lightly floured surface or bed sheet until ready to cook.

Preheat oven to 350° F.

Bring a large pot of water to a boil. Add salt to taste and slowly add the lasagne, stirring frequently. Cook for 2 minutes if fresh or until just under al dente if dried. Plunge into a pan of cold water with 2 tablespoons olive oil added to prevent further cooking and sticking. Drain lasagne and set aside.

In a large bowl, combine the ricotta, pecorino or Parmesan, egg, parsley, salt, and pepper. Set aside.

In a medium saucepan, heat sauce of your choice over medium heat. Let simmer for 5 to 10 minutes.

In a 10-by-14-inch ungreased baking pan, spread a thin layer of sauce, just enough to coat bottom of pan. Add a layer of lasagne, ⅓ of the ricotta mixture, a light layer of sauce (about 4 to 6 tablespoons dotted here and there), and ¼ of the mozzarella. Continue layering in that order, ending with lasagne, sauce, and mozzarella. There should be 4 layers of pasta.

Bake uncovered for 45 to 50 minutes, or until bubbly and the cheese has melted and is golden brown. Let set for 5 minutes to ease cutting. Pass remaining sauce at table.

Serves 8 to 10

Sagne Chjine
Calabrian Lasagne with Vegetables and Tiny Meatballs

This classic masterpiece, worthy of the most elegant occasion, is Calabria's finest version of lasagne. Also called *sagne chine*, it is layered with porcini mushrooms, artichoke hearts, fresh peas, tiny meatballs, hard-boiled eggs, and two cheeses. Unquestionably a spectacular, scrumptious dish, it is perfect for New Year's dinner. Because it is so rich, it comfortably serves as many as 12 as a first course and even more for a buffet. Although the recipe is lengthy and may appear complicated, it really isn't, and much can be done in advance. The sauce and meatballs can be made ahead or frozen; the lasagne, vegetables, and eggs can be cooked and the dish assembled and refrigerated early in the day. An added glory of this exquisite dish is fresh lasagne, either homemade or purchased at an Italian specialty store. A good-quality dried lasagne is acceptable.

1	pound fresh or dried lasagne
1	recipe *Salsa Marinara, Pronto!* (Mariner's Style Tomato Sauce—Quick, Easy, and Perky, page 130)

MEATBALLS:

2	slices dry bread, crusts removed
3 to 4	tablespoons water
¾	pounds very lean, finely ground beef
1	egg, lightly beaten

2 tablespoons freshly grated pecorino or Parmesan cheese
1 tablespoon fresh Italian parsley, finely chopped
1 clove garlic, finely minced
1 teaspoon salt
¼ teaspoon freshly ground black pepper
2 tablespoons olive oil

VEGETABLES:

1 tablespoon olive oil
1 ounce dried porcini mushrooms,
  soaked in warm water for 20 to 25 minutes
1 medium onion, finely chopped
1 10-ounce package frozen artichoke hearts,
  thawed and thinly sliced
1 10-ounce package frozen baby peas, slightly thawed
½ teaspoon salt
¼ teaspoon freshly ground black pepper

OTHER INGREDIENTS:

3 hard-boiled eggs, thinly sliced
12 ounces fresh mozzarella, shredded
½ cup freshly grated pecorino cheese
2 tablespoons olive oil

Making the lasagne: Whether using a pasta machine or rolling by hand, cut rolled strips into pieces 3-inches wide by 14-inches long. Place cut strips onto a lightly floured surface or bed sheet until ready to cook.

Preparing the sauce: In a medium saucepan, heat sauce over medium heat. Let simmer for 5 to 10 minutes.

Preparing the meatballs: In a medium-sized mixing bowl, soak bread in water for several minutes until softened. Squeeze until almost dry and discard liquid. Shred bread and add the beef, egg, cheese, parsley, garlic, salt, and pepper. Mix thoroughly. Shape uniformly into ½-inch meatballs and set aside. Add the olive oil to a large, heavy skillet over medium-high heat. Sauté the meatballs for 5 to 7 minutes, turning frequently, or until lightly browned on all sides and cooked through. Remove, drain on paper towels, and set aside. Wipe skillet clean, but do not wash.

Preparing the vegetables: In the same skillet, heat the oil over medium-high heat. Drain the mushrooms, rinse, and place on paper towels. Sauté the onion for 3 to 4 minutes or until translucent. Slice mushrooms thinly and add to skillet. Add artichoke hearts, peas, salt, and pepper. Sauté for 5 minutes or until vegetables are tender but not mushy. Remove from heat and set aside.

Cooking the pasta: Bring a very large pot of water to a boil over high heat. Add salt to taste and 2 tablespoons olive oil. (This is the exception to the rule that oil should not be added to the water when cooking pasta. In this case, the sauce will not slide off the pasta because it lies flat.) Add pasta, stirring constantly, and cook for 2 minutes, if fresh, or until just under al dente if dried. Have a large bowl of cold water with 2 tablespoons olive oil ready. Remove cooked pasta and plunge into cold water to prevent further cooking and sticking. Drain lasagne and set aside.

Preheat oven to 375° F.

Assembling the Sagne Chjine: Spread a thin layer of sauce over the bottom of a deep 10-by-14-inch baking pan. Add a layer of pasta, ⅓ of the meatballs, ⅓ of the vegetables, 1 sliced egg, a thin layer of sauce, ⅓ of the mozzarella, and ¼ of the pecorino. Continue layering in that order, ending with lasagne and a light covering of sauce. Sprinkle remaining pecorino cheese over the top. There should be 4 layers of pasta.

Bake uncovered for 50 to 60 minutes or until the cheese is lightly browned. Insert a knife tip into center to make sure that the lasagne is cooked through. Let set for 5 to 10 minutes to ease cutting. Cut into desired portions and serve immediately.

Serves 10 to 12

Pasta con Alici e Mollica
Pasta with Anchovies and Toasted Bread Crumbs

Here is proof of yet another way in which Calabrians combine the right amount of the simplest ingredients and work wonders with them. Never wasting a thing, stale bread found its way into sauces, soups, and stuffings. The toasted bread crumbs in this dish provide the crunchy, crowning touch to this pasta topping. It was probably concocted when meat was not affordable and before tomatoes reached Italy. It has withstood the test of time and still has wide appeal.

1   **pound spaghetti or linguine**
¼   **cup reserved pasta water**
4   **tablespoons olive oil, divided**
1   **small onion (optional)**

3 cloves garlic, finely minced

6 anchovy fillets, mashed

3 tablespoons fresh Italian parsley, finely chopped

¼ teaspoon crushed red pepper

½ cup coarse bread crumbs, toasted

Bring a large pot of water to boil over high heat. Add salt to taste. Stir in the pasta and cook al dente. Reserve ¼ cup water before draining.

Meanwhile, in a medium skillet over medium heat, add 3 tablespoons olive oil. Sauté onion, if using, for 3 to 4 minutes or until translucent. Sauté the garlic and anchovies for 1 to 2 minutes or until the garlic is light golden brown and the anchovies are melted. Return reserved water to skillet, add parsley and crushed red pepper. Mix well.

In a small skillet over medium heat, add the remaining olive oil. Add bread crumbs. Stir constantly for 1 to 2 minutes. Remove from heat immediately.

Drain pasta and put in a serving bowl. Drizzle the anchovy mixture over it slowly while at the same time mixing it in to prevent the macaroni from becoming gummy. Divide into individual servings and sprinkle tops with toasted bread crumbs. Serve immediately.

Serves 4

Pasta con Carciofi e Pancetta
Pasta with Artichokes and Pancetta

My cousins told me that this ancient, appetizing dish is still enjoyed in Calabria. The recipe works only with tender artichoke hearts. It is a fast-food favorite. Artichokes and pancetta, similar to our bacon, complement each other, producing a delicious, near-meatless pasta topping. In a pinch, lean bacon can be substituted for the pancetta.

1 16-ounce can artichoke hearts

1 to 2 ounces pancetta, chopped

2 tablespoons olive oil

2 cloves garlic, finely minced

1 pound spaghetti or linguine

¼ cup reserved pasta water

3 tablespoons freshly grated pecorino or Parmesan cheese

2 tablespoons Italian parsley, finely chopped

Drain artichoke hearts and reserve juice.

In a medium skillet over medium high heat, add pancetta. Sauté for 3 to 4 minutes or until medium golden brown. Remove most of the fat and discard, but do not wash the skillet. Add olive oil and garlic and sauté for 1 to 2 minutes or until light golden brown. Add artichokes and sauté for 2 to 3 minutes or until heated through.

Bring a large pot of water to a boil over high heat. Add salt to taste. Stir in the pasta and cook al dente. Drain pasta and reserve ¼ cup water. Return the reserved pasta water to the pot and add the reserved artichoke juice and the artichoke mixture. Sprinkle with cheese and parsley. Mix thoroughly and serve immediately.

Serves 4

Pasta con Broccoli
Pasta with Broccoli, Anchovies, Pine Nuts, and Pecorino Cheese

A classic Calabrian dish, this tangy and nutritious vegetable pasta topping is one of the few widely known outside the province. Most recipes remain within the village or family, but this dish has such wide appeal it defies confinement. Wise Calabrian cooks tell me the secret to its special flavor lies in cooking the pasta in the same water in which the broccoli is cooked. The addition of anchovies, pine nuts, pecorino cheese, and crushed red pepper adds zest without overpowering. Ideal pastas for this dish are those that will entrap pine nuts, such as farfalle or shells, but rotini also work. Serve this from a large serving platter to ensure including pine nuts on every plate. Final approval on this recipe came from a tasting by son John, his wife Amy, and grandson Spencer.

1 to 1½	pounds fresh broccoli
4	cups reserved broccoli water
½	teaspoon salt
1	pound farfalle, shells, or rotini
4	tablespoons extra-virgin olive oil, divided
4	cloves garlic, finely minced
6 to 8	anchovy fillets, mashed
3	tablespoons pine nuts
½	teaspoon crushed red pepper

¼ cup reserved pasta water
¼ cup freshly grated pecorino cheese

Separate broccoli into long stalks and cut into 4-inch stems. Separate into bite-sized florets. Peel remaining bottom stems and cut into ¼-inch slices. Rinse carefully.

Bring a medium pot with about 4 cups of water to a boil. Add broccoli and salt. Lower heat and cook uncovered for 3 to 4 minutes or until cooked but still crisp. Do not overcook. Remove broccoli with a slotted spoon and set aside. Reserve broccoli water.

Bring a large pot with 4 quarts of water and the reserved broccoli water to a boil over high heat. Stir in the pasta and cook al dente. Drain pasta and reserve ¼ cup water.

Meanwhile, in a large, heavy skillet, heat 2 tablespoons olive oil over medium heat. Sauté garlic, anchovies, pine nuts, and crushed red pepper for 1 to 2 minutes or until garlic is light golden brown and anchovies are nearly dissolved. Gently stir in the broccoli. Remove from heat and set aside.

Return the pasta water to the pot and add the broccoli mixture and the remaining 2 tablespoons olive oil. Mix gently. Sprinkle with cheese and toss again.

Serves 4

Pasta alle Vongole in Bianco
Pasta with White Clam Sauce

Here is a traditional Christmas Eve dish served in many parts of Calabria and considered by many to be the "queen of pasta and seafood dishes." Savory and satisfying, it also graced tables on special occasions and on Friday nights when Catholics abstained from meat. *Vongole* are the small, tasty clams of the Mediterranean. To replicate the taste, try to find the smallest clams available.

2 pounds fresh cherrystone or littleneck clams
4 tablespoons olive oil, divided
4 cloves garlic, finely minced
½ teaspoon crushed red pepper
½ cup bottled clam juice or fish broth
4 tablespoons fresh Italian parsley, finely chopped, divided
¼ teaspoon salt

1   pound spaghettini or cappellini
¼   cup reserved pasta water

Wash and scrub fresh clams thoroughly in cold, salted water. Pat dry with paper towels. In a large heavy pot, add 2 tablespoons olive oil over high heat. Add clams, cover, and cook 8 to 10 minutes or until clams open, shaking pan frequently. The exact cooking time depends on the size of the clams. Discard any that do not open. Remove clams with a slotted spoon. Strain pan juice through a doubled cheesecloth and reserve. Remove clams from shells, chop coarsely, and put in a medium bowl.

In a large, heavy skillet over medium heat, add the remaining 2 tablespoons olive oil. Add garlic and crushed red pepper. Sauté for 1 to 2 minutes or until garlic is light golden brown. Lower heat and add the reserved pan juice, clams, clam juice, 2 tablespoons parsley, and salt. Stir thoroughly with a wooden spoon. Simmer for 3 to 5 minutes.

Bring a large pot of water to a boil over high heat. Add salt to taste. Stir in the pasta and cook al dente. Drain and reserve ¼ cup pasta water. Add the pasta and water to the skillet and mix thoroughly. Let stand for 1 or 2 minutes to allow pasta to absorb the flavor of the sauce. Mix again, put in individual dishes, and sprinkle with the remaining 2 tablespoons parsley.

Serves 4 to 6

TIP: For best flavor, do not add grated cheese to fish dishes.

VARIATIONS:
- Fresh clams are preferable, but a 12-ounce can of baby clams can be substituted. Add clams and juice to skillet with sautéed onion and garlic and simmer 2 or 3 minutes only.
- Add 1 or 2 tablespoons of bread crumbs along with the clams to thicken the sauce.

Timballo di Maccheroni e Melanzane
Baked Macaroni and Eggplant

Eggplant is a Calabrian favorite and is used extensively in a variety of ways. Here it is combined with macaroni and cheese and baked to produce a satisfying and sumptuous dish. This is a good party dish to prepare in advance and bake just before serving time.

2	medium eggplants, about 1 pound each
4 to 5	tablespoons olive oil
1	recipe *Salsa Marinara, Pronto!* (Mariner's Style Tomato Sauce—Quick, Easy, and Perky, page 130)
1	pound ziti
4	ounces grated pecorino or Parmesan cheese, divided
8	ounces mozzarella cheese, thinly sliced or shredded, divided

Preheat oven to 350° F.

Peel and cut eggplant lengthwise into uniform ¼-inch slices. In a small bowl, add 4 tablespoons olive oil. With a pastry brush, lightly brush both sides of sliced eggplant with oil and place on broiler pan in a single layer. Add remaining olive oil if needed. Broil for 10 minutes, or until lightly browned, turning once. Do not leave unattended.

In a medium saucepan, heat sauce over medium heat. Let simmer for 3 minutes. Bring a large pot of water to a boil over high heat. Add salt to taste. Stir in the pasta and cook al dente. Drain and set aside.

Working quickly, in a 9-by-13-inch baking pan, spread a thin layer of tomato sauce, just enough to coat bottom of pan. Add about ⅓ of the pasta, ½ of the eggplant, ⅓ of each of the cheeses, and a thin layer of sauce. Continue layering in that order until all ingredients are used up, ending with a layer of cheeses. There will be 3 layers of pasta.

Bake uncovered for 45 to 50 minutes, or until the top is golden brown and eggplant is tender. Let stand for 5 minutes to ease cutting. Pass additional sauce at table.

Serves 6 to 8

Pasta Aglio, Olio, e Peperoncino
Pasta with Garlic, Oil, and Hot Red Pepper

This pasta dish goes from stove to table in less than 30 minutes. Its success depends on a good-quality olive oil. Start cooking the pasta before you begin making the sauce. Popular in all of Calabria and in southern Italy, this dish represents home-cooking simplicity at its best. Immigrants brought it to the United States, where it remained their little secret for quite some time. However, it's difficult to keep a good thing hidden for too long.

1	pound spaghetti or linguine
¼	cup reserved pasta water
3	tablespoons extra-virgin olive oil
4	cloves garlic, finely minced
1	hot red pepper, finely chopped, or ½ teaspoon crushed red pepper
3	tablespoons fresh Italian parsley, finely chopped
3	tablespoons freshly grated pecorino or Parmesan cheese (optional)

Bring a large pot of water to a boil over high heat. Add salt to taste. Stir in the pasta and cook al dente.

Meanwhile, in a large, heavy skillet, heat olive oil over medium heat. Sauté the garlic and red pepper for 1 to 2 minutes or until garlic is light golden brown.

Drain pasta and reserve ¼ cup water. Return pasta and the reserved water to the skillet. With two forks, toss once or twice to prevent sticking. Sprinkle with parsley and with cheese, if using. Mix thoroughly and serve immediately.

Serves 4

Pasta alla Pastora, Uno
Pasta with Ricotta, Shepherd Style I

Ready in less than 30 minutes, this version of *Pasta alla Pastora* is an ideal choice for some night when you want a short-order, home-cooked entrée. And this version, unlike others, does not require baking. The pasta is drained, mixed with the other ingredients, and served. Eye-catching little dots of green parsley and crushed red pepper adorn the pasta, adding to its visual appeal.

1 pound ziti, penne, or fusilli
¼ cup reserved pasta water
1 pound ricotta
½ cup freshly grated pecorino or Parmesan cheese
1 teaspoon fresh Italian parsley, very finely chopped
¼ teaspoon crushed red pepper

Bring a large pot of water to a boil over high heat. Add salt to taste. Stir in the pasta and cook al dente.

Meanwhile, in a medium mixing bowl, add ricotta, grated cheese, parsley, and crushed red pepper. Mix thoroughly.

Drain the pasta, reserving ¼ cup water. In a shallow serving casserole large enough to hold the pasta and ricotta, add the pasta. Add the reserved water to the cheese mixture and mix thoroughly. Fold cheese mixture into pasta and serve immediately.

Serves 4 to 6

VARIATION: Thinly slice 4 ounces of hot or mild sausage. In a medium skillet, over medium-high heat, sauté sausage, turning frequently until no pink remains. Remove with slotted spoon and drain on paper towels. Add to the cheese mixture.

Pasta alla Pastora, Due
Pasta with Spinach, Ricotta, and Mozzarella, Shepherd Style II

I had this typical Calabrian pasta dish in a *tavola calda* ("hot table" eatery) in Calabria. I enjoyed it and tried to get the recipe, but the chef had left. The following evolved from memory and some research. It took several testings to make it perfect. This version includes spinach and is baked. It is an ideal party dish. It can be assembled early in the day and refrigerated. Remove from refrigerator 1 hour prior to baking.

1 pound ziti, penne, or rotelli
¼ cup reserved pasta water
6 ounces fresh spinach
1 pound ricotta
3 tablespoon fresh Italian parsley, finely chopped
½ teaspoon salt

¼ teaspoon crushed red pepper
1 egg, lightly beaten
4 ounces mozzarella cheese, thinly sliced or shredded
⅓ cup freshly grated pecorino or Parmesan cheese

Preheat oven to 350° F.

Bring a large pot of water to a boil over high heat. Add salt to taste. Stir in the pasta and cook until just under al dente. Drain pasta and reserve ¼ cup water. Transfer half of the pasta to an oiled 8-by-12-inch casserole.

While the pasta is cooking, put spinach in a double boiler or steamer. Steam for 1 to 2 minutes or just long enough to wilt. Drain, squeeze dry, chop coarsely, and set aside.

In a medium mixing bowl, add ricotta, parsley, salt, and crushed red pepper. Cover pasta with the ricotta mixture. Dot evenly with the spinach, half the mozzarella, and half the grated cheese. Cover with remaining pasta.

In a small bowl, with a whisk, lightly beat the egg and the reserved water. Pour evenly over the pasta. Sprinkle top with remaining mozzarella and grated cheese.

Bake uncovered for 35 to 40 minutes, or until cooked through and cheese is golden brown. Let stand for 10 minutes to ease cutting.

Serves 6 to 8

VARIATION: Thinly slice 4 ounces of hot or mild sausage. In a medium skillet, over medium-high heat, sauté sausage, turning frequently until no pink remains. Remove with slotted spoon and drain on paper towels. Add to the spinach.

Pasta con le Sarde e Finocchio
Pasta with Sardines and Fresh Fennel

Mediterranean sardines, plentiful in the waters off Calabria and Sicily, are small and tasty with little fat. Fresh sardines in the United States are equally good. If you can't find fresh, this recipe is worth preparing with frozen sardines, which are preferable to the canned. The unusual combination of sardines and fennel is such a prized creation that this is one of the dishes served in Italy on the March 19th feast of St. Joseph. Opinions vary about whether this savory dish was originated by the Calabrians, the Sicilians, or the Greeks, who colonized parts of southern Italy.

1 pound fresh small sardines
1 large bulb fennel (about 1 pound)
2 tablespoons plus 1 teaspoon olive oil, divided
1 small onion, finely chopped
2 cloves garlic, finely minced
¼ cup white wine
6 anchovy fillets, coarsely chopped
4 tablespoons pine nuts
½ teaspoon freshly ground black pepper or crushed red pepper
¼ teaspoon salt
   pinch of nutmeg (optional)
1 pound macceroncelli or bucatini
½ cup bread crumbs

Wash sardines and cut off heads. Slit lengthwise and remove guts and backbone. Rinse thoroughly in salted water. Pat dry with paper towels.

Discard any tough outer parts of the fennel bulb. Cut off the green fern top, cut the bulb in quarters, and rinse. In a large pot, add enough water to cover fennel. Bring to a boil over high heat. Add fennel bulb, fennel top, and salt. Lower heat and simmer for 10 minutes or until fennel is just tender. Remove with slotted spoon, reserving the water, and let cool. Discard the top and chop the bulb coarsely.

In a large, heavy skillet, add 2 tablespoons olive oil over medium heat. Add onion and sauté for 3 to 4 minutes or until translucent. Add garlic and sauté for 1 to 2 minutes or until light golden brown. Add sardines and sauté for 3 to 4 minutes, allowing them to break up at will. Add fennel, wine, anchovies, pine nuts, pepper, salt, and nutmeg, if using. Lower heat and simmer gently for 5 minutes or until fennel is tender.

In a small skillet, add remaining 1 teaspoon olive oil over medium heat. Add bread crumbs and sauté for 2 minutes, stirring constantly, until lightly browned. Remove from heat and set aside.

Add more water to the pot in which the fennel was cooked. Bring to a boil over high heat. Add salt to taste. Stir in the pasta and cook al dente. Drain and add to the skillet with sardines and fennel. Mix gently. Divide among serving dishes and sprinkle with toasted bread crumbs. Serve immediately.

Serves 4 to 6

VARIATION: Good-quality canned sardines can be substituted. Add two 3½-ounce cans and the oil to the skillet and heat for 2 to 3 minutes, stirring occasionally.

Pasta con Calamari e Pomodori
Pasta with Squid and Tomatoes

Squid is included in a variety of Calabrian dishes. I love its chewy texture and distinctive flavor. It's great stuffed or marinated, alone or with other seafood. Here squid combines with tomatoes, yielding a robust pasta topping. Sometimes you can buy squid already cleaned. If not, don't fret—it's easy to do. A typical tasty, tangy southern Italian dish, you can spice it up or down with crushed red pepper, according to your own taste.

1   pound small squid, fresh or frozen
3   tablespoons extra-virgin olive oil
1   small onion, finely chopped
4   cloves garlic, finely minced
1   16-ounce can Italian plum tomatoes, coarsely chopped
4   tablespoons fresh Italian parsley, coarsely chopped, divided
½   teaspoon salt
½   teaspoon crushed red pepper
1   pound linguine

Cut tentacles from the head of the squid just below the eyes and discard the mouth, which is hidden in the tentacles. Peel off outer skin. Squeeze out insides and pull out center bone. Wash all parts under cold running water. Cut tentacles in half and cut squid body into ½-inch rings. Drain on paper towels and set aside.

In a large, heavy skillet, heat olive oil over medium heat. Add onion and sauté for 3 to 4 minutes or until light golden brown. Add garlic and sauté for 1 to 2 minutes or until light golden brown. Lower heat and add tomatoes, 1 tablespoon parsley, salt, and crushed red pepper. Simmer for 20 minutes. Add squid and simmer for 4 to 5 minutes or until just tender.

Bring a large pot of water to a boil over high heat. Add salt to taste. Stir in pasta and cook al dente. Drain and place on a serving platter. Ladle some sauce over pasta and mix well. Put remaining sauce on top of pasta, sprinkle with remaining parsley, and serve immediately.

Serves 4

TIP: Try to buy small squid of equal size; they are the most tender.

VARIATIONS:
• Add ⅓ cup dry red wine along with the tomatoes.
• Add ½ cup fresh or 5 ounces frozen peas along with the tomatoes.

Penne Arrabbiata
Penne with a Hot Tomato Sauce

What a difference a sauce makes! Here is a truly delectable, fiery tomato sauce, spicier than most. Adding pancetta enhances the flavor even more. In a pinch, lean bacon can be substituted. Literally, *arrabbiata* means "enraged" or "angry," but in this recipe it means "hot" to the taste.

       2   tablespoons olive oil, divided
       2   ounces pancetta, coarsely chopped
       1   medium onion, coarsely chopped
       3   cloves garlic, finely minced
       1   28-ounce can Italian plum tomatoes, coarsely chopped
     ½   teaspoon salt
       3   tablespoons fresh Italian parsley, coarsely chopped, divided
     ½   teaspoon crushed red pepper
       1   pound penne, ziti, or rigatoni
           freshly grated pecorino or Parmesan cheese, to taste

In a large pot, add 1 teaspoon olive oil over medium heat. Sauté the pancetta for 5 to 6 minutes or until crisp, turning occasionally. Remove with slotted spoon, drain on paper towels, and set aside. Remove fat from skillet and wipe clean with paper towel, but do not wash.

Return skillet to heat and add remaining oil. Sauté onion for 3 to 4 minutes or until translucent. Add garlic and sauté for 1 to 2 minutes or until garlic is light golden brown. Lower heat and return pancetta to the skillet. Add tomatoes, salt, 2 tablespoons parsley, and the crushed red pepper. Simmer uncovered for 20 minutes. Add remaining parsley, stir, and simmer 2 to 3 minutes.

Bring a large pot of water to a boil over high heat. Add salt to taste. Stir in the pasta and cook al dente. Drain, put on individual serving dishes and ladle a small amount of sauce on pasta. Pass extra sauce and cheese at the table.

Serves 4

Ravioli Calabrese
Ravioli, Calabrian Style

Ravioli are served in some parts of Calabria at Christmas, a custom dating back to the twelfth century when they were also given to priests and monks as Christmas gifts. Ravioli are also popular year-round. Making ravioli at home is fun family fare. The dough is made in much the same way as homemade pasta. Forming and filling ravioli is quite easy with molds or wheels as described below. Ricotta is the favored filling. Calabrians sometimes add bits of sopressata, a nicely flavored cured meat for which they are well known. Serve ravioli with a hearty sauce such as *Ragu con Carne Tritata* (Tomato Sauce with Ground Meat, page 131).

DOUGH:

2 cups unbleached or all-purpose flour
1 teaspoon salt
3 large eggs, lightly beaten
1 teaspoon olive oil

FILLING:

8 ounces whole-milk ricotta
3 tablespoons freshly grated pecorino or Parmesan cheese
1 ounce sopressata, sliced and cut into ¼-inch pieces (optional)
1 egg
⅛ teaspoon salt
¹⁄₁₆ teaspoon freshly ground black pepper

Mound flour and salt on a floured surface. Make a well in the center, gradually add eggs and olive oil, and with a fork beat lightly. Gradually pull in flour until it is absorbed. If dough is too sticky, add a bit more flour; if too hard and doesn't mix easily, add a few drops of water. Mix dough well and form into a ball.

Using pasta machine: Pasta machines have two parts; one for rolling and one for cutting. For ravioli, you use only the rolling part. Set machine at its widest setting, break off dough the size of a golf ball, and pass it through the machine 8 times to knead, folding the dough in half and lowering the setting 1 notch each time until you reach the next-to-last notch. Put on floured surface or bed sheet and sprinkle lightly with flour. Repeat process until all dough is rolled out. Let rest for at least 15 minutes to make cutting easier. Meanwhile, prepare filling.

Rolling by hand: Place dough on floured surface; knead for 7 minutes or until dough is smooth, evenly golden colored, and elastic. Break off dough the size of a golf ball. With a rolling pin, roll each piece to about 1/16-inch thickness. Put on floured surface or bed sheet and sprinkle lightly with flour. Repeat process until all dough is rolled out. Let rest for at least 15 minutes to make cutting easier. Meanwhile, prepare filling.

In a large bowl, mix the ricotta, pecorino or Parmesan, sopressata if using, egg, salt, and pepper. Set aside.

Cutting and filling the ravioli:

Using ravioli tray molds: The bottom tray contains twelve 2-inch squares. Each square has a 1½-inch-round depression. The top tray is made of hard plastic and has twelve 1-inch depressions. To form the ravioli, sprinkle bottom tray lightly with flour and cover it with a strip of dough a bit larger than the size of the tray. Put the top tray over the dough and press evenly to form even depressions in the dough. Remove top tray. Dip a pastry brush into a small bowl of water and brush flat dough surface so top dough will adhere well. Fill each hole with a heaping teaspoon of the ricotta filling. Lay second sheet of dough over top. With a rolling pin, roll back and forth over the top of the dough until the raised fluted edges appear and the 12 squares are well formed. Continue process until all dough is used. Remove to a floured surface in a single layer for at least 30 minutes, turning over once to let them dry.

Using ravioli wheel: A fluted ravioli wheel allows you to make ravioli any size you wish. Some wheels also seal the dough as you cut it. Put a strip of dough on a floured surface. For small ravioli, place heaping teaspoons of filling evenly 1½-inches apart. For larger ones, double the filling and gently flatten. Dip a pastry brush into a small bowl of water and brush dough surfaces around fillings. Place a second strip of dough over fillings. With your fingers, press areas around each filling to seal. Roll the wheel between fillings, making either round or square ravioli. Remove to a floured surface in a single layer for at least 30 minutes, turning over once to let them dry.

Using ravioli press: A round, etched press with a wooden handle uniformly cuts and seals the dough at the same time. Put a strip of dough on a floured surface. Put heaping teaspoons of filling evenly 1½-inches apart. Put another strip of dough over fillings. Put the press securely over the filling and press evenly until it cuts through the dough. Gather up pieces of unused dough edges, roll again and repeat the process until all ravioli are made. Remove to a floured surface in a single layer for at least 30 minutes, turning over once to let them dry.

Bring a large pot of water to a boil over high heat. Add salt to taste. Gently add ravioli a few at a time and stir frequently with a wooden spoon. Cook for about 5 to 8 minutes or until just tender. The exact time depends on the thickness of the dough.

Serves 4

TIPS:
- Ravioli can be frozen. Freeze them in a single layer, not touching. Do not defrost to cook. Add 2 to 4 minutes to above cooking time.
- Tray molds and wheels are available in Italian specialty stores, special kitchen equipment stores, and some department stores. I bought my etched ravioli press in Calabria, but these may now be available in the United States in Italian specialty stores.

Salsa al Pomodori Secchi
Sun-Dried Tomato Sauce with Artichoke Hearts, Pine Nuts, and Capers

Sun-dried tomatoes take center stage in this sauce. When combined with a supporting cast of artichoke hearts, pine nuts, and capers, they create a winning, aromatic sauce. The sauce is ready in minutes, so start boiling the water first. Sun-dried tomatoes are a long-time staple of Calabrians, especially the tiny cherry ones. Of them they say, "tiny but with big taste." Sun-dried tomatoes are available in Italian specialty stores and most supermarkets, but if you would like to try your hand at drying your own or packing store-bought dried ones in oil, refer to *Pomodori Secchi sott' Olio* (Sun-dried Tomatoes in Oil, page 240).

½ cup dry or oil-packed sun-dried tomatoes
2 tablespoons extra-virgin olive oil
½ small onion, finely chopped
3 cloves garlic, finely chopped
2 tablespoons pine nuts
1 16-ounce can Italian plum tomatoes, coarsely chopped
1 6-ounce can artichoke hearts, drained and chopped
4 tablespoons dry white wine
1 tablespoon capers
1 tablespoon fresh Italian parsley, finely chopped
½ teaspoon salt
¼ teaspoon crushed red pepper

If you are using dry-packed tomatoes, put in a small bowl and add boiling water to cover. Let stand until soft, 2 to 4 minutes. Drain, slice coarsely, and set aside. If you are using oil-packed tomatoes, remove from container with a slotted spoon, slice coarsely, and set aside.

In a small skillet over medium heat, add olive oil. Sauté onion for 3 to 4 minutes or until translucent. Add garlic and pine nuts and sauté for 1 to 2 minutes or until garlic is light golden brown. Add canned and sun-dried tomatoes, artichoke hearts, wine, capers, parsley, salt, and crushed red pepper. Mix well. Simmer for 2 to 3 minutes, stirring constantly.

Makes 2½ to 3 cups sauce

Salsa di Pomodoro
Tomato Sauce

There are many variations on this basic tomato sauce. Every village has a preference, each with its own little twist. What they all have in common is that it is a long-simmering version, giving it depth and character. It is the kind of sauce most familiar to immigrants from Calabria and southern Italy. It is one of the sauces my mother prepared most frequently. It contains no meat since it often precedes a meat dish, such as roasted chicken. Like all tomato sauces, it freezes well. It traditionally calls for a little tomato paste, resulting in heightened flavor and color. My mother canned her own tomatoes (we all helped) and made her own tomato paste, which she called *conserva*. She simmered tomatoes slowly until they reached a highly concentrated state.

3 tablespoons olive oil
1 small onion, coarsely chopped
3 cloves garlic, finely minced
1 28-ounce can Italian plum tomatoes, coarsely chopped
3 ounces tomato paste
4 tablespoons fresh Italian parsley, coarsely chopped, divided
4 tablespoon fresh basil, coarsely chopped, divided
½ teaspoon salt
¼ teaspoon freshly ground black pepper

In a large, heavy saucepan, add olive oil over medium heat. Sauté onion for 3 to 4 minutes or until translucent. Add garlic and sauté for 1 to 2 minutes or until light golden brown. Add tomatoes, tomato paste, 2 tablespoons each of the parsley and basil, salt, and pepper. Simmer slowly for 2½ to 3 hours. Two minutes before serving, add remaining parsley and basil and stir thoroughly.

Makes 3 to 3½ cups sauce

Salsa di Pomodori con Due Formaggi
Tomato Sauce with Two Cheeses

I can't recall my mother ever adding cheese to the sauce itself, though I know it is done. At our home, it was always passed at the table, to be freshly grated. I am probably one of the few people who doesn't sprinkle cheese on pasta. I love it on soup, vegetables, salads, and various dishes, but not on pasta. So why then do I love this sauce? Maybe because even though it has a rich, assertive flavor, it doesn't overpower the more important flavor of tomatoes.

> 3 tablespoons extra-virgin olive oil
> 4 cloves garlic, finely minced
> 1 28-ounce can Italian plum tomatoes, coarsely chopped
> 3 tablespoons fresh basil, finely chopped, divided
> 3 tablespoons fresh Italian parsley, finely chopped, divided
> ½ teaspoon salt
> ¼ teaspoon freshly ground black pepper
> 2 tablespoons freshly grated Parmesan cheese
> 2 tablespoons freshly grated pecorino cheese

In a large saucepan, add olive oil over medium heat. Sauté garlic for 1 to 2 minutes or until light golden brown.

Lower heat and add tomatoes, 2 tablespoons each of the basil and parsley, salt, and pepper. Simmer for 20 minutes. If mixture seems thick, add a little hot water. Add the grated cheeses and the remaining basil and parsley, and stir.

Makes 3 to 3½ cups sauce

Salsa alla Norma
Sauce Norma with Tomatoes and Eggplant

Tradition tells us that this classic dish was created to honor the debut of Vincenzo Bellini's operatic masterpiece, *Norma*, and so two classics were created on December 26, 1831. Southern Italians are noted for adding vegetables to their sauces. In this popular Calabrian and Sicilian sauce, eggplant stars. I had the pleasure of dining in the famed Ristorante Bonaccorso in Reggio Calabria, where I enjoyed this famous dish. Chef-owner Antonio Bonaccorso, whose recipes have appeared in *Gourmet* and who is also a noted sculptor, painter, and poet, graciously contributed his recipe. His version is my favorite.

3	tablespoons olive oil, divided
1	small onion, coarsely chopped
3	cloves garlic, finely minced
1	medium eggplant, about ¾ pound
2½	pounds fresh tomatoes
4	tablespoons fresh basil, coarsely chopped, divided
½	teaspoon salt

In a large, heavy skillet add 1 tablespoon olive oil over medium heat. Sauté onion for 3 to 4 minutes, or until translucent. Add garlic and sauté for 1 to 2 minutes or until light golden brown. Remove garlic and onion with slotted spoon and reserve.

Wash and cut unpeeled eggplant into ½-inch pieces. Add remaining olive oil and the eggplant to the skillet. Sauté for 4 to 5 minutes, or until golden brown, stirring frequently. Return onion and garlic to skillet, add tomatoes, 2 tablespoons basil, and salt. Lower heat and simmer, uncovered, for 20 minutes. Add the remaining basil, stir, and simmer for 2 minutes.

Makes 3½ to 4 cups sauce

VARIATIONS: For more tangy taste, add 2 tablespoons capers with the remaining basil.

Salsa con Porcini di Due C Ristorante

Tomato Sauce with Porcini Mushrooms from the Due C Restaurant

One night while in Calabria, I decided to find a hotel and trattoria in the little town of Luzzi. Luckily, I stumbled upon a wonderful place. It had fine Calabrian food, a great owner, Dino Leone, and a whole bunch of friendly Calabrian diners. I ordered farfalle with this distinctive sauce and asked Mr. Leone if he would give me the recipe. He willingly consented. If you can find only dried porcini, no problem. The woodsy flavor of even a small amount of dried, wild porcini mushrooms is imparted to the button mushrooms, transforming this great dish into an extraordinary one. Before I left, Mr. Leone consented to having his picture taken but insisted on having mine taken with his family as well!

3	tablespoons olive oil, divided
1	small onion, coarsely chopped
2	cloves garlic, finely minced
½	pound fresh porcini mushrooms, quickly rinsed and coarsely chopped, or ½-ounce dried, soaked in warm water to cover for 20 to 25 minutes
½	pound button mushrooms, rinsed quickly or brushed clean, coarsely chopped
1	28-ounce can Italian plum tomatoes, coarsely chopped
¼	cup chicken or beef broth
3	tablespoons fresh Italian parsley, coarsely chopped, divided
½	teaspoon crushed red pepper

In a large saucepan, add 1 tablespoon olive oil over medium heat. Sauté onion for 3 to 4 minutes or until translucent. Add garlic and sauté for 1 to 2 minutes, or until light golden brown. Remove with slotted spoon to a medium bowl and set aside. If using dried mushrooms, drain and reserve liquid. Increase heat to medium-high. Add 1 tablespoon olive oil and fresh or dried porcini mushrooms and sauté for 3 to 4 minutes, or until lightly browned. Remove with slotted spoon and put into bowl with onions. Add remaining olive oil and button mushrooms. Sauté for 3 to 4 minutes or until lightly browned.

Raise heat, add the porcini liquid if using dried, and cook until the liquid is reduced by about half. Add tomatoes, broth, 2 tablespoons parsley, and crushed red pepper. Lower heat and simmer uncovered for 20 minutes. Use remaining parsley for garnish.

Makes 3 to 3½ cups sauce

Salsa con Porcini, Prosciutto, e Olive
Tomato Sauce with Porcini, Prosciutto, and Olives

Just north of Calabria in Paestum is Il Cantinone Ristorante, owned by Mario Sabello and Pasquale D'Angelo. Meeting them and their families was a pleasant experience. This incredibly flavorful sauce is one of their favorite Calabrian recipes and is now one of mine. They served it with penne, but ziti or rotini would be fine. And this is another sauce that is ready in about the time it takes to cook the pasta.

- 3 tablespoons olive oil
- 1 small onion, coarsely chopped
- 2 cloves garlic, finely minced
- 2 ounces sliced prosciutto, coarsely chopped
- ½ pound fresh porcini mushrooms, quickly rinsed and coarsely chopped, or 2 ounces dried, soaked in warm water to cover for 20 to 25 minutes
- 1 28-ounce can Italian plum tomatoes, coarsely chopped
- 3 tablespoons fresh Italian parsley, coarsely chopped, divided
- ½ teaspoon salt
- ½ teaspoon crushed red pepper
- ¼ cup black olives, brine-cured, pitted and halved
- 2 tablespoons freshly grated pecorino or Parmesan cheese

In a large pot add 1 tablespoon olive oil over medium heat. Sauté onion for 3 to 4 minutes or until translucent. Add garlic and prosciutto and sauté for 1 to 2 minutes or until garlic is light golden brown. Remove with slotted spoon and set aside. If using dried mushrooms, drain and reserve liquid. Increase heat to medium-high. Add 1 tablespoon olive oil and fresh or dried mushrooms. Sauté for 3 to 4 minutes or until lightly browned.

Raise heat, add the porcini liquid if using dried, and cook until the liquid is reduced by about half. Add tomatoes, 2 tablespoons parsley, salt, and crushed red pepper. Lower heat and simmer, uncovered, for 20 minutes. Add the remaining parsley, olives, and cheese. Mix well. Simmer for 2 to 3 minutes.

Makes 3 to 3½ cups sauce

Salsa di Pomodori con Olive alla Bova Marina

Tomato Sauce with Olives, Bova Marina Style

One of the tastiest sauces I had in Calabria was this one in La Primula Ristorante. The rest of the meal was equally good; is it any wonder I returned the following year? Located in Bova Marina where most of my cousins now live, La Primula commands a fine view of the Ionian Sea. The young couple who manage it are delightful and accommodating. Isabella is the daughter of the owner, Dinnaro di Dellavilla, and Pasquali is her *fidanzato* (fiancé). The tomatoes, vegetables, and herbs were grown in their own garden and picked fresh that day, and the bread was homemade. I raved about it so that they gave me a whole loaf when I left! Isabella gladly contributed this recipe and let me take pictures of them, too.

2	tablespoons olive oil
1	small onion, coarsely chopped
3	cloves garlic, finely minced
2 to 2½	pounds ripe tomatoes, coarsely chopped, or 1 28-ounce can Italian plum tomatoes, coarsely chopped
¼	cup black olives, brine-cured, pitted and halved
3	tablespoons fresh basil, coarsely chopped
3	tablespoons fresh Italian parsley, coarsely chopped
½	teaspoon salt
½	teaspoon crushed red pepper

In a large pot, add olive oil over medium heat. Sauté onion for 3 to 4 minutes or until translucent. Add garlic and sauté for 1 to 2 minutes or until light golden brown. Add tomatoes, lower heat, and simmer uncovered for 20 minutes. Add olives, basil, parsley, salt, and red pepper. Stir and simmer for 3 to 4 minutes.

Makes 3 to 3½ cups sauce

Salsa Puttanesca
Tomato Sauce with Olives, Anchovies, Capers, and Hot Red Pepper

Also known as *salsa con olive e alici*, the Romans are but one group who claim this hot and spicy sauce as their own. The Greeks who settled southern Italy and the Neapolitans also take credit for it, but the flavor-laden ingredients spell Calabria. The most popular version of how this hot, robust sauce got its name is that it was often prepared by the ladies of the night for their clients. If you are not accustomed to hot food, use less crushed red pepper. Calabrians often serve this sauce over fusilli. Do not serve cheese with this piquant sauce.

2	tablespoons extra-virgin olive oil
1	medium onion, coarsely chopped
3	large cloves garlic, finely minced
4 or 5	anchovy fillets, mashed
1	28-ounce can Italian plum tomatoes, coarsely chopped
4	tablespoons fresh Italian parsley, finely chopped, divided
½	teaspoon crushed red pepper
12	Italian black olives, brine-cured, pitted and halved
2	tablespoons capers

In a large saucepan, add olive oil over medium heat. Add onion and sauté for 3 to 4 minutes or until translucent. Add garlic and anchovies, sauté for 1 to 2 minutes, or until garlic is light golden brown and anchovies are dissolved. Add tomatoes, 2 tablespoons parsley, and crushed red pepper. Simmer for 15 minutes. Add olives, capers, and remaining parsley. Mix thoroughly.

Makes 3 to 3½ cups sauce

Salsa di Pomodori con Peperoni
Tomato Sauce with Peppers

This is an especially tasty version of a tomato and pepper sauce. It has a chunky texture and is rich in flavor. I personally prefer it without the carrot, which tends to sweeten the sauce, but that is simply a matter of taste.

2	tablespoons extra-virgin olive oil
1	small onion, coarsely chopped

        1   clove garlic, finely minced
        2   medium red peppers, seeded and thinly sliced
        1   small carrot, finely chopped (optional)
        1   28-ounce can Italian plum tomatoes, coarsely chopped
        ½   teaspoon salt
        ¼   teaspoon crushed red pepper
        2   tablespoons fresh Italian parsley, finely chopped

In a large, heavy skillet add olive oil over medium heat. Add onion and sauté for 3 to 4 minutes or until translucent. Add garlic and sauté for 1 to 2 minutes or until light golden brown. Remove onions and garlic and reserve.

Add peppers and carrot, if using, and stir to coat with oil. Sauté for 5 to 6 minutes or until peppers just begin to brown. Lower heat and sauté for 10 to 12 minutes, or until tender, stirring frequently. Return onions and garlic to the skillet, add tomatoes, salt, and crushed red pepper. Mix well. Simmer for 20 minutes. Add parsley and mix thoroughly. If sauce seems too thick, add a little hot water.

Makes 3 to 3½ cups sauce

Salsa di Pomodori, Prosciutto, e Capperi
Tomato Sauce with Prosciutto and Capers

Parma prosciutto, which is now exported to the United States, has a fresh, subtle taste that distinguishes it from our domestic brands. It is air cured first and then salted ever so lightly. The technique of curing ham is attributed to the Spanish who once occupied southern Italy. This is a popular choice for Easter, birthdays, anniversaries, and any other special occasion you can think of! Serve with fresh or dried tagliarini, ¼-inch-wide noodles.

        3   tablespoons extra-virgin olive oil
        1   medium white onion, halved and thinly sliced
        2   cloves garlic, finely minced
   2 to 3   ounces thinly sliced Parma prosciutto, coarsely chopped
        1   28-ounce can Italian plum tomatoes, coarsely chopped
        4   tablespoons fresh basil, coarsely chopped, divided
        2   tablespoons capers
        ½   teaspoon salt
        ¼   teaspoon freshly ground black pepper

In a large saucepan add olive oil over medium heat. Add onion and sauté for 3 to 4 minutes or until translucent. Add garlic and chopped prosciutto. Sauté for 1 to 2 minutes or until garlic is light golden brown. Lower heat, add tomatoes and 2 tablespoons basil, and simmer uncovered for 25 minutes. If the mixture seems thick, add a little hot water. Stir in the remaining basil, capers, salt, and pepper. Simmer for 2 minutes.

Makes 3 to 3½ cups sauce

Salsa di Pomodori Fresca e Basilico
Tomato Sauce with Fresh Tomatoes and Basil

When fresh tomatoes are in season, they produce a fresh tasting, flavorful, fabulous sauce. The tomatoes must be ripe, very ripe, and the basil fresh, if you want perfection.

- 2½ pounds ripe tomatoes
- 2 tablespoons extra-virgin olive oil
- ½ medium onion, coarsely chopped
- 3 cloves garlic, finely minced
- 3 tablespoons fresh basil, finely slivered, divided
- ½ teaspoon salt
- ¼ teaspoon freshly ground black pepper

Plunge tomatoes into boiling water for 10 to 15 seconds. Make a cross on the bottom of each tomato for ease in removing skin. Peel each tomato, cut in half, squeeze to remove some seeds, and chop coarsely. Do not puree. Put tomatoes into a bowl.

In a large, heavy skillet add olive oil over medium heat. Sauté onion for 3 to 4 minutes or until translucent. Add garlic and sauté for 1 to 2 minutes or until light golden brown. Lower heat and add tomatoes, half the basil, salt, and pepper. Simmer uncovered for 45 minutes or until sauce is thickened. Add remaining basil and simmer for 1 to 2 minutes. Serve immediately.

Makes 3 to 3½ cups sauce

TIP: For a milder garlic flavor when cooking fresh tomatoes, add garlic uncooked directly to the sauce.

Salsa Marinara, Pronto!
Mariner's Style Tomato Sauce—Quick, Easy, and Perky

Quicker than takeout, easier than shopping for a jar, and so much tastier, this sauce is ready in about the time it takes to cook the pasta. I get requests for this recipe from just about everyone who has ever tasted it. It was the creation of fishermen aboard ship who could not bear to be without their favorite comfort food, pasta. They needed to create a sauce for it that was flavorful, yet quick and easy. This sauce also serves as a base for many recipes throughout this book. It can be doubled and frozen in varying size containers to be ready when you are. Serve with your favorite pasta—but shells take on more meaning with this sauce.

> 3 tablespoons extra-virgin olive oil
> 1 small sweet onion, coarsely sliced
> 3 cloves garlic, finely minced
> 1 28-ounce can Italian plum tomatoes, coarsely chopped
> 3 tablespoon fresh basil, coarsely chopped, divided
> 3 tablespoon fresh Italian parsley, finely chopped, divided
> ½ teaspoon salt
> ¼ teaspoon freshly ground black pepper

In a large saucepan add olive oil over medium heat. Add onion and sauté for 3 to 4 minutes or until translucent. Add garlic and sauté for 1 to 2 minutes or until light golden brown.

Lower heat and add tomatoes, 2 tablespoons each of the basil and parsley, salt, and pepper. Simmer uncovered for 20 minutes. If mixture seems thick, add 2 to 3 tablespoons hot water. Add remaining basil and parsley, and simmer for 2 minutes.

Makes 3 to 3½ cups sauce

TIP: This sauce is ideal for pizza. Follow directions, except reduce cooking time to 10 minutes. Cool slightly before spreading on pizza dough.

Ragu con Carne Tritata
Tomato Sauce with Ground Meat

This is a quick-and-easy meat sauce commonly used with sturdy pasta such as rigatoni or ziti, or with baked pasta such as lasagne. It came into use in Calabria and southern Italy at varying times as meat became affordable. The meat and tomatoes blend beautifully to create a great tasting, satisfying sauce. Some recipes call for ½ to 1 pound of ground meat. I find 1 pound too much and ½ pound not quite enough. It's simply a matter of taste, so use more or less to suit your own.

- 2 tablespoons plus 1 teaspoon olive oil
- 1 small onion, coarsely chopped
- 3 cloves garlic, finely chopped
- 1 28-ounce can Italian plum tomatoes, coarsely chopped
- ½ teaspoon salt
- ¼ teaspoon freshly ground black pepper
- 2 tablespoons fresh Italian parsley, coarsely chopped, divided
- 2 tablespoons fresh basil, coarsely chopped, divided
- ¾ pound lean ground beef, veal, pork, or any combination of same
- ¼ cup dry red wine (optional)

In a large, heavy skillet add 2 tablespoons olive oil over medium heat. Sauté onion for 3 to 4 minutes or until translucent. Add garlic and sauté for 1 to 2 minutes or until light golden brown. Add tomatoes, salt, pepper, and 1 tablespoon each of parsley and basil. Simmer uncovered for 20 minutes.

In another large, heavy skillet add 1 teaspoon olive oil over medium-high heat. Add the ground meat, stirring constantly with a wooden spoon to break up any clumps. When no pink remains and the meat is lightly browned, remove and strain fat. Add meat to the sauce, and wine, if using. Simmer for 30 to 35 minutes. One or two minutes before serving, add the remaining parsley and basil.

Makes 3½ to 4 cups sauce

Ragu con Carne Varie
Tomato Sauce with a Variety of Meats

This elaborate, slow-simmering old world *ragu* is perhaps the one most familiar to southern Italian immigrants. It is an important ingredient for a traditional Calabrian Sunday dinner—the *ragu* to cook the meat and to dress the pasta. The variety of meats transforms it into a wonderfully aromatic *ragu* quite different from northern Italian sauces, which usually contain small amounts of meat cut into tiny pieces. Calabrians insist on some form of pork—a pork butt or sausage—believing that pork flavors a sauce best. My mother shared that view. Often an inexpensive cut of beef is added, transfiguring itself into a tender morsel, although meatball lovers may opt for these instead. Feature glorious beef (or veal) *braciole* and your family and friends will love you forever! Traditionally, the pasta was eaten first and the meat reserved for the second course, to be eaten with a side dish of vegetables or salad. Today, however, it is often served alongside the pasta, combining the first and second course, followed only by a salad. This recipe can easily be doubled and the other half frozen.

1   recipe *Salsa di Pomodoro* (Tomato Sauce, page 121)
2   tablespoons olive oil
½   pound pork butt, all fat removed, or ½ recipe *Salsiccia Piccante di Casa* (Homemade Spicy Sausage, page 161)
½   pound piece of lean beef roast, all fat removed, or ½ recipe *Polpette* (Meatballs, page 152)
1   pound *Braciole di Manzo alla Calabrese* (Rolled Stuffed Beef, Calabrian Style, page 148), or 1 pound *Braciole di Vitello alla Calabrese* (Rolled Stuffed Veal, Calabrian Style, page 165)

In a large pot over medium heat, add the tomato sauce. Cover and let simmer slowly.

Add olive oil to a large, heavy skillet over medium-high heat. If using pork or beef, sauté each for 8 to 10 minutes or until nicely browned, turning occasionally. Set aside. If using sausages, meatballs, or *braciole*, prepare according to their recipes and add to the sauce. Simmer sauce slowly for 2½ to 3 hours, or until all meat is cooked and tender, stirring occasionally.

Remove meat, slice, and arrange on a warmed serving platter.

Makes 3 to 3½ cups sauce (excluding meat)

Salsa di Capra alla Bova Superiore
Goat, Tomato, and Wine Sauce, Bova Superiore Style

To serve this dish, you will have to find an Italian or Mediterranean specialty store that carries goat. Goat is a traditional Calabrian wedding entrée served over ziti (which means bridegroom). It is also a choice for Easter. Buy ridged ziti; it holds sauce better. I had the good fortune to have several outstanding meals in La Primula Restaurant in Bova Marina on both trips to Calabria. I asked Isabella Dellavilla, the proprietor's daughter, about preferred choices for wedding dinners celebrated at the restaurant. She named this dish among today's choices.

3 pounds young goat
2 cups red wine vinegar
3 tablespoons olive oil, divided
1 pound onions, coarsely chopped
4 ounces dry white wine
1 28-ounce can Italian plum tomatoes, coarsely chopped
4 tablespoons tomato paste
1 bay leaf
½ teaspoon fresh rosemary
¼ teaspoon salt
¼ teaspoon crushed red pepper

Wash the meat well and cut into 1-inch cubes. Put meat in a large saucepan with sufficient water to cover. Add the vinegar and stir the meat well. Drain and rinse thoroughly until water is clear. Remove meat and pat dry with paper towels.

In a large, heavy skillet, add 1 tablespoon olive oil over medium heat. Add onion and sauté for 4 to 5 minutes or until translucent. Remove and set aside. Add remaining olive oil and meat. Brown for 8 to 10 minutes, stirring frequently. Add wine and continue to simmer until most evaporates.

Add tomatoes, tomato paste, bay leaf, rosemary, salt, and crushed red pepper. Mix well. Lower heat and simmer for 4 to 6 hours or until meat is tender, stirring occasionally. The length of time will vary depending on the age of the goat. If the sauce begins to thicken too much, add a little water.

Remove bay leaf before serving.

Serves 6 to 6½ cups sauce

Salsa di Capretto alla Calabrese

Roast Kid in Onion, Cheese, and Tomato Sauce, Calabrian Style

Not many cookbooks in the United States include recipes for kid, but in Calabria, there are several. To serve this interesting dish, you will have to find an Italian or Mediterranean specialty store that carries kid. Kid and goat are still traditional entrees for weddings and Easter in many parts of Calabria. I therefore decided to include a recipe for each because of their continued traditional use. Of course, ziti is the pasta choice for weddings, since the word means bridegroom.

2½	pounds kid
6	tablespoons olive oil, divided
2	large white onions, coarsely sliced
1	cup dry white wine
1½	pounds fresh tomatoes, coarsely chopped, or 1 28-ounce can Italian plum tomatoes, coarsely chopped
½	cup water
3	tablespoons grated pecorino cheese
½	teaspoon salt
½	teaspoon dried oregano
¼	teaspoon freshly ground black pepper

Preheat oven to 350° F.

Wash and dry the meat. Cut into 1-inch cubes.

In a large, heavy skillet, add 2 tablespoons olive oil over medium heat. Add onion and sauté for 4 to 5 minutes or until translucent. Remove and set aside. Add 2 tablespoons olive oil and about half the meat in a single layer. Do not crowd. Brown for 8 to 10 minutes, stirring frequently. Remove and set aside. Add remaining 2 tablespoons olive oil and the remaining meat and brown as above. Return meat to skillet and add wine. Simmer until most of the wine evaporates.

Transfer meat to a lightly oiled 10-by-14-inch casserole. Distribute the onions and tomatoes over all and drizzle with the water. Sprinkle with the cheese, salt, oregano, and pepper. Cover and bake for 1½ to 2 hours, or until meat is tender. The baking time will depend on the age of the kid. If sauce begins to thicken too much, add a little water.

Makes 6 to 6½ cups sauce

VARIATION: Some Calabrian cooks add 3 medium potatoes, cut into 1½-inch cubes, along with the tomatoes.

Polenta con Formaggio
Polenta with Cheese

Creamy polenta with cheese is a great side dish served creamy hot. It also can be chilled, cut into squares, and then fried, baked, or broiled. It is a good vegetarian choice. Italian-style polenta is readily available in supermarkets these days, but American cornmeal can be substituted. Cooking polenta can be tricky. Add it slowly to cool or warm water and stir constantly. Adding it to boiling water produces lumps that do not dissolve.

- 4 cups water
- 1 cup polenta or yellow cornmeal
- ½ teaspoon salt
- 4 ounces mozzarella or provolone, cut into ¼-inch cubes
- ⅓ cup freshly grated pecorino or Parmesan cheese
- ¼ teaspoon freshly ground black pepper

In a large saucepan, add water over low to medium heat. Slowly add polenta and salt, stirring constantly with a wooden spoon to avoid lumps. Stirring constantly, cook for 45 to 50 minutes or until polenta thickens, is smooth, and comes away from the side of the pan. If using a quick-cooking polenta, follow the cooking directions on the package; some cook in as little as 8 to 10 minutes. Remove polenta from heat and mix in the mozzarella or provolone, grated cheese, and pepper. Stir vigorously until the cheese melts.

To serve hot and creamy: Spoon immediately onto plates.

To serve at room temperature or chilled: Turn onto a wooden board and spread to a ½-inch thickness. Let cool and cut into 3-inch square pieces. Pieces can either be fried in olive oil just long enough for each side to brown and be heated through, or they can be broiled for 3 minutes, 1 to 1½ minutes each side or until browned. In either case, do not leave unattended.

Serves 4 to 8

Polenta con Salsìcce e Pomodori
Polenta with Sausage and Tomatoes

When, in the sixteenth century, polenta arrived in southern Italy from Spain, it was the main meal—an inexpensive substitute when pasta was not available. Today, polenta can serve as an appetizer, a side dish, or if topped with meat or cheese as here, even as an entrée.

½ pound sweet or hot Italian sausage
2 tablespoons plus 1 teaspoon olive oil
½ small onion, finely chopped
2 cloves garlic, finely minced
1 16-ounce can Italian plum tomatoes, coarsely chopped
1 tablespoon fresh basil, coarsely chopped
½ teaspoon salt
¼ teaspoon freshly ground black pepper
4 cups water
1 cup polenta or yellow cornmeal
1 teaspoon salt
¼ cup freshly grated pecorino or Parmesan cheese

Remove sausage meat from casing. In a large, heavy skillet add 1 teaspoon olive oil over medium heat. Add loose sausage and sauté until all pink disappears. Remove with slotted spoon and drain on paper towels. Set aside. Remove fat from skillet with paper towels, but do not wash.

Add the 2 tablespoons olive oil to the skillet. Add onion and sauté for 3 to 4 minutes or until translucent. Add garlic and sauté for 1 to 2 minutes or until light golden brown. Add tomatoes, basil, salt, and pepper. Lower heat and simmer for 15 minutes.

Preheat oven to 375° F.

In a large saucepan, add water over low to medium heat. Slowly add polenta and salt, stirring constantly to avoid lumps. Stirring constantly, cook for 45 to 50 minutes, or until polenta thickens, is smooth, and comes away from the side of the pan. If using quick-cooking polenta, follow the cooking directions on the package; some cook in as little as 8 to 10 minutes. Remove polenta from heat and allow to cool slightly.

Spread half the polenta in a lightly greased, 12-inch-square baking dish. Distribute sausage evenly over top and ladle ⅓ to ½ of the tomato sauce over the sausage. Spread remaining polenta over sausage. Sprinkle with cheese and bake for 20 to 25 minutes or until set and top is golden brown. Cut into 3-inch squares and serve immediately. Pass remaining sauce at the table.

Serves 4 to 8

CUISINE

A dieta ugni male queta.

The diet minimizes all ailments.
<small>CALABRIAN PROVERB</small>

To Italians, food is far more than nourishment for the body. It is an expression of love, a ritual closely linked to tradition. All meals in the Italian family are treated with reverence. Eating is almost sacred in Italy; meals are an occasion, a celebration. Love and attention are lavished in the preparation of even the simplest and humblest dish. Family life in Calabria centers around the dining table, where the family gathers at midday for the most important meal of the day and again in the evening for somewhat lighter fare. The family eats together daily and talks, taking time, taking pleasure. Family values are inculcated and reinforced, and traditions are forged that continue for generations and span continents.

Even in today's busier, changing times, the extended Calabrian family, here and abroad, still comes together on holidays and special occasions as it has done for countless generations. They believe that food keeps the family close, that it is a means of bonding, and that it nourishes both the body and the soul. Eating together and preparing the foods our ancestors ate are ways of maintaining family ties and keeping Italian-American families close to their heritage.

In the *Mezzogiorno*, creativity begins in the kitchen. Even the most humble Calabrians, who are as imaginative as they are sentimental about their food, treat it with special reverence and appreciation. They take nature's abundance and present it at its best. Nothing is wasted; everything is put to good use. Here more than anywhere applies the saying "They have made a virtue of necessity." Their skill in the kitchen historically disguised poverty with ingenuity.

I invite you to take a culinary journey with me into the world of irresistible Calabrian food. It is exciting and diverse, home cooking at its best—spontaneous, creative, beguiling, and robust. Although Calabrian cooking was and to a certain extent still is frugal it should not be misinterpreted as limited or unappetizing. Its straightforward simplicity can be misleading. Natural, fresh foods are enhanced with just the right amount of distinctive ingredients and herbs—such as capers, anchovies, crushed red pepper, basil, parsley, sage—

to create an appetizing, savory, colorful cuisine that truly reaches great heights. Ingredients are brought together in a perfect harmony of flavors.

Calabrians have a wonderful way with all food but especially with vegetables, which are an important part of their diet. They prepare them in an infinite variety of delectable ways, never plain, with as much care and reverence as if creating a work of art. They know intuitively which ingredients go well together and which herbs and in what amounts will enhance them, producing dishes with intense flavor and flair. They do not smother their food in sauces but rather let the flavor and color come through, preserving its identity.

Perhaps one of many reasons why Italian food is so widely loved is that it represents a style of home cooking that suits the majority of people everywhere. As Joyce Goldstein stated in her excellent book *Back to Square One*, "What they knew, they knew." She could have been talking about my ancestors.

Gabriella Mari and Christina Blasi of the Scuola de Arte Culinaria Cordon Bleu of Florence teach that "Cooking is first a science, then an art." This, they explain, is because before one can become an artist, one must first understand the physical and chemical principles of food and the techniques of food preparation. Italian cooks understand this and weave this technical and creative knowledge into their everyday creations. Italian restaurants, in fact, are often a family affair. The owner's mother is still found behind the scenes working alongside the trained chef, each learning from the other.

Some recipes in this cookbook go back to ancient times. The foundations of Italian cooking were laid by the Etruscans in the north, the Greeks in the south, and later the Saracens. Perhaps none were more knowledgeable than the Romans, however. They contributed expertise to food preparation, cooking, and dining as well as to preservation, salting, and drying. It wasn't until the Middle Ages that the rest of Europe learned these skills. The Romans were also quick to learn culinary secrets from other countries, including Greece and Asia Minor. A book devoted to the art of cooking, *De re Coquinaria* (*Concerning Cooking*) by Apicius, is the most ancient of European cookbooks. All subsequent food literature in Europe was influenced by Apicius. Particularly notable was a fifteenth century cookbook author named Bartolomeo Platina.

Roman meals consisted of at least three courses: an appetizer, the main course, and a dessert, mostly fruit. And, of course, all meals included bread. Food writer Serafino Amabile Guastella (could we be related?) explained that in the seventeenth and eighteenth centuries, hunger was so rampant in southern Italy and Sicily that sometimes even bread was not available to peasants in abundance.

A staple dish of the Romans was a mush made from a primitive kind of wheat or chickpea flour. When eaten immediately it had the consistency of oatmeal; allowed to harden, it was sliced and fried or eaten cold. It was the precursor of today's polenta, still eaten in all of Italy though preferred by northern Italians.

Romans raised sheep for food and wool. Other early food sources included cheese made from ewe's milk. In time, they came to learn that the goat, sheep, and ox could serve to plow and seed the soil and later, thresh grain. Romans were the first to consider sanitation of their water supply. They constructed a vast system of aqueducts to bring the clean waters of the Apennine Mountains into Rome and built basins and filters to ensure clarity of the water.

Outdoor/indoor markets have existed in Italy since the second century. Shopping as well as eating *al fresco* (outdoors) came early to the Romans. The multilevel market built by Emperor Trajan was located in Rome near the Forum. Its remains are evidence of imperial grandeur. The semicircle indoor/outdoor building with arches contained various shops selling meats, local fish, wheat, oil, spices, wine, and cosmetics. Prior to this "super market," suppliers of these products were scattered about the city. Now each owned and ran his own shop in one place, to the gratitude of the people.

Today in Italy, outdoor markets still thrive. Going to market is a part of everyday life in most cities. Even in little villages, a market is available once or twice a week. Noisy and fragrant, markets carry fresh foods in season as well as olive oils, an infinite variety of dried pastas, dried or preserved foods, and canned foods.

Italians have always been considered good cooks. From early Roman days to Italy's glorious Renaissance during the fourteenth through sixteenth centuries, Italy led the world in gastronomic arts. The first fully developed cuisine in Europe was Italian. Attaining that status was painstakingly slow—from a humble beginning, it had taken around 1,500 years to reach that stage. Outside of Italy, however, the art of cooking was still in the Middle Ages, according to sixteenth-century French culinary historian Georges Blond. Italian chefs brought to France by Catherine de Medici in the early 1500s taught cooking to the French. The torch was then passed to the rest of Europe. By the end of the sixteenth century, Europe began to be transformed in many ways, not the least of which included a dramatic change in food crops, significantly improving the versatility and nourishment of cuisine. Meanwhile, housewives in Italy were busy creating culinary wonders of their own.

Even in the poorest villages, the ingenuity and creativity of housewives in Calabrian kitchens is now recognized as remarkable. Not content only to serve new foods alongside the old, they skillfully incorporated them and new spices into their time-honored cuisine, transforming them into an unforgettable blend of flavors while preserving their identity. They added potatoes to flour and created gnocchi; transformed corn into polenta; added vegetables to main dishes, sauces, and soups; and found many uses for fresh and dried beans. Italians invented pizza, were first to introduce the world to sugar, first to perfect espresso, and first to create ice cream.

One of the greatest creations of them all, however, is their beloved pasta. Various forms of pasta were served during ancient times. The Romans served some form of lasagne and gnocchi. The Chinese had their *mein*, the Japanese their *udon*, the French their *nouilles*, the Polish their *pierogi*, the Germans their *spaetzle*, and the Italians their *maccheroni*. Some say the word *maccheroni* is derived from *ma, che carini*—my, what little dears—others say it is a derivation of the Greek word, *makar*, which means divine. Either definition is delightful. The same care and devotion are given to pasta dishes served daily in Italy as they receive for special occasions.

The Spanish introduced several vegetables to Europe, including potatoes and most important, the tomato about the sixteenth century. It had traveled from Peru, Equador, and Bolivia to Mexico and the rest of Central America. It was then brought to Spain by the Conquistadors. Most of Europe did not know what to do with it. Southern Italians found the greatest use of the tomato and were the first to acknowledge its greatness and diversity. Dressing pasta with a tomato sauce was a major achievement, and combining it with other foods quickly followed. Eventually, the tomato became a fundamental part of their diet.

Tomatoes were primarily confined to the south until Garibaldi (revered for his role in helping to unite Italy in 1871) stopped in Melito in Calabria and had pasta with a tomato sauce. When he and his soldiers returned north, they took the recipe for the tomato sauce with them. Slowly, the combination spread to northern Italy and Europe. It is still served most frequently in the south.

Calabria's extended 485-mile coastline yields a wealth of seafood for the second course, some varieties of which are unknown to America. However, swordfish, fresh tuna, mussels, clams, squid, red mullet, eels, and even the famous *baccala* (dried cod) can be found in most American markets. Each province of Italy has its own recipes for fish.

Although each province believes its cuisine to be the best, Calabrian cooking rivals that of any other part of Italy. As more and more people discover it, the reputation of the area's excellent cuisine grows. In the United States, southern Italian food is fast being discovered. This ties in with emphasis on the "Mediterranean diet," with its heavy emphasis on bountiful fresh vegetables, fresh fruit, legumes, grains, complex carbohydrates, fish, light use of olive oil, and sparing use of meat. In 1993, a conference was held in Cambridge, Massachusetts entitled "Traditional Diets of the Mediterranean." A group of experts on diet and health, scientists and scholars from around the world, assembled to evaluate the Mediterranean diet. After about a year of deliberation, a document was published featuring a dietary pyramid similar to the United States Department of Agriculture (USDA) pyramid, but with vastly different recommendations. The main difference is that the Mediterranean diet places meat at the top of the pyramid and recommends it be eaten in small amounts only several times per month. The USDA had placed meat, poultry, fish, and eggs at the bottom, with the recommendation of two to three servings daily. The Mediterranean diet recommends the use of olive oil, which was not included in the USDA pyramid.

The experts made known to the world what Italians had known for years. The world now recognized that the *cucina povera* diet of Mediterranean countries, with their excellent health statistics, was and had been the "Mediterranean diet." Its message is one of variety, balance, and moderation, not deprivation.

Few adjustments needed to be made at the tables of Italians, north or south, regarding the sparing use of red meat. At one time meat was absent from the tables of poor Italians. Even today, when economics may no longer be a factor, meat mainly plays a supporting role to the vegetable and pasta dishes which star in Calabrian cooking. As for the use of olive oil, Italians cannot cook without it. However, a significant step toward improving our health is to reduce the amount of all fat in our diet. The recipes in this book have done that without sacrificing taste. The secret is to reduce, not eliminate, as the experts announced. As we strive to eat more healthfully, we can look to Calabria for its tempting treasures to sustain and delight us. Good, old-fashioned, family-style home cooking, peasant cooking, is being acclaimed good for you!

Fruits, vegetables, and spices were brought to Italy from a variety of sources, including the Middle East, Greece, Spain, Portugal, India, and China. Each of these peoples left their trade-mark in Italy. Some were brought to Europe by Christopher Columbus in his voyages. Hunger, ever present in daily life for millennia, continually spurred the peasants to adopt new sources of food.

Yet even into the early 1900s, for the most part, southern Italian cooking was unknown in northern Italy, and vice versa. Only recently, for example, provincial cooking is becoming known and appreciated throughout the country as the tradition of handing down recipes from one generation to the next began to include the recording of measurements. It seemed that for centuries, Calabrians passed on recipes outside the family only reluctantly and only in whispers, almost as though they were jealously guarding them from the rest of the country.

Some of that division between provinces in Italy persists to this day, though it is slowly changing. The tangy intensity and richness of Calabrian and southern Italian food ranks among the most adventurous and diversified of all the regional cuisines of Italy. Recipes from Calabria are beginning to trickle up into other provinces, where they are being adopted enthusiastically. Likewise, Calabrians are beginning to incorporate certain northern delicacies with their own. Slowly, very slowly, all are learning that each region of Italy has its own specialties, its own delights.

Some say that for a time French cuisine surpassed that of Italy. But for some years now, Italian food has re-invaded France to the expressed delight of the French and pride of the Italians. Pasta and other Italian dishes can be found in some of the very best restaurants in Paris and in the south of France. They often replace butter with olive oil or reduce it substantially, grill or roast meats free of rich sauces, replace shallots with garlic and chervil with Italian parsley. Italy's savory food is still considered by many to be the most diversified and tempting of any European country.

Southern Italians' affinity with the land and deep love for cultivating the soil assumes an almost religious devotion. Their very soul is tied to the land. Their skill in gardening has long been recognized and praised. In Calabria, farming was carried out under very difficult conditions. Much of the terrain is mountainous or rocky, and there is not much water. Irrigation existed only in northern Italy for centuries. It was only through strong motivation and persistence that farmers were able to produce ample vegetables and fruits to feed the nation, even while they were left with little enough for themselves. When peasants eventually were able to have land of their own, no matter how small, they planted their beloved vegetables. They knew vegetables must be picked at just the right time, must not travel far, and must be cooked immediately. Nor did they believe in adding preservatives to prolong the vegetable beyond its natural time.

When Calabrians and southern Italians immigrated to the United States, they brought their cuisine with them. Even while beginning to adapt to their new country, they tenaciously maintained and followed time-honored concepts and methods. They had to give up country, village, home, and often the extended family, but they did not have to give up their food, which was perhaps most important to their ethnic identity. At first, they had to grow their own vegetables and herbs, since many were not available in the new world.

Soon neighborhood Italian stores began to sprout, providing immigrants with their native foods. If no such stores were yet available, there were peddlers with truckloads of wonderful Italian delicacies—olives, meats, cheeses, fresh vegetables, and fruits. As a child, I recall my confirmation godmother Josephine's father, Pasquale Ciccui, delivering from his truck, 25-pound wooden boxes of various pastas, whole salami, prosciutto, capocollo, luscious muted green and wrinkled black olives, imported olive oil, and many cheeses, stocking our walk-in pantry with the foods essential to our cuisine. Gone now are the peddlers, but most supermarkets carry many Italian delicacies, and thriving Italian specialty stores carry just about everything.

Because the growing season in the northeastern United States is much shorter than in southern Italy, preserving food in our home was essential—and frugal. Our pantry was stocked with jars of canned tomatoes, vegetables, and fruits that sprang forth from my father's garden to my mother's busy hands. Canning the many tomatoes, however, was a family undertaking. Dad coordinated the process while he, my mom, my sister, and I did various tasks in assembly-line fashion. I didn't realize it then, but my parents taught me many values that have served me my entire life. Among them, Dad taught me to love the earth and its abundance. I have always had a vegetable and herb garden, no matter how small. Mom taught me to love to cook and how to do it well.

Most of us, here and abroad, no longer preserve, can, or freeze food to the extent we once did, but some of my relatives in Bova Superiore, Bova Marina, and Reggio Calabria still preserve some of their own meats, grow vegetables and herbs, bake their own bread, make homemade fusilli, and make their own pecorino cheese. Even though some shortcuts are taken, the Calabrian table, a true mosaic of cuisines, survives beautifully.

It has been said that you can't have a bad meal in all of Italy. Great food and great scents await you everywhere. Many fine restaurants serve spectacular food, but you need not go only to renowned restaurants in major cities for outstanding food. Even small restaurants and trattorias do not disappoint. Often a tiny village has a trattoria that presents unbelievably good meals at modest prices. What may have sounded like a simple, straightforward dish becomes exquisite as each bite mixes pleasure with amazement. Owner and staff welcome you warmly—happy to see you and eager to please. When you leave, you realize a fair exchange has occurred. You are as fortunate to have been there as they are to have had your business.

Likewise, wherever you travel in the United States, you will find many good Italian restaurants. They are the most popular ethnic restaurant even though Italian descendants rank fifth in population among European immigrants after the English, German, Irish, and French. My hometown of Marblehead, Massachusetts, with a population of about 22,000, has eight Italian restaurants and several pizza parlors. Most are quite good.

For some time, most Italian restaurants in this country were a mere facsimile of authentic Italian fare, north or south. Restaurants were split between a limited variety of northern Italian fare and few southern Italian dishes other than spaghetti and meatballs with one tomato sauce. In time, chefs began to implement a more authentic Italian style and attitude, observing response. So well received were they that today, more and more menus contain a wider variety of southern Italian and Calabrian dishes.

One thing Italians here and in Italy have in common is that they never rush meals at home or in restaurants. Food is to be savored. They don't squeeze time to eat between other things, they take time before other things to sit down with the family, relax, talk over the day's events, and enjoy a good meal. Few Italians "eat and run" even in today's faster world. Food is an important part of their identity, and they are passionate about it. It provides them with a deep sense of cultural connection.

Calabrian food is truly an adventure. To those whose experience with it is somewhat limited, I hope this book will entice you to join in the adventure, exposing you to new and delectable dishes from soup to desserts from a region not extensively explored. To those of Calabrian descent, may you discover dishes you have not eaten or thought about in years, some you may have never seen on paper and some new ones. To those with ancestors from Abruzzi, Basilicata, Apulia, Campania, Molise, Sicily, and Sardinia, may you find some familiar-sounding recipes. To all others who love Italian food, you're in for a treat as well.

Whatever your background, this book is designed to encourage you to try dishes that may be new and exciting and, in some cases, filled with memories of food that are penetratingly familiar. You will be delighted with the infinite variety and originality of Calabrian cuisine, from the simple to the elegant.

CARNE E POLLAME

MEAT AND POULTRY

Gallina e porcelli per la bocca si fan belli.

The chicken and the pig are wonderful to eat.
Calabrian proverb

In Italy, a small serving of meat, poultry, or fish is served after the pasta course. At one time, meat was only for the rich, and fish was only available to those living directly on the coast. Except on special occasions or holidays, meat was absent from the tables of all poor Italians, north or south. Even today, when economics may be less of a factor for most, meat mainly plays a supporting role. To most Italians, in fact, meat is a side dish rather than the focus. When meat is served in Calabria, however, it is prepared and seasoned in as creative and delicious a manner as can be found anywhere.

Pork was the common centerpiece of medieval feasts. Regal and proud, the suckling pig surrounded by mountains of vegetables was a welcome sight to the multitude. Since its domestication between 8000 to 6000 B.C., the pig, common in China and Sumeria, was a boon. Small in size, it could be kept in or about the house and fed scraps, potatoes, and chestnuts (which grow wild). It matured in one year and was prolific—capable of having two litters of up to twelve piglets each—and produced excellent tasting meat. For some time in ancient Greece and Italy, only the rich could afford to raise pigs, sheep, or goat other than for sacrificial occasions. In time, however, pigs became more readily available to them and like the Chinese, they recognized their culinary potential and adopted them as their own.

Pork still ranks high in the cuisine of all southern Italians, and Calabrians transform it into such princely fare! *Porchétta Arrostito* (Roast Suckling Pig, page 160), is still a traditional endeavor for very special occasions. However, roast pork is so desirable that roasting an entire pig evolved into the more manageable *Maiale Arrosto con Patate* (Roast Herbed Pork with Golden Roasted Potatoes, page 159). The seasonings mingle with the potatoes, culminating in a heavenly, delectable meal.

Famous throughout all of Italy are southern Italian hot-and-spicy, fresh-and-dried sausages. Calabrian dried sopressata is made with cut-up pork rather than ground, seasoned with herbs, and dried in various shapes and sizes. Other pork products include salami, one of the most popular; capicola, which also ranks high; prosciutto; and pancetta. Sliced meats are most often served as an antipasto at lunch rather than dinner.

Prosciutto is a heavenly dry-cured ham from the pig's hind leg. There are many varieties, but Parma prosciutto is considered by many the king of prosciuttos. If you have never tasted it, you are missing out on an extraordinary culinary experience. Air dried, it has a sweet, subtle, delicate, and unique taste that is cherished! Served as an antipasto, it is paired with melon or fresh figs, and it is added to pasta sauces, entrées, and vegetable dishes. And, of course, it is heaped between two slices of crusty Italian bread or onto a hard roll, with or without cheese or vegetables.

Pancetta is similar to our bacon but is milder, unsmoked, and salt cured. If you must substitute bacon for pancetta, blanch the bacon for 2 or 3 minutes first to reduce the smoked flavor.

Taming wild goats and sheep is said to have been comparatively easy. Domestication began about 9000 B.C. in Romania and almost simultaneously in Iraq. Sheep and goats were readily available in Palestine, and kid, a young goat, sweet and tender, adorned tables at the court of the Caliphs in the Persian Empire. *Capra* (goat) and *capretto* (kid) are still served in Calabria, often at weddings to observe ancient traditions. They are obtainable in Italian specialty stores in certain areas.

Highly regarded for centuries, chicken has been domestically raised for thousands of years. Domestication may have begun with the Indian jungle fowl in Pakistan at about the fourth millennium B.C. The Roman food writer Apicius cited recipes for chicken in his cookbook.

I read with interest how making a wish on the chicken's "wishbone," or collarbone, evolved. The custom appears to have begun with the Etruscans over 2,000 years ago. Chickens were believed capable of providing answers to questions through priests' interpretation of their pecking at grains. The chicken was cooked and eaten, and the collarbone was then dried and stroked, but not broken. The Romans were the first to begin breaking the *forcella* to make a wish. Getting the longer half meant your wish would come true. And we've been doing it ever since!

In Italy, chickens are sold whole, and all parts are used. For example, chicken feet are added to broth for stronger flavor. Calabrians living in rural areas often still raise their own chickens and pigs. Chicken has always been a bargain. It is versatile and easy to prepare. It is considered one of the most popular of all proteins throughout the world.

Chicken is classified according to its age and size. Year-old stewing hens or fowls produce the most flavorful soup, but roasters are also suitable for soup, as well as for roasting or braising. Fryers can be fried, sautéed, roasted, or braised. The younger broiler/fryers are not flavorful enough for soup and are best suited for broiling, grilling, or roasting.

Capon, lamb, rabbit, and veal, are also included in Calabrian cuisine. Tastier than turkey and a bit more impressive than chicken, roast capon is a top choice at Christmas. Roast baby lamb is a traditional Easter choice and a good source of B vitamins. One can still see shepherds and their flocks lingering in the hills of Calabria.

Although extremely popular in Europe, rabbit—low in fat and high in protein, bred by the early Romans—has not caught on in the United States except for the adventurous. My cousins Mimma Dieni Favasuli and Maria Dieni Cuppari served a delicious stewed rabbit with tomatoes, peppers, and onions one evening while I was in Calabria researching this book.

Each meat or chicken dish in the chapter is designed to complement in taste, texture, and color the pasta dishes in the preceding chapter, as well as other foods. One expects nothing less from Calabrians, who create simple, satisfying, and scrumptious meals with the patience of a chemist and the eye of an artist.

Scaloppine di Manzo alla Calabrese
Beef Cutlets, Calabrian Style

While in Calabria one night, I decided to find a hotel and a nearby trattoria where I was rather than go back into town. Luckily, I stumbled upon a great restaurant with fine Calabrian food and wonderful people. Dino Leone, the owner of the Due C Ristorante in the town of Luzzi, willingly gave me some recipes. A short time later, his sister and brother-in-law, Amelia and Giuseppe Pirri, introduced themselves and graciously contributed this recipe as well. After dinner, their two adorable young daughters, Lea and Daniella, came to meet me. Before long, I found myself encircled by members of their family and other friendly diners.

  1 **pound thinly sliced (⅛-inch) fillets of beef**
  ½ **cup all-purpose flour**
  3 **tablespoons fresh Italian parsley, finely chopped, divided**
  ½ **teaspoon salt**

¼ teaspoon freshly ground black pepper
2 tablespoons extra-virgin olive oil
½ cup dry white wine
6 ounces button mushrooms, thinly sliced

Pound beef slices to tenderize and make them even thinner, being careful not to tear the meat. In a large flat dish, add flour, 2 tablespoons parsley, salt, and pepper. Dredge beef lightly on both sides, shake excess, and set aside.

In a large, heavy skillet, add olive oil over medium-high heat. Sauté beef for 2 to 3 minutes, turning once. Lower heat, add wine and mushrooms, and simmer for 2 to 4 minutes or until meat is tender. Put meat on serving platter. Pour mushrooms and liquid over top. Sprinkle with remaining parsley and serve hot.

Serves 4

TIP: When freezing slices of beef, put a piece of wax paper between each slice. In this way, it is easy to remove only as many as you need.

Braciole di Manzo alla Calabrese
Rolled Stuffed Beef, Calabrian Style

Braciole is a traditional Calabrian Christmas dish. Mom served it every Christmas and on other special occasions. It is a dish I eagerly learned from her. When my sons and their families come to visit, they invariably ask for it. *Braciole*, with its flavorful stuffing, makes a scrumptious entrée. Use the heavenly-flavored sauce to dress your pasta, or dribble it on top of the rolls and serve alongside vegetables.

BRACIOLE:
1½ pounds top round steak, sliced ¼-inch thick
2 hard boiled eggs, peeled and chopped finely
½ cup dried bread crumbs, coarsely ground
6 tablespoons freshly grated pecorino or Parmesan cheese
4 tablespoons fresh Italian parsley, finely chopped
3 cloves garlic, finely minced
1 tablespoon olive oil
½ teaspoon salt
¼ teaspoon freshly ground black pepper

2 tablespoons olive oil

1 small onion, coarsely chopped

1 clove garlic, finely minced

1 16-ounce can Italian plum tomatoes, coarsely chopped

2 tablespoons fresh basil, coarsely chopped

2 tablespoons fresh Italian parsley, coarsely chopped

¼ teaspoon salt

Pound slices of meat with a *battecarne* (mallet) to tenderize, being careful not to tear the meat. Cut into pieces about 8-inches long. Spread them on a flat working surface.

In a medium bowl, mix the chopped eggs, bread crumbs, cheese, parsley, garlic, olive oil, salt, and pepper. Divide mixture evenly among the slices. Using the shorter side of the meat, gently roll up the slices, jelly-roll fashion. Tie the rolls securely in several places with kitchen string.

In a large, heavy skillet over medium heat, add olive oil. Sauté onion for 3 to 4 minutes or until translucent. Add garlic and sauté for 1 to 2 minutes or until light golden brown. Remove from heat and set aside.

Raise heat to medium-high. Using tongs, put meat in the skillet. Do not crowd. Sauté for 6 to 8 minutes, turning to brown all sides. Add onion and garlic, tomatoes, basil, parsley, and salt. Lower heat, cover, and simmer gently for 1 hour, turning occasionally, or until meat is tender to the probing touch of a fork. Do not overcook, or meat will fall apart. Transfer to a serving platter, remove string, and cut into 2-inch slices. Serve immediately.

Serves 4 to 8

Cotolette di Manzo in Padella con Limone
Beef Slices with Lemon

What makes this quick-and-easy sautéed dish different is the addition of lemon while cooking. It adds a tartness I like. It's the kind of fast entrée that works well if you forgot to remove something from the freezer early in the morning. Bottom round is a good choice, but you can use your favorite cut. Veal also works well here. The important thing is that the slices be very thin.

1 pound ⅛-inch-thick slices of bottom round beef,
6 to 8 inches long

          2 tablespoons olive oil
          ½ clove garlic, coarsely chopped
          ½ lemon, juiced
          2 tablespoons hot water
          ¼ teaspoon salt
          ⅛ teaspoon freshly ground black pepper
          1 tablespoon fresh Italian parsley, finely chopped
          1 lemon, cut into 4 wedges

Pound beef slices to tenderize them and to make them even thinner, being careful not to tear the meat.

In a large, heavy skillet add olive oil over medium heat. Add garlic and sauté for 1 to 2 minutes or until light golden brown. Remove and discard. Raise heat to medium-high. With tongs, put in only as many meat slices as fit comfortably; otherwise they will not brown. Sauté for 3 to 4 minutes or until lightly browned, turning once. Remove from skillet and keep warm. Repeat process until all slices are cooked.

Add lemon juice and hot water to skillet, scraping the bottom and sides with a wooden spoon. Return meat to skillet, sprinkle with salt and pepper, and let simmer for 1 to 2 minutes. Transfer to a serving platter, sprinkle with parsley, garnish with lemon wedges, and serve immediately.

Serves 4

Bistecca alla Pizzaiola
Beef Steak with Tomatoes

Calabrians don't eat a lot of red meat, but this flavorful dish is becoming more popular for special occasions. The beef, cooked gently in tomatoes and spices to absorb their flavor, makes an elegant, enticing entrée.

       1½ pounds sirloin steak, ⅜-inch thick
          2 tablespoons extra-virgin olive oil
          1 small onion, coarsely chopped
          3 cloves garlic, finely minced
          1 pound ripe tomatoes, coarsely chopped, or
             1 16-ounce can Italian plum tomatoes, coarsely chopped
          ¼ cup black olives, oil-cured, pitted and halved (optional)

¼ teaspoon dried oregano

¼ teaspoon salt

¼ teaspoon freshly ground black pepper

Trim steak of fat, then pound with a *battecarne* or mallet for 1 to 2 minutes, taking care not to tear the meat.

In a large, heavy skillet, add olive oil over medium heat. Sauté onion for 3 to 4 minutes or until translucent. Add garlic and sauté for 1 to 2 minutes or until light golden brown. Remove onion and garlic and set aside.

Raise heat to high. Sear the steak for 2 to 3 minutes to lock in the juices, turning once with tongs so as not to pierce it and allow the juices to escape. Lower heat. Add onions and garlic, tomatoes, olives if using, oregano, salt, and pepper. Simmer uncovered for 5 to 8 minutes, depending on desired doneness. Remove steak to a platter and cut into wedges. Ladle pan juices over meat and serve at once.

Serves 4 to 6

Stufato di Manzo
Beef Stew, Simmered Slowly in Red Wine

When southern Italians were able to afford beef, it didn't matter if the cut was tender or not. They let it cook slowly, enhanced with the addition of wine, vegetables, and herbs. This produced a tender and tasty stew.

¾ cup burgundy wine

1 clove garlic, finely minced

1 teaspoon sage

1 teaspoon rosemary

2 pounds boneless lean beef, cut into 1-inch pieces

2 tablespoons all-purpose flour

2 teaspoons fresh Italian parsley, finely chopped

1 teaspoon salt

½ teaspoon freshly ground black pepper

2 tablespoons olive oil

1 large onion, coarsely sliced

2 stalks celery, thickly sliced

1½ cups beef stock or water

2   teaspoons tomato paste
1   large potato, cut into 1-inch cubes

In a small bowl, mix wine, garlic, sage, and rosemary. Put the beef in a glass baking dish and add the marinade. Cover and let marinate, refrigerated, for at least 2 hours or overnight.

Remove meat from marinade and reserve marinade. Pat meat dry with paper towel. In a flat dish, mix flour, parsley, salt, and pepper. Roll meat in flour and set aside.

Add olive oil to a large, heavy skillet over medium-high heat. Sauté onion and celery for 3 to 4 minutes or until onion is translucent. Remove and reserve. Add meat and brown on all sides. Add marinade, beef stock, and tomato paste to skillet. Simmer slowly for 2 hours. Return onion and celery to skillet, add potato, and simmer for 1 hour more or until meat is tender, stirring occasionally.

Serves 6

Polpette
Meatballs

No matter how sophisticated Americans have become about trying the infinite variety of southern Italian food, their desire for meatballs has not diminished. Several factors may dramatically change the texture of meatballs, such as whether you use bread crumbs or dry stale bread, and whether you fry or bake them or simmer them in sauce. Using bread crumbs and frying them produces crusty meatballs. Fried meatballs are heavenly as is, make great sandwiches, and can be enlisted as an entrée. Baking meatballs made with bread soaked in water and squeezed dry produces softer-textured meatballs. If meat is extra-lean, meatballs also can be dropped uncooked right into a simmering sauce. For years I have used an ice-cream scoop to form meatballs; it saves time and ensures uniform size. I just round them off slightly by hand.

4   large slices day-old Italian bread, or
     ¾-cup dry bread crumbs plus 2 tablespoons water
1   pound extra-lean ground beef
     (or any combination of beef, lean pork, and veal)
2   large eggs, lightly beaten
2   tablespoons freshly grated pecorino or Parmesan cheese

2 cloves garlic, finely minced
2 tablespoons fresh Italian parsley, finely chopped
¾ teaspoon salt
¼ teaspoon freshly ground black pepper
4 tablespoons olive oil for frying

If using bread instead of bread crumbs, put slices in a small bowl, add water to soften, and let stand for several minutes. Squeeze dry and break into bits.

In a large mixing bowl, add bread, or add bread crumbs plus 2 tablespoons water. Add meat, eggs, cheese, garlic, parsley, salt, and pepper. Knead until well blended. Make balls about the size of a large egg and roll in the palm of your hands until they are firm and fully rounded (or use an ice-cream scoop).

To fry: In a large, heavy skillet, heat olive oil over medium-high heat. Add meatballs and, with a small wooden spoon, roll gently for 20 to 25 minutes or until all sides are uniformly crisp and brown and no pink remains in center. Add to tomato sauce.

To bake: Preheat oven to 350° F. Put meatballs on a lightly oiled cookie sheet. Bake 20 to 25 minutes, or until no pink remains in center. Add to tomato sauce.

To cook in sauce: Simmer in sauce for 30 to 35 minutes or until no pink remains in center.

Makes about 10 meatballs

Agnello al Forno con Patate
Roast Baby Lamb with Golden Roasted Potatoes

Lamb is one of the most traditional Calabrian entrées served at Easter. It has a deep-rooted heritage and an ancient religious significance. The Jewish custom of sacrificing a lamb to God is said to have been the basis for Italians and Greeks serving it at Easter. Later, lamb came to symbolize Christ. Lamb should weigh no more than about 18 pounds; past that it is mutton and has a heavy taste.

1 6- to 8-pound half baby lamb, or one 4- to 5-pound leg of lamb
½ cup fresh Italian parsley, coarsely chopped
2 teaspoons dried rosemary
4 cloves garlic, finely minced
5 to 6 tablespoons olive oil, divided
1½ teaspoons salt

½	teaspoon freshly ground black pepper
6 to 8	potatoes, peeled and cut into large wedges
½	teaspoon salt
⅛	teaspoon freshly ground black pepper

Preheat oven to 400° F.

Trim meat of any fat. With a sharp knife make slits in the form of Xs throughout the meat. Mix parsley, rosemary, garlic, 1 tablespoon of olive oil, salt, and pepper. Force mixture into the slits. With a pastry brush, coat meat with 2 tablespoons olive oil. Put in an oiled 13-by-15-inch roasting pan.

In a large mixing bowl, add potatoes and drizzle with remaining olive oil. Mix thoroughly until all sides of potatoes are coated. Scatter potatoes around meat in a single layer; do not crowd. Roast lamb for about 15 minutes per pound, about 1½ hours to 1¾ hours, or until internal temperature on a thermometer reaches 140° to 150° F for rare or 150° to 155° F for medium. Turn roast over once and turn potatoes occasionally with a sturdy spatula to brown all sides. Season potatoes with salt and pepper about 5 to 10 minutes before meat is done. If roast is done but potatoes are not golden brown, remove roast and keep warm. Raise oven temperature to 450° F. Put potatoes back in oven for 5 to 10 minutes or until deep golden brown.

Put roast in center of serving platter and surround with the potatoes. Serve immediately.

Serves 6 to 8

Costolette di Agnello con Mollica di Pane
Lamb Chops with Seasoned, Crunchy Crumb Topping

Lamb chops lovingly smothered with this crusty topping are smashing! And they can be prepared in minutes.

2	tablespoons olive oil, divided
1¼	pounds baby lamb chops (about 8)
2	cloves garlic, finely minced
½	cup fine bread crumbs
2	tablespoons fresh Italian parsley, finely chopped
¼	teaspoon salt
¼	teaspoon freshly ground black pepper

Preheat broiler for 5 minutes, with oven door slightly ajar.

Heat 1 tablespoon olive oil in a large, heavy skillet over medium to high heat. Quickly sear and brown the chops on both sides for 2 to 3 minutes. Lower heat and continue sautéing for 3 to 5 minutes or until chop centers are pink or reach the desired doneness. Set aside.

In a medium skillet add remaining olive oil over medium heat. Sauté garlic for 1 to 2 minutes or until light golden brown. Add bread crumbs, parsley, salt, and pepper. Mix constantly for 1 minute until just lightly toasted. Remove from heat and set aside.

Remove lamb chops from skillet and arrange on broiler pan. Sprinkle the crumb topping over each lamb chop. Put under broiler and brown for up to 1 minute, watching carefully to avoid burning the crumb topping. Serve immediately.

Serves 4

Morzeddu

Liver, Heart, and Lung in a Tomato Wine Sauce

A dish with a long past attributed to the city of Catanzaro, this medley of liver, heart, and lung called *morzeddu,* "big bite," is served on or with small, bite-sized pieces of flatbread or crostini. I was surprised to learn that it is not uncommon in some parts of Calabria for this dish to be served at breakfast, although it is more generally served at lunch or dinner. Some supermarkets and most Italian specialty markets carry these meats. For those who enjoy spicy food, increase crushed red pepper to taste.

½ pound veal liver
½ pound veal lung
½ pound veal heart
2 tablespoons olive oil
1 medium onion, coarsely chopped
3 cloves garlic, finely minced
1 16-ounce can Italian plum tomatoes, coarsely chopped
¼ cup dry red wine
½ teaspoon salt
¼ teaspoon crushed red pepper

Remove fat from veal liver, lung, and heart; and wash thoroughly. Put lungs and heart only in a large bowl filled with cold water and salt and let soak for 30 minutes. Remove, rinse, drain on paper towels, and pat dry. Finely chop liver, lung, and heart. Set aside.

In a large, heavy skillet over moderate heat, add olive oil. Sauté onion for 3 to 4 minutes or until translucent. Sauté garlic for 1 to 2 minutes or until light golden brown. Remove onion and garlic and reserve. Add the liver, heart, and lung to skillet. Sauté for 5 to 7 minutes, turning frequently, until lightly browned. Return onion and garlic to the skillet and add the tomatoes, wine, salt, and crushed red pepper. Lower heat, cover, and simmer for 35 to 40 minutes or until all meats are tender. Serve immediately.

Serves 6 to 8

Costolette di Maiale al Limone
Pork Chops Sautéed with Lemon

In ancient times, the Greeks sacrificed pigs to their goddess Maia, hence *maiale* for pork. The pig traveled to Sumeria, China, Egypt, Italy, and many other countries. It was domesticated and therefore looked upon as a good omen, and southern Italians began raising and consuming it. Although they do not eat meat in large quantities, pork is most often the preferred choice. This is a near effortless way to serve savory pork chops.

> ¼ cup flour
> ½ teaspoon salt, divided
> ½ teaspoon freshly ground black pepper, divided
> 4 loin pork chops, ¾-inch thick, trimmed of fat
> 2 tablespoons olive oil
> 1 clove garlic, finely minced
> ¼ cup dry white wine
> 1 lemon, freshly juiced
> ¼ teaspoon fresh sage, finely chopped
> 1 lemon, quartered, for garnish

In a small bowl, mix flour, ¼ teaspoon salt, and ¼ teaspoon pepper. Dredge pork chops in the flour mixture.

In a large, heavy skillet add olive oil over medium heat. Sauté garlic for 1 to 2 minutes or until light golden brown. Remove and discard. Sauté the chops for 6 to 8 minutes, turning once, until lightly browned. Lower heat and add wine, lemon, sage, and remaining salt and pepper. Cover and simmer for 35 to 40 minutes, basting periodically, until golden brown and fully cooked through. If liquid evaporates, add a little water. Chops are done when no pink remains in the meat. Transfer pork chops to a serving platter, pour pan juices over top, and serve immediately with lemon wedges.

Serves 4

Costolette di Maiale alla Pizzaiola
Pork Chops with Tomatoes, Peppers, and Mushrooms

Pork has played an important role in Calabrian cuisine since ancient times. In this recipe, pork chops are combined with vegetables, producing a contrast in color and flavor that is as aesthetically pleasing as it is satisfying.

  2 tablespoons olive oil, divided
  2 cloves garlic, finely minced
  4 loin pork chops, ¾-inch thick, trimmed of fat
  ¼ cup dry white wine
  ½ teaspoon salt
  ¼ teaspoon crushed red pepper (optional)
  ⅛ teaspoon dried oregano
  1 cup fresh or canned Italian plum tomatoes, coarsely chopped
  1 large red or green pepper, seeded and cut into ¼-inch strips
  8 ounces button mushrooms, coarsely sliced

In a large, heavy skillet add 1 tablespoon olive oil over medium heat. Sauté garlic for 1 to 2 minutes or until light golden brown. Remove and discard. Sauté the pork chops for 6 to 8 minutes, turning once, until lightly browned. Remove and set aside. Raise heat and add wine, salt, crushed red pepper if using, and oregano. Continue to cook until wine is reduced by about half.

Add tomatoes and return chops to the skillet. Lower heat, cover, and simmer for 35 to 40 minutes, basting periodically, until chops are fully cooked through. Chops are done when no pink remains in the meat.

Meanwhile, in a medium skillet, add remaining olive oil over medium heat. Sauté red or green pepper for 6 to 8 minutes, stirring frequently. Add mushrooms and sauté for 2 minutes, turning frequently. Transfer peppers and mushrooms to the skillet with the cooked chops and mix thoroughly. Simmer for 2 or 3 minutes to allow ingredients to blend. Transfer pork chops to a serving platter, pour pan juices and vegetables over top, and serve immediately.

Serves 4

Costolette di Maiale con Peperoni sott' Aceto
Pork Chops with Vinegar Peppers

Combining flavorful pork chops with tart vinegar peppers was a clever idea. They complement each other nicely. Vinegar peppers are available in Italian specialty stores and most supermarkets.

> 2 tablespoons olive oil
> 1 clove garlic, finely minced
> 4 loin pork chops, ¾-inch thick, trimmed of fat
> ½ cup white wine vinegar
> ½ cup water
> 5 vinegar peppers, coarsely chopped
> 4 anchovy fillets, coarsely chopped (optional)
> 2 tablespoons fresh Italian parsley, finely chopped
> ¼ teaspoon freshly ground black pepper

In a large, heavy skillet, add olive oil over medium heat. Sauté garlic for 1 to 2 minutes or until light golden brown. Remove and reserve.

Raise heat to medium-high. Add pork chops and cook for 6 to 8 minutes, turning once, until lightly browned. Lower heat and add vinegar and water. Cover and cook for 35 to 40 minutes basting periodically, until golden brown and fully cooked through. Chops are done when no pink remains in the meat.

Remove pork chops and keep warm. Return garlic to the skillet and add vinegar peppers, anchovies if using, parsley, and pepper. Stir and simmer for 2 to 3 minutes or until anchovies are dissolved. Return chops to skillet and heat through. Transfer chops to a serving platter, pour pan juices over top, and serve immediately.

Serves 4

Maiale Arrosto con Patate
Roast Herbed Pork with Golden Roasted Potatoes

Roast pork is always served for the Feast of St. Anthony the Abbot on January 17th. This method of stuffing the pork with such highly flavorful ingredients is common in the province of Campania as well as in Calabria and is the way my late mother-in-law, Stella Mauriello Palmer Palleschi, prepared it as well. The aroma emitted from the oven while the meat is roasting is enticing; the golden potatoes absorb flavor from the herbs and pan juices; and the result is taste perfection!

1	4 to 4½ pounds boned pork loin or pork butt
½	cup fresh Italian parsley, coarsely chopped
6	cloves garlic, finely minced
2	tablespoons grated pecorino or Parmesan cheese
4	tablespoons olive oil, divided
1¾	teaspoons salt, divided
½	teaspoon plus ⅛ teaspoon freshly ground black pepper, divided
6 to 8	potatoes, peeled and cut into large wedges

Preheat oven to 350° F.

With a sharp knife, make slits in the form of Xs throughout the meat. Mix the parsley, garlic, cheese, 1 tablespoon olive oil, 1½ teaspoons salt, and ½ teaspoon pepper and force into the slits. Set aside.

Put potatoes in a bowl, add remaining olive oil, and mix well until all sides are coated.

Put meat in a lightly oiled 12-by-15-inch roasting pan. Scatter potatoes around the meat in a single layer; do not crowd. Roast pork for approximately 30 minutes per pound, covered for 1 hour and uncovered for an additional 1 to 1½ hours or until internal temperature reaches 170°F on a meat thermometer. Turn roast over once and turn potatoes occasionally with a sturdy spatula to brown on all sides. Pork is done when no pink remains. Season meat and potatoes with ¼ teaspoon salt and ⅛ teaspoon pepper about 5 minutes before meat is done.

If roast is done but potatoes are not sufficiently browned, remove roast to a warm platter and cover lightly with foil. Raise over temperature to 450° F. Turn potatoes over and return pan to oven. Bake for 5 to 6 minutes or until a deep golden brown. Carve roast just before potatoes are done. Remove potatoes from oven and arrange them around the roast. Serve immediately.

Serves 6 to 8

Porchétta Arrostito
Roast Suckling Pig

Spit-roasting a pig is a traditional southern Italian endeavor. Of course, it can also be roasted in the oven. The ideal weight for a *porceddu*, as it is called in Calabrian dialect, is under 15 pounds when the pig is about 6 weeks old. In the United States, you will have to order a pig from an Italian specialty market or from your supermarket. The pig was often the centerpiece of medieval feasts throughout much of the ancient world. Roast Suckling Pig served with *Patate al Forno* (Golden Roasted Potatoes, page 235) and *Maiale Arrosto con Patate* (Roast Herbed Pork with Golden Roasted Potatoes, page 159) are choices for Christmas dinner and for the Feast of St. Anthony the Abbot on January 17th. St. Anthony is often depicted with a friendly pink pig at his side; among other things, he is patron saint of domestic animals.

> 1   suckling pig, 10 to 15 pounds
> ½ cup olive oil, or more as needed
> 2   tablespoons salt
> 2   teaspoons freshly ground black pepper
> 2   cloves garlic, finely minced

Clean pig or have your butcher do so. Remove entrails and wash thoroughly inside and out with warm water. Pat dry with paper towels. In a small bowl, mix olive oil, salt, and pepper. Rub the outside of the pig with some of the olive oil. Add garlic to remaining oil and with a pastry brush, also coat inside. Tie front legs together with kitchen string and tie hind legs together stretched backward. Cover ears and tail with foil to prevent burning. Slash pig on either side of the backbone to prevent it from bursting.

To cook on a spit: Impale pig on a large skewer and put on spit, 18 inches away from the fire. Baste pig with remaining olive oil from time to time, adding more if needed. Turn occasionally to brown evenly. Cook for 3½ to 5 hours (20 to 22 minutes per pound) or until the internal temperature reaches 170° F and the pig is a rich golden brown. Cut into its meatiest part to insure that no pink remains. Remove pig from spit, remove skewer, and put pig on a large platter to let rest for 10 to 15 minutes for ease in carving. Slice and serve hot.

To roast in the oven: Preheat oven to 350° F.

Place pig in a large, oiled roasting pan and roast uncovered. Baste pig with remaining olive oil from time to time, adding more if needed. Turn occasionally to brown evenly. Periodically, remove pan from oven, pour off fat, and return to oven. Cook 3½ to 5 hours (20 to 22 minutes per pound) or until pig is a rich golden brown and the internal temperature reaches 170° F. Cut into its meatiest part to ensure that no pink remains. Remove, place on a large platter, and let rest for 10 to 15 minutes to make carving easier. Slice and serve hot.

Serves 10 to 15

Salsìccia Piccante di Casa
Homemade Spicy Sausage

Making your own sausage is not hard. The immediate advantages are that you can use less fat and you can season it to your personal taste. If you are unaccustomed to hot foods, begin with less crushed red pepper. Packed in salt, sausage casing is available in various size packages at most supermarkets and at Italian specialty stores. If you do not have a special sausage funnel, you can buy one with a ½- or ¾-inch opening at an Italian specialty store. You can sauté, bake, broil, or grill the sausage. Whichever method you choose, be sure to cook it until no trace of pink remains.

> 1   **package of sausage casing**
> 1   **pound lean pork, coarsely ground**
> 1   **teaspoon fennel seeds**
> ½   **teaspoon crushed red pepper or freshly ground black pepper**
> ½   **teaspoon salt**

Wash the sausage casing thoroughly in cold water. In a large mixing bowl, combine all other ingredients and mix well. Push one casing over the sausage funnel end. Gently stuff the meat into the wide end of the funnel. As the casing loosens from the funnel filled with the sausage meat, prick it periodically with a needle to eliminate air bubbles. Twist every 3½ inches to mark the length of each sausage link. Continue this process until all meat is used.

To sauté: Prick each sausage link on all sides with a fork to allow fat to escape. In a large, heavy skillet add water over medium-high heat with water halfway up sausage. As the water begins to evaporate, the sausages will begin to brown. Continue to simmer for 30 to 40 minutes, or until no pink remains, turning occasionally. Drain on paper towels and serve hot.

To bake: Preheat oven to 325° F.

If you are cooking a large quantity of sausage, it is easier to bake them. Prick each sausage link on all sides with a fork to allow fat to escape. Put sausages on top of a broiler pan to allow fat to drip into lower pan and bake for 30 to 40 minutes, or until no pink remains, turning occasionally. Drain on paper towels and serve hot.

To broil: Preheat broiler for 5 minutes with door ajar. Prick each sausage link on all sides with a fork to allow fat to escape. In addition, you may cut each link in half to ensure thorough cooking and to ensure a larger crustier surface. Put sausages on top of a broiler pan to allow fat to drip into lower pan. Lower broiler temperature to 350° F. Broil for 30 to 35 minutes if whole, or 15 to 20 minutes if cut in half, or until no pink remains, turning occasionally. Drain on paper towels and serve hot.

To grill: Prick each sausage link on all sides with a fork to allow fat to escape. In addition, you may cut each link in half to ensure thorough cooking and to ensure a larger crustier surface. Put sausages on an oiled grid 4 to 6 inches above hot coals. Grill for about 30 minutes if whole, or about 15 minutes if cut in half, or until no pink remains, turning occasionally. Drain on paper towels and serve hot.

Serves 4

Salsìcce, Peperoni, e Cipolle
Sausage, Peppers, and Onions

No festival, here or in Italy, takes place without the classic combination of savory sausage, peppers, and onions. Wrapped with a cut hard roll, these compatible ingredients represent the true essence of "street food."

> 2 large red bell peppers
> 2 large green bell peppers
> 3 tablespoons olive oil, divided
> 2 medium or 1 large onion, thinly sliced
> 2 cloves garlic, finely minced
> 8 Italian sausages, hot or sweet
> 8 Italian sandwich rolls

Wash and dry all 4 peppers. Cut out stems, remove seeds, and cut into 1-inch pieces.

In a large, heavy skillet, add 1 tablespoon olive oil over medium heat. Add onion and sauté for 3 to 4 minutes or until translucent. Add garlic and sauté for 1 to 2 minutes or until light golden brown. Remove with slotted spoon and reserve.

Add remaining 2 tablespoons olive oil. Add peppers and sauté for 5 to 6 minutes, turning frequently, until the peppers just begin to brown. Lower heat and continue sautéing for 10 to 12 minutes or until tender. Remove with slotted spoon and reserve.

Meanwhile, prick each sausage link with a fork to allow fat to escape. Add to skillet and raise heat to medium-high. Add water halfway up the sausage. As the water begins to evaporate, the sausages will begin to brown. Continue to simmer for 30 to 40 minutes, turning occasionally until no pink remains. Drain on paper towels.

Drain fat from skillet and wipe clean, but do not wash. Return onion, garlic, peppers, and sausage to the skillet and mix thoroughly. Let simmer for 2 or 3 minutes to allow ingredients to mingle.

Put 1 sausage, smothered with peppers and onions, into a hard roll and serve while hot or warm.

Serves 8

VARIATION: Add 1 cup fresh or canned Italian plum tomatoes, coarsely chopped, to peppers halfway through cooking.

Coniglio con Verdura alla Contadina
Rabbit with Vegetables, Peasant Style

Do try this recipe if you have never tasted rabbit before. Available in Italian specialty stores and some supermarkets, it has a unique, sweet taste. In this Calabrian dish, rabbit is combined with vegetables and simmered slowly so the flavors have plenty of time to mingle. Tomato paste is added for color as well as for taste. Serve with *Patate al Forno* (Golden Roasted Potatoes, page 235), a green vegetable, and crunchy Italian bread to soak up the sauce for a satisfying meal.

    1   3- to 3½-pound rabbit, cut into 10 serving pieces
    3   tablespoons olive oil
    1   medium onion, coarsely chopped
    1   celery stalk with leaves, thinly sliced
    1   carrot, thinly sliced
    2   cloves garlic, finely minced
    ¼   cup red wine vinegar
    ½   cup water
    1   tablespoon tomato paste

3 tablespoons fresh Italian parsley, finely chopped
1 bay leaf
½ teaspoon salt
¼ teaspoon freshly ground black pepper

Wash rabbit pieces thoroughly and rinse in cold salted water. Drain on paper towels and pat dry.

In a large, heavy skillet add olive over medium heat. Add rabbit and sauté for 8 to 10 minutes, turning frequently, until nicely browned. Add onion, celery, and carrot and sauté for 4 to 6 minutes or until onions are translucent. Add garlic and sauté for 1 to 2 minutes or until light golden brown.

Combine the vinegar, water, and tomato paste. Stir into the skillet. Add parsley, bay leaf, salt, and pepper. Lower heat and continue to simmer for 40 to 45 minutes, turning rabbit once or twice, until it is tender to the probing touch of a fork and no pink remains near the bones. Do not overcook, or it will become dry. If too much of the liquid has evaporated, add a few teaspoons of water. Remove bay leaf and serve immediately.

Serves 4 to 6

TIP: A timesaving, efficient way to handle a can of tomato paste is to line a pie tin with waxed paper, measure out tablespoons of paste, put on paper, and freeze. When frozen, remove and pop into a zippered plastic bag. When a recipe calls for tomato paste, it is premeasured, easy to spot, and waiting for you.

VARIATION: Add 2 ounces chopped pancetta when sautéing the onion, but reduce the olive oil by 1 tablespoon.

Trippa con i Diavuliddi e Pomodori
Tripe in a Peppery Hot Sauce

For those who enjoy tripe, this recipe should please. For those who like it hot, this recipe will delight. *Diavuliddi* in Calabrian dialect refers to the "devilish" hot peppers. Because the dish requires time to simmer, you may want to make it early in the day or even the day before.

1 pound tripe
2 tablespoons olive oil
½ large onion, coarsely chopped

1 clove garlic, finely minced
1 medium red pepper, seeded and coarsely chopped
1 stalk celery, coarsely chopped
1 16-ounce can Italian plum tomatoes, coarsely chopped
2 tablespoons fresh Italian parsley, finely chopped, divided
1 bay leaf
½ teaspoon crushed red pepper
¼ cup freshly grated pecorino cheese

Wash tripe thoroughly under cold running water. Rinse in cold salted water. In a large soup pan over high heat, add tripe and enough cold water to cover. Cover pan and bring to a boil. Immediately lower heat and cook for 1½ to 2 hours or until just tender. Drain and rinse with cold water. Cut into ½ inch strips.

In a large, heavy skillet add oil over medium heat. Add onion and sauté for 3 to 4 minutes or until translucent. Add garlic and sauté for 1 to 2 minutes or until light golden brown. Add pepper and celery and sauté for 6 to 8 minutes or until lightly browned. Lower heat and add tripe, tomatoes, 1 tablespoon parsley, bay leaf, and crushed red pepper. Simmer for 25 to 30 minutes, or until tripe is tender. Stir in cheese and remaining parsley, then cook for 2 minutes to allow ingredients to blend.

Remove bay leaf and serve hot with crusty Italian bread.

Serves 4

Braciole di Vitello alla Calabrese
Rolled Stuffed Veal, Calabrian Style

Veal rolls have a variety of names, including *rollatini*, depending on the province. The origin of this dish proved hard to trace. I suspect it is reasonably new to the province of Calabria, but several Calabrians happily shared their recipes with me. It is a welcomed variation for serving veal. To enhance the veal's mild taste, prosciutto is added to the stuffing. Veal rolls are equally at home accompanied by a side order of pasta or an assortment of vegetables.

1½ pounds of boneless veal cutlets, sliced ¼-inch thick
½ cup dried bread crumbs, coarsely ground
2 ounces provolone cheese, coarsely chopped
2 ounces prosciutto, coarsely chopped

- 2 tablespoons fresh Italian parsley, finely chopped
- 3 tablespoons olive oil, divided
- 1 clove garlic, finely minced
- ¼ teaspoon salt
- ¼ teaspoon freshly ground black pepper
- ¼ cup dry white wine
- ¼ cup chicken or vegetable broth or hot water

Pound slices of meat with a *battecarne* (mallet) to tenderize them, being careful not to tear the meat. Cut into pieces 6- to 8-inches long. Spread them on a flat working surface.

In a medium bowl, mix the bread crumbs, cheese, prosciutto, parsley, 1 tablespoon olive oil, garlic, salt, and pepper. Divide mixture evenly among the slices. Using the shorter side of the meat, gently roll up the slices, jelly-roll fashion. Tie the rolls securely in several places with kitchen string.

In a large, heavy skillet over medium heat, add the remaining 2 tablespoons olive oil. Using tongs, add meat to the skillet. Do not crowd. Sauté for 6 to 8 minutes, turning to brown all sides.

Add ½ cup each of the wine and broth. Lower heat and continue cooking for 20 to 25 minutes or until veal is tender, turning occasionally and adding remaining liquid as needed. Do not overcook, or meat will fall apart. Transfer to a serving platter, remove string, and cut into 2 inch slices. Serve immediately.

Serves 4 to 8

Vitello con Peperoni, Patate, e Pomodori
Veal with Peppers, Potatoes, and Tomatoes

Here is a wonderful, savory combination of ingredients that has been a favorite of mine since childhood. When my sons come to visit, they often ask me to make it, and I am always happy to oblige them (and me). Serve this with crusty Italian bread and a green salad.

- 1 pound boneless stew veal
- 1 large red bell pepper
- 1 large green bell pepper
- 5 tablespoons of olive oil, divided

1   large onion, coarsely sliced
2   cloves garlic, finely minced
1   16-ounce can Italian plum tomatoes, coarsely chopped
1   tablespoon fresh Italian parsley, coarsely chopped
1   tablespoon fresh basil, coarsely chopped
½   teaspoon salt
¼   teaspoon freshly ground black pepper
2   potatoes, peeled, halved, and cut into thin slices

Remove fat from veal, cut into 1-inch cubes, and set aside.

Wash and dry both peppers. Cut out stems, remove seeds and cut into 1-inch pieces. Set aside.

In a large, nonstick skillet, heat 1 tablespoon olive oil over medium heat. Add onion and sauté for 3 to 4 minutes, or until translucent. Add garlic and sauté for 1 to 2 minutes, or until light golden brown. Remove both with a slotted spoon and reserve.

Increase heat to medium-high. Add 2 tablespoons olive oil. Add veal in small batches without overcrowding. Sauté for 5 to 6 minutes or until lightly browned on all sides, turning constantly. Remove and set aside. Continue process until all veal is sautéed. Return all veal to the skillet along with the cooked onion and garlic, tomatoes, parsley, basil, salt, and pepper. Lower heat and simmer for 1 to 1½ hours or until veal is almost tender.

Meanwhile, in another large, nonstick skillet, add the remaining 2 tablespoons olive oil over medium heat. Sauté peppers, stirring constantly, for 5 to 6 minutes, or until peppers just begin to brown, stirring occasionally. Lower heat and continue sautéing for 10 to 12 minutes or until tender. Remove with a slotted spoon and set aside.

Add potatoes and sauté for 10 to 12 minutes, stirring constantly until browned on all sides. Add a little more olive oil if needed. Combine peppers with potatoes and sprinkle with salt. Mix thoroughly.

When veal is tender, add the peppers and potatoes. Mix thoroughly and let simmer for 2 or 3 minutes to allow ingredients to blend. Serve immediately.

Serves 4 to 6

Vitello con Pomodori e Vino Rosso
Veal Stewed in Tomatoes and Red Wine

Calabrians do not eat much meat, but when they do, this is one recipe they choose. Once you try it, you will know why. This versatile, delectable veal stew can be served alongside of pasta such as linguine or fettuccine or next to vegetables such as broccoli or roasted peppers. It works anywhere. This special, great-tasting treat evokes warm and loving memories. Tasted at my home, Linda Bassett, a food writer and teacher, wrote: "A bite of this stew brought back memories of my grandma's cooking."

2	pounds stewing veal, boned
3	tablespoons olive oil
1	onion, coarsely chopped
2	large cloves garlic, finely minced
1	16-ounce can Italian plum tomatoes, coarsely chopped
½	cup dry red wine
3	tablespoons fresh Italian parsley, finely chopped, divided
1	teaspoon salt
1	bay leaf

Remove any fat from veal and cut into 1-inch cubes.

In a large, heavy skillet, add olive oil over medium heat. Add onion and sauté for 3 to 4 minutes or until translucent. Add garlic and sauté for 1 to 2 minutes or until light golden brown. Remove both and set aside.

Increase heat to medium-high. Add veal without crowding to permit it to brown. Sauté for 8 to 10 minutes or until browned, turning frequently, then set aside. Continue until all veal is sautéed, then return all browned veal to skillet. Add tomatoes, wine, 2 tablespoons parsley, salt, and bay leaf. Lower heat, cover, and simmer for 1½ to 2 hours, stirring occasionally, or until veal is tender. If sauce seems too thick, add a little water. Return onions and garlic to the skillet, add remaining parsley, and mix well. Let simmer for 5 minutes to allow ingredients to blend. Remove bay leaf and serve at once.

Serves 6 to 8

TIP: This dish tastes even better if made a day ahead.

Cappone Arrosto con Patate
Roast Capon with Golden Roasted Potatoes

Capon is a favored choice for Christmas dinner in Calabria and all of Italy. It is more flavorful and festive than chicken. Capons are available in most supermarkets or in Italian specialty stores. Save every precious bone and bit of meat and use them to make *Brodo di Pollo* (Chicken Broth, page 68), as capon makes an excellent broth. To stuff the capon, see *Pollo Ripieno Arrosto con Patate* (Roast Stuffed Chicken with Golden Roasted Potatoes, page 175).

1	6- or 7-pound capon
3	tablespoons olive oil, divided
¼	teaspoon salt
⅛	teaspoon freshly ground black pepper
6 to 8	large all-purpose potatoes, peeled and cut into large wedges
½ to ¾	cup dry white wine

Preheat oven to 350° F.

Wash capon thoroughly but quickly under cold running water. Pat dry with paper towels. Brush inside and out with about 1 tablespoon olive oil. Rub with salt and pepper.

Put potatoes in a bowl, add remaining 2 tablespoons olive oil, and mix well until all sides are coated.

Put capon, breast side up, in a lightly oiled 12-by-15-inch roasting pan. Scatter potatoes around capon in a single layer; do not crowd. Cover with a loose tent of foil to prevent breast from overcooking (dark meat takes longer to cook than white). Roast capon for about 25 to 30 minutes per pound. After 1 hour, baste capon with half the wine. Roast for an additional hour and baste with remaining wine. Roast for a total of 3 to 3½ hours or until internal temperature reaches 170° F for the breast meat and 185° F for the thigh. Capon will be a deep golden brown. Turn potatoes over occasionally with a sturdy spatula to brown on all sides.

If capon is done but potatoes are not browned, remove capon to a warm platter and cover lightly with foil. Raise oven temperature to 450° F. Turn potatoes over and return pan to oven. Bake for 5 to 10 minutes or until a deep golden brown. Just before potatoes are done, carve capon and put meat on a serving platter. Then remove potatoes from oven and put around the capon. Serve immediately.

Serves 6 to 8

Pollo alla Griglia, Marinato in Limone e Capperi
Grilled Chicken Marinated in Lemon and Capers

Summer is the ideal time to prepare chicken in this simple but savory way. The tangy marinade delivers a refreshing, light taste.

1	2½- to 3½-pound chicken
½	cup lemon juice, freshly juiced
⅓	cup olive oil
2	cloves garlic, thickly sliced
2	tablespoons capers
1	tablespoon fresh Italian parsley, finely chopped
½	teaspoon crushed red pepper
¼	teaspoon salt
	lemon wedges, for garnish

Cut up chicken into 8 serving pieces. Rinse thoroughly but quickly under cold running water. Pat dry with paper towels.

Combine lemon juice, olive oil, garlic, capers, parsley, and crushed red pepper. Pour marinade into a flat glass baking dish large enough to hold chicken in one layer. Immerse chicken and let marinate for at least 30 minutes, turning once. To marinate longer, for a maximum of 2 hours, refrigerate and turn every hour. Remove from refrigerator ½ hour before grilling.

Preheat grill.

Put chicken on an oiled grid 5 to 6 inches above coals. Grill over hot coals for 30 minutes, turning and basting occasionally, until chicken is cooked through. Chicken is done when a thigh is pierced with the tip of a knife and its juice runs clear.

Put on warm serving dish and sprinkle with salt. Serve immediately with lemon wedges.

Serves 4

TIP: Do not add salt to a marinade. It draws out the juice of fish or meat and makes the cooked dish drier.

Pollo alla Cacciatora

Hunter-Style Chicken

A Calabrian restaurateur once told me, "If it has tomatoes, peppers, and onions in it, it's Calabrian." That description certainly applies to this popular dish as well as to many others. When added to the sauce for this chicken, they absorb the chicken juices and the herbs and almost magically create a glorious topping for pasta or for soaking up with crusty Italian bread. Rabbit can be substituted for the chicken.

1	2 ½- to 3-pound chicken fryer
1	large green bell pepper
1	large red bell pepper
4	tablespoons olive oil, divided
1	medium sweet onion, coarsely chopped
2	cloves garlic, finely minced
4 to 6	ounces button mushrooms, coarsely chopped (optional)
1	16-ounce can Italian plum tomatoes, coarsely chopped
2	tablespoons fresh Italian parsley, coarsely chopped
½	teaspoon salt
¼	teaspoon crushed red pepper

Cut up chicken into 8 serving pieces and remove skin. Rinse thoroughly but quickly under cold running water. Drain on paper towels and pat dry.

Cut out stems from both peppers, remove seeds, and cut into 1-inch pieces.

In a large, heavy skillet, heat 1 tablespoon olive oil over medium-high heat. Add onion and sauté for 3 to 4 minutes or until translucent. Add garlic and sauté for 1 to 2 minutes or until light golden brown. Remove both with slotted spoon and set aside.

Add 1 tablespoon olive oil and peppers and sauté for 10 to 12 minutes or until light golden brown. Remove with slotted spoon and add to onions and garlic. If adding mushrooms, sauté for 2 to 3 minutes and add to onion, garlic, and peppers.

Add remaining 2 tablespoons olive oil and sauté chicken for 10 minutes or until nicely browned, turning frequently. Lower heat and add tomatoes, parsley, salt, and crushed red pepper. Simmer slowly for 45 minutes, turning chicken and sauce occasionally.

Return onion, garlic, peppers, and mushrooms if using, to the skillet and simmer for 8 to 10 minutes or until chicken is tender. Turn chicken occasionally. Chicken is done when a thigh is pierced with the tip of a knife and its juice runs clear.

Serves 4 to 6

Pollo con Funghi e Vino Bianco
Chicken with Mushrooms and White Wine

Here is a delectable dish that is prepared with ease. Tasters included two of the best cooks in the Albany–Schenectady, New York area, Renee and Fran Federighi. It is an excellent choice for a dinner party because much can be done ahead. Prepare the chicken for cooking, sauté the onion and garlic, and have the mushrooms ready. About an hour before serving time, sauté the vegetables, brown the chicken, and then have it simmering slowly when the guests arrive, tempting them with the tantalizing aroma.

1	2½- to 3-pound chicken fryer
2	tablespoons all-purpose flour
4	tablespoons olive oil, divided
1	medium onion, coarsely chopped
1	large clove garlic, finely minced
½	pound button mushrooms, coarsely sliced
1	cup dry white wine
½	cup chicken broth or water
½	teaspoon salt

Cut up chicken into 8 serving pieces and remove skin. Rinse thoroughly but quickly under cold running water. Pat dry with paper towels. Dust lightly with flour.

In a large, heavy skillet, add 1 tablespoon olive oil over medium-high heat. Sauté the onion for 3 to 4 minutes or until translucent. Add garlic and sauté for 1 to 2 minutes or until light golden brown. Add mushrooms and sauté lightly for 3 to 4 minutes. Remove all with a slotted spoon and set aside.

Add remaining olive oil to skillet. Sauté chicken for 10 minutes or until nicely browned, turning frequently. Reduce heat to low and add the wine. Partially cover pan and simmer for 45 minutes, basting chicken occasionally. When the wine evaporates, add chicken broth or water. Return cooked onion, garlic, and mushrooms to skillet, add salt, and simmer 10 minutes or until chicken is cooked. Chicken is done when a thigh is pierced with the tip of a sharp knife and its juice runs clear.

Serves 4 to 6

Pollo con Olive e Alici
Chicken with Olives and Anchovies

This is quite an unusual but flavorful medley. It is cooked in a skillet, so once you get the ingredients into the pan and lower the heat, you can sit back, have an aperitif or a glass of wine, and let the magic happen. Serve with vegetables and a salad.

- 1   2½- to 3-pound chicken
- 3   tablespoons olive oil
- 1   medium onion, coarsely chopped
- 2   cloves garlic, finely minced
- ½   cup dry white wine
- ¼   teaspoon dried oregano
- 1   bay leaf
- ½   teaspoon salt
- ¼   teaspoon freshly ground black pepper
- 1   cup chicken broth, divided
- ¼   cup black olives, brine-cured, pitted and sliced
- 3   anchovy fillets, coarsely chopped

Cut up chicken into 8 serving pieces and remove skin. Rinse quickly but thoroughly under cold running water. Pat dry with paper towels.

In a large, heavy skillet add olive oil over medium heat. Sauté onion for 3 to 4 minutes or until translucent. Add garlic and sauté for 1 to 2 minutes or until light golden brown. Remove both and set aside.

Raise heat to medium-high. Sauté chicken for 10 minutes or until golden brown, turning frequently. Add wine, oregano, bay leaf, salt, and pepper. Scrape any browned bits of chicken sticking to the pan. Lower heat, cover, and simmer for 15 minutes or until most of the wine has evaporated. Add ½ cup chicken broth. Simmer slowly for 40 to 45 minutes, basting occasionally, or until chicken is cooked. Chicken is done when a thigh is pierced with the tip of a sharp knife and its juice runs clear. Remove chicken and put on a large serving platter. Keep warm.

Working quickly, raise heat, remove bay leaf, and add remaining broth. Bring to a boil. Stir in olives and anchovies and cook for 1 minute or until anchovies melt. Pour pan juices over chicken and serve immediately.

Serves 4 to 6

Pollo con Prosciutto e Salvia
Chicken with Prosciutto and Sage

Sweet prosciutto and musty, minty sage team nicely with chicken to make this dish enticing.

1	2½- to 3-pound chicken fryer
3	tablespoons olive oil
1	cup dry white wine
4	thin slices prosciutto, coarsely chopped
1	tablespoon fresh sage leaves, coarsely chopped
½	teaspoon salt
¼	teaspoon freshly ground black pepper
8 to 10	whole fresh sage leaves, for garnish

Cut up chicken into 8 serving pieces and remove skin. Rinse thoroughly but quickly under cold running water. Pat dry with paper towels.

In a large, heavy skillet, add olive oil over medium-high heat. Sauté chicken for 10 minutes or until nicely browned, turning frequently. Lower heat and add wine, prosciutto, chopped sage, salt, and pepper. Partially cover skillet and simmer for 45 to 50 minutes, turning occasionally, until chicken is cooked. Chicken is done when a thigh is pierced with the tip of a sharp knife and its juice runs clear.

Remove chicken, put on serving dish, and garnish with sage leaves. Serve immediately.

Serves 4 to 6

Pollo Ripieno Arrosto con Patate
Roast Stuffed Chicken with Golden Roasted Potatoes

Roasted chicken is one of several favored Calabrian choices for Christmas Day. Roasting uncovered or only loosely covered produces the best tasting, best looking, evenly browned, crispy bird. The amount of stuffing depends on the size of the bird, but figure on about 1 cup of cubed bread for each pound of chicken. Be sure to add an extra ½ hour of cooking time for the stuffing. A small *tacchino* (turkey) can be substituted for chicken.

1	4- to 5-pound roasting chicken
3	tablespoons olive oil, divided
2	hot or sweet Italian sausage links, about ¼ pound (optional)
½	loaf day-old sliced Italian bread, cubed (4 cups)
½	cup coarsely chopped onion
½	cup coarsely chopped celery with leaves
1	tablespoon fresh Italian parsley, finely chopped
½	teaspoon poultry seasoning or minced sage
½	teaspoon salt
¼	teaspoon freshly ground black pepper
½	cup broth or water
6 to 8	large all-purpose potatoes, peeled and cut into large wedges

Preheat oven to 325° F.

Wash chicken thoroughly but quickly under cold running water. Pat dry with paper towels. Brush inside and out with about 1 tablespoon olive oil.

If using sausage, remove casing. In a small skillet over medium heat, sauté sausage until all pink disappears. Drain on paper towels. In a large bowl, combine sausage if using, bread, onion, celery, parsley, poultry seasoning or sage, salt, and pepper. Add up to ½ cup broth or water, depending on how dry the bread is, and mix until moistened. If stuffing is too loose and does not stick together, add more water. Spoon stuffing lightly into the chicken and skewer shut.

Put potatoes in a bowl, add remaining 2 tablespoons olive oil, and mix well until all sides are coated.

Put chicken, breast side up, into a lightly oiled 12-by-15-inch roasting pan. Scatter potatoes around chicken in a single layer; do not crowd. Cover with a loose tent of foil to prevent breast from overcooking (dark meat takes longer to cook than white). Roast chicken for about 25 minutes per pound. Baste chicken every hour with its own juices. Roast for a total of 2½ to 3 hours, or until internal temperature reaches 170° F for the breast and 185° F for the thigh. Chicken will be a deep golden brown. Turn potatoes over occasionally with a sturdy spatula to brown on all sides.

If chicken is done but potatoes are not browned, remove chicken to a warm platter and cover lightly with foil. Raise oven temperature to 450° F. Turn potatoes over and return pan to oven. Bake for 5 to 10 minutes or until a deep golden brown. Just before potatoes are done, remove stuffing from chicken and put in deep serving bowl. Carve chicken and put on serving platter. Remove potatoes from oven and place around the chicken. Serve immediately.

Serves 6 to 8

TIPS:
- You can make the stuffing a day ahead but do not stuff the bird until immediately before roasting to prevent bacteria from growing inside the bird. Remove leftover stuffing immediately and store separately.
- If adding sausage to the stuffing, you can cook it the day before but do not combine it with the stuffing until just before stuffing the bird.

VARIATION: If baking stuffing separately, add an additional ½ cup broth or water, place in greased casserole, cover, and bake for 25 to 30 minutes, timed to be ready when chicken is done.

Anatra alla Calabrese
Duck with Tomatoes and Marsala, Calabrian Style

Wild duck has been around in Italy for at least a couple of thousand years. First-century Roman food writer and gastronome Apicius included several recipes for it in his book *De re Coquinaria*. Duck was domesticated in Central America sometime during the sixteenth century. This nicely seasoned dish produces a savory sauce with which can dress your favorite pasta.

1	3- to 3½ pound duck, cut into 8 serving pieces
3	tablespoons olive oil
½	medium onion, coarsely chopped
1	clove garlic, finely minced
4	ounces dry Marsala wine
1	16-ounce can Italian plum tomatoes, coarsely chopped
½	teaspoon salt
¼	teaspoon freshly ground black pepper
8	ounces button mushrooms, coarsely sliced
2	tablespoons fresh Italian parsley, coarsely chopped

Remove skin from duck and rinse thoroughly but quickly under cold running water. Put pieces in colander to drain. Pat dry with paper towels and set aside.

In a large, heavy skillet add olive oil over medium heat. Sauté the onion for 3 to 4 minutes or until translucent. Add the garlic and sauté for 1 to 2 minutes or until light golden brown. Remove both and set aside. Sauté duck for 5 to 6 minutes or until browned on all sides. Lower heat, drain fat, add wine, and simmer for 15 minutes. Add the tomatoes, salt, and pepper. Simmer for 45 minutes, basting occasionally.

Add mushrooms and parsley and simmer for 4 to 5 minutes longer. Duck is cooked when a thigh is pierced with the tip of a sharp knife and its juice runs clear. Serve immediately.

Serves 4

PESCE

FISH

U pesce nata sempre: intra l'acqua, intra l'oglio, e intra 'u vinu.

The fish swims forever: in water, in oil, and in wine.

<small>CALABRIAN PROVERB</small>

For centuries the rugged coastline along the Ionian and Tyrrhenian seas has yielded Calabrians with a wealth of seafood. And for centuries, many families have made their living as fishermen. Some ancient methods for catching fish are still practiced. About 20 percent of all swordfish are still harpooned off the coast of Bagnara Calabra and in Scilla (made immortal in Homer's *Odyssey*) with the same techniques used by the Greek colonists as far back as 12,000 B.C. Each morning as the dawn mists slowly rise, small fishing boats called *ontri* or *paranze* can be seen bringing in their daily catch.

It is believed that as far back as 25,000 B.C. a fishhook with a line was developed. Post-Ice Age humans used clubs, spears, or traps such as thick branches to capture fish. Lures came later in the form of thorns. In 12,000 B.C. fishermen in France and Spain began using harpoons and shortly thereafter, bows and arrows. Dugout canoes and reed rafts used in prehistoric times were not reliable until oars came into existence in the Neolithic era at about 8000 B.C. Supplementing the hunting of animals and gathering of wild foods, fish became an important dietary addition.

Ancient Romans had access to a large variety of fish. However, fresh fish did not travel very far inland. Slow means of transportation and lack of refrigeration made it impractical. Fish was dried in the sun and/or salted to preserve what could not be eaten at once, a tradition that continues today with *baccala* (dried, salted cod). Other parts of the world also salted fish and some countries, among them Egypt and Spain, exported it as well.

Today, most fish in Italy is only hours old when bought and prepared both in the home and in restaurants. In some restaurants, live selections can be made from a watertank; in others, preparation on a wood-fired grill can be viewed. It is not unusual for a whole fish to be served for two at one table. Deftly, the waiter removes the head and tail and fillets the fish with panache, transfers it to the dinner plates, and pours its juices over the fillets.

Traditionally, southern Italians and Calabrians eat seven different dishes on Christmas Eve for the seven sacraments, nine for the trinity multiplied by three, or thirteen for the twelve apostles and Christ. Because no meat is eaten on Christmas Eve, fish appears in every course of the elaborate dinner—from antipasti to soups, pasta toppings, and entrées, and even salads. That presents no problem, for Calabria's extended 485-mile coastline yields a wealth of seafood.

Most varieties of Italian fish are available in the United States: swordfish, fresh tuna, anchovies, trout, clams, sardines, mussels, red mullet, squid, lobster, shrimp, crab, eel, dried cod, and a variety of flatfish. Swordfish is still favored in Italy, but no fish is ignored. Anchovies, however, fresh and salted, are a hallmark of Calabrian and southern Italian cuisine. The technique of adding mashed anchovies to a wide variety of foods adds a piquant note of interest and richness of flavor without being overpowering. Their use goes back to Roman times, when anchovies or other fish were preserved as a substitute for salt because salt taxes were prohibitive.

Each province of Italy has its own recipes for preparing fish. Most Italians, however, favor simple preparations that allow the fresh, subtle flavor of the fish to come through. Fish, they hold, should not be smothered in sauces or overpowered with too many flavors. Grilling over a wood fire or roasting with freshly squeezed lemon juice, a splash of olive oil, and a sprinkling of herbs are perhaps the best and oldest methods of cooking fresh fish. Another ancient method, attributed to alchemist Maria de Cleofa, is "wet cooking." Her invention, the first double boiler, became known as *Bagno Maria*, Mary's Bath. The container holding the food to be cooked is set over a larger pan holding water. The name has come to mean both a pan and a method of cooking.

It is best to purchase fish the day you plan to serve it. All fish should be white and firm with shiny skin and no odor; fresh whole fish has bright eyes. Rinse immediately, pat dry with paper towels, place on a plate, and cover loosely with paper towels, *not* plastic wrap. Put a few ice cubes on top to keep it ice cold and refrigerate. If whole, most of us (except for practiced experts) cut off tails and fin with sharp scissors. To skin, first cut lengthwise with a thin sharp knife. Place fillet side down on cutting board and cut close along skin to remove.

If baking fish, it is important to remember that because oven heat is dry, it can sap the moisture from it. To prevent that, brush lightly with olive oil or coat with seasoned bread crumbs. The rule for baking fish is if it is thick, the oven temperature should be 350° F; if it is thin, bake quickly at 425° F. Baking fish requires little fat, which is a plus.

Dried cod (*baccala*) can be purchased or ordered at many American markets, especially during the Christmas season. Eel and *baccala* are often served on Christmas Eve.

Directions for soaking *baccala* are as follows: Purchase *baccala* two to three days before serving. Try to buy pieces uniform in size. If it is very thick at one end and thin at the other, as soon as it has softened sufficiently, slice the thick part horizontally to hasten the elimination of salt. Put in a large bowl, cover with cold water, and refrigerate. Soak for three days to remove excess salt. Turn the pieces periodically and change the water every six to eight hours. At the end of soaking period, the fish will be plump, soft, fleshy, and well hydrated. Rinse again, drain and pat dry, and proceed with the recipe.

Baccalà al Forno con Patate e Pomodori
Baked Cod with Potatoes and Tomatoes

The medley of ingredients in this casserole combine to make it a fine dish, which Calabrians often serve on Christmas Eve and Good Friday. Easy to prepare, this traditional dish needs no tending. Once assembled, it frees you to concentrate on other parts of the important meal.

1	pound dried cod, soaked (see page 181)
2	tablespoons olive oil, divided
3	medium potatoes, peeled and thinly sliced
2	medium to large onions, thinly sliced
8 to 10	Italian plum tomatoes, peeled and coarsely chopped, or 1 16-ounce can Italian plum tomatoes, coarsely chopped
3	tablespoons fresh Italian parsley, coarsely chopped, divided
1	teaspoon fresh rosemary, divided
¼	cup green olives, brine-cured, pitted and sliced
¼	teaspoon freshly ground black pepper

Remove any skin and bones from fish and pat dry with paper towels. Cut into 4 pieces.

Preheat oven to 350° F.

In an 8-inch square baking dish, brush bottom with 2 teaspoons olive oil. Layer ⅓ of the potato slices, ½ of the onion slices, ½ of the cut cod, and ½ of the tomatoes. Sprinkle with half the parsley and rosemary. Add olives, if using. Repeat for a second layer of potatoes, onion, cod, and tomatoes, ending with a third layer of potatoes. Sprinkle with remaining parsley and rosemary and the pepper. Drizzle remaining olive oil over top and bake for 40 to 45 minutes or until the potatoes are cooked through and a golden brown.

Serves 6

Baccalà Fritto
Fried Cod with Lemon

This simple *baccalà* dish can be served as an appetizer as well as an entrée. If using as an antipasto, cut into bite-sized pieces before cooking. *Baccalà* is available in Italian specialty stores and in most supermarkets during the holiday seasons.

- 1 pound dried cod, soaked (see page 181)
- ½ cup all-purpose flour
- ¼ teaspoon freshly ground black pepper
- 4 tablespoons olive oil, divided
- 2 cloves garlic, finely minced
- 1 lemon, freshly juiced
- 1 lemon, sliced for garnish
  fresh Italian parsley leaves for garnish

Remove any skin and bones from fish and pat dry with paper towels. Cut into 8 to 10 pieces.

Combine flour and pepper on a flat plate. Using tongs or two forks, dredge the fish in the flour on both sides and place on a platter until all pieces are coated.

In a large, heavy skillet, add 1 tablespoon olive oil over medium heat. Sauté garlic for 1 to 2 minutes or until light golden brown. Remove with slotted spoon and discard. Add remaining 3 tablespoons olive oil over medium-high heat. Sauté fish for 8 to 10 minutes, turning once, or until cooked through and golden brown. The exact cooking time will depend on the thickness of the fish.

Transfer fish to a warm serving platter. Remove all the drippings but 1 to 2 tablespoons, add the lemon juice, scrape the bottom of the skillet, and heat through. Pour pan juices over fish. Garnish with lemon slices and parsley leaves and serve immediately.

Serves 4 to 6 as an entrée, or up to 12 as an antipasto

Anguille con Vino Bianco
Eel in White Wine

The use of eels for food dates back to the Etruscans. It is said that the female eel is tastier than the male. If eels are not available in your supermarket, try an Italian specialty store. Eel is traditionally served on Christmas Eve and greatly appreciated in Calabria. Sautéed in wine and simmered slowly in a spicy tomato sauce, they produce this savory dish.

1 pound small eels (skinned or unskinned)
2 tablespoons olive oil, divided
1 large onion, thinly sliced
2 cloves garlic, finely minced
½ cup dry white wine
½ cup tomato sauce
3 anchovy fillets, coarsely chopped
1 tablespoon fresh Italian parsley, coarsely chopped
½ teaspoon crushed red pepper
¼ teaspoon dried oregano
¼ teaspoon salt

If eels are whole, remove heads and tails. Wash thoroughly under cold running water. Cut into 3-inch pieces and drain on paper towels. Pat dry and set aside.

In a large, heavy skillet add 1 tablespoon olive oil over medium heat. Sauté the onion for 3 to 4 minutes or until translucent. Add garlic and sauté for 1 to 2 minutes or until garlic is light golden brown. Remove both and set aside.

Add remaining tablespoon olive oil to skillet, raise heat to high, and add eel. Cook until the water from the eel evaporates. Lower heat, add wine, and cook for 10 minutes. Add all remaining ingredients. Cover skillet and let simmer for 20 to 25 minutes or until eels are tender, turning once. Serve immediately.

Serves 4 to 6

Crocchette di Luccio
Pike Croquettes with Cheese, Parsley, and Nutmeg

Although less common than many other fish in the United States, pike is available at most supermarkets or can be special ordered. The interesting combination of seasonings that makes this pike dish worth trying includes nutmeg, an Arabian contribution to Europe.

1	pike, about 1¼ to 1½ pounds
1	cup fine dried bread crumbs, divided
3	tablespoons fresh Italian parsley, finely chopped, divided
2	tablespoons pecorino or Parmesan cheese, freshly grated
¼	teaspoon nutmeg
½	teaspoon salt, divided
¼	teaspoon freshly ground black pepper
3	eggs
½	cup all-purpose flour
4 to 5	tablespoons olive oil
1	lemon cut into wedges, for garnish

Wash and debone fish. Process through a food processor or chop finely. Put in a large mixing bowl. Add ¾ cup bread crumbs, 2 tablespoons parsley, cheese, nutmeg, ¼ teaspoon salt, and pepper, and mix. In a small bowl, beat 2 eggs lightly with a whisk. Add beaten eggs to the fish mixture and mix well.

On a flat plate, spread the flour and ¼ teaspoon salt. In a small bowl, lightly beat the last egg. On another flat plate, spread the remaining ¼ cup bread crumbs. Dip hands into the flour and shape about 3 tablespoons of the fish mixture into a croquette. Carefully dredge each croquette in the flour, then in the egg, and last press into the bread crumb mixture. Set aside on a large floured plate. Do not crowd.

In a large, heavy skillet, heat 3 tablespoons olive oil over medium-high heat. Sauté the croquettes for 3 to 5 minutes, turning until all sides are golden brown. Add more oil as needed. Lower heat to medium-low and sauté for 10 to 12 minutes or until cooked through, turning occasionally. Test by cutting one in half. Remove with slotted spoon and drain on paper towels. Place on a warm serving platter and surround with lemon wedges. Sprinkle with remaining parsley and serve immediately.

Serves 6

Triglie con Olive e Capperi
Red Mullet with Olives and Capers

Red mullet is a striking bright pink in color, and one lovely variety has bright yellow bands from head to tail. When fully grown, it weighs between 2 and 3 pounds. Delicate in flavor, its flesh is firm and white. Traditionally, this fish was served whole, and often it is still served that way in Italy. In the United States, the fish is very often sold already filleted.

1 pound red mullet
2 tablespoons olive oil
2 tablespoons fresh lemon juice, divided
3 tablespoons black olives, brine-cured, pitted and sliced
3 tablespoons capers
¼ teaspoon dried oregano
¼ teaspoon salt
¼ teaspoon freshly ground black pepper
1 tablespoon fresh Italian parsley, finely chopped, for garnish

Preheat oven to 400° F.

Wash fish thoroughly under cold running water and drain on paper towels. Pat dry and place in an 8-by-12-inch casserole. Drizzle evenly with oil and 1 tablespoon lemon juice. Distribute the olives and capers over the top and sprinkle with oregano. Bake on middle rack for 14 to 17 minutes, or until fish is golden, cooked through, but moist, basting once in between.

Remove to a warm serving platter, drizzle with remaining lemon juice, and garnish with parsley. Serve at once.

Serves 4

Eperlani al Limone
Smelts Baked with Lemon

This dish is made with fresh anchovies in Calabria, but smelts have been used in their place by Italian-Americans for some time now. The recipe for this nicely crusted dish was given to me by an elderly woman at an outdoor vegetable market in Calabria. She said any small fish could be used. Before she finished, two or three other women joined in to voice their slightly different opinions of spice measurements. But they were unanimously delighted that an Italian-American was writing a Calabrian cookbook. With little modification I think I got it so they would approve!

 1 pound smelts
 1 cup dried bread crumbs
 1 clove garlic, finely minced
 ½ teaspoon crushed red pepper
 ½ teaspoon salt
 ¼ teaspoon dried oregano
 3 tablespoons olive oil, divided
 1 lemon, halved
 1 tablespoon fresh Italian parsley, finely chopped, for garnish

Preheat oven to 350° F.

If smelts are whole, remove heads. Wash fish thoroughly under cold running water. Slit each down one side and remove the backbone. Rinse again and drain on paper towels. Pat dry.

In a small bowl, combine bread crumbs, garlic, crushed red pepper, salt, and oregano. Using 1 tablespoon olive oil, grease a 10-by-14-inch baking dish. Arrange fish in one layer. Sprinkle with the bread crumb mixture. Drizzle remaining olive oil and the juice from ½ lemon over top. Bake for 18 to 20 minutes, or until cooked through and the top has formed a golden crust. The exact cooking time will depend on the size of the fish.

Cut remaining ½ lemon into wedges. Sprinkle fish with parsley and serve immediately with lemon wedges.

Serves 4 to 6

Eperlani Fritti
Fried Smelts

In Italy, sardines are the traditional choice for this dish. But fresh sardines are not readily available in the United States, and at some point smelts took their place with equal success. Many avoid fried foods, but this traditional dish is such a tempting treat, I give in to the desire on occasion.

- 1 pound smelts
- ½ cup all-purpose flour
- 2 tablespoons fresh Italian parsley, finely chopped, divided
- ½ teaspoon salt
- ¼ teaspoon freshly ground black pepper
- 3 tablespoons olive oil
- 1 lemon, quartered, for garnish

If smelts are whole, remove heads. Wash fish thoroughly under cold running water. Slit each down one side and remove the backbone. Rinse again and drain on paper towels. Pat dry.

On a flat plate, combine flour, 1 tablespoon parsley, salt, and pepper. Dredge fish in the flour mixture and set aside.

In a large, heavy skillet, heat olive oil over medium-high heat, until almost smoking. If oil is not hot enough, fish will absorb more oil. Sauté the fish without crowding, for 8 to 10 minutes, turning frequently, until cooked through and golden. Remove and drain on paper towels.

Put fish on individual warmed plates, sprinkle with the remaining parsley, add lemon wedges, and serve immediately.

Serves 4

Pesce all' Acqua Pazza
Flat Fish Cooked in Crazy Water

This delectable fish recipe with its delightful name was contributed by Mario Sabello and Pasquale D'Angelo, owners of Il Continoni, a fine restaurant in Paestum, slightly north of Calabria. I think the water is called crazy because all ingredients are put in a pot with the water and, crazy as it seems, the result is perfect. While I was dining, both owners came and sat at my table and willingly talked to me for some time about Italian food and customs and also allowed me to take pictures of them. Shortly after finishing an excellent dinner, Chef Gennaro Buono and his daughters Manuela and Fabrizia came and introduced themselves. The girls shared their views on many things American and on all great Calabrian food.

¼ pound mussels
¼ pound clams
1 pound fillet of flat fish, such as sole
1 large ripe tomato, peeled and coarsely chopped
½ cup white wine
2 tablespoons olive oil
1 tablespoon fresh Italian parsley, coarsely chopped
2 cloves garlic, finely minced
1 teaspoon salt
½ teaspoon freshly ground black pepper

Thoroughly scrub mussels and clams and rinse under cold water. Rinse sole quickly and cut into 4 pieces.

In a large pot over high heat, add 3½ cups water and bring to a boil. Immediately lower heat, add all ingredients, and simmer slowly for 12 to 15 minutes.

Remove mussels and clams and shell them. Discard any that are unopened. Return shelled mussels and clams to the pot and mix thoroughly. Drain, reserving liquid for *Brodo di Pesce* (Fish Broth, see page 69), and serve fish immediately.

Serves 4 to 6

Grìgliata di Pesce Spada
Grilled Swordfish Marinated in Lemon and Oregano

In this simply prepared grilled dish, the tangy marinade enhances the sword-fish, creating a tasty and satisfying entrée. In inclement weather, the fish can be cooked in the oven. Preheat broiler for 5 minutes with oven door slightly ajar and broil 8 to 12 minutes. Tuna can be substituted for the swordfish.

- 1 pound swordfish, ½ to ¾ inch thick
- 3 tablespoons olive oil
- 2 cloves garlic, thickly sliced
- 1 lemon, freshly juiced
- 1 tablespoon fresh Italian parsley, finely chopped
- ¼ teaspoon dried oregano
- ¼ teaspoon freshly ground black pepper
- ¼ teaspoon salt
- 1 lemon cut into wedges, for garnish

Preheat grill.

Wash swordfish under cold running water and pat dry with paper towels. Cut into 4 pieces.

Combine olive oil, garlic, lemon juice, parsley, oregano, and pepper. Mix and pour marinade into a flat glass baking dish large enough to hold fish in one layer. Immerse swordfish and let marinate for at least 30 minutes, turning once. To marinate longer, for a maximum of 2 hours, refrigerate and turn after 1 hour. Remove from refrigerator ½ hour before grilling.

Put fish on an oiled grid 4 to 6 inches above hot coals. Grill fish for 8 to 12 minutes, depending on thickness, basting and turning once with long handled tongs (not a fork) until fish is golden and cooked through. (Turning fish or meat with a fork pierces it and releases juices and flavor.)

Transfer fish to a serving dish, sprinkle with salt, and serve immediately with lemon wedges.

Serves 4

Pesce Spada al Capperi e Limone
Swordfish with Capers and Lemon

If your travels take you to Bagnara Calabra in Calabria in July, be sure to catch the celebration in honor of swordfish. At the same time, search out an *ontri* (fishing boat) with its tall mast and protruding lookout platform from which sailors seek out the large fish. When one is spotted, the boat rushes to its side and from the ship's deck, the fisherman spears it with a long harpoon as it has been done since ancient times. This recipe, enhanced by the wonders of pungent capers and by refreshing lemon juice, presents swordfish at its sumptuous best.

> 1 pound swordfish, ½-inch thick, cut into 4 pieces
> 2 tablespoons extra-virgin olive oil
> 2 cloves garlic, finely minced
> ¼ teaspoon salt
> ¼ teaspoon freshly ground black pepper
> 2 tablespoons capers, drained
> 1 lemon, freshly juiced
> 1 tablespoon fresh Italian parsley, finely chopped
> ¼ teaspoon dried oregano

Wash swordfish under cold running water. Drain on paper towels and pat dry.

In a large, heavy skillet, add olive oil over medium heat. Add garlic and sauté for 1 to 2 minutes or until light golden brown. Remove and reserve.

Add the swordfish to the skillet and sauté for 8 to 10 minutes, turning once, or until fish is golden and cooked through. Remove and place on a warm platter. Sprinkle lightly with salt and pepper.

Add the reserved garlic, capers, lemon juice, parsley, and oregano to the skillet. Heat briefly and pour juices over the fish. Serve immediately.

Serves 4

Pesce Spada al Pomodori e Alici
Swordfish with Tomatoes and Anchovies

A combination of nicely proportioned ingredients complements the swordfish in this recipe. It was on the rugged coast of Scilla, an ancient seaside village built at the base of a rock on which a castle stands, that Homer told of ships lured by sirens, of sailors who met their doom by crashing on the Scilla rock, of Odysseus who met the monster Charybdis (actually a whirlpool), all made immortal in Homer's epic poem *The Odyssey,* written in 700 B.C. (In Calabria, legend and mythology blend with history.) Scilla and Bagnara Calabra provide much of Italy with fresh swordfish. If a visitor is an early riser, he or she will be rewarded with a beautiful sunrise and may also see Calabrian fisherman harpooning swordfish the same way that Greek settlers did in ancient times.

    1   pound fresh swordfish, cut into 4 pieces
    ½   cup bread crumbs, divided
    ½   teaspoon dried oregano
    ¼   teaspoon salt
    ¼   teaspoon freshly ground black pepper
    1   small onion, thinly sliced into rings
    2   cups fresh or canned Italian plum tomatoes, coarsely chopped
    4   anchovy fillets, mashed
    1   tablespoon fresh basil, finely chopped

Preheat oven to 425° F.

Wash swordfish under cold running water. Drain on paper towels and pat dry. On a flat plate, add ¼ cup bread crumbs, oregano, salt, and pepper. Mix well. Dredge fish lightly with bread crumbs and set aside.

In a large, heavy skillet, add olive oil over medium heat. Add onion rings and sauté for 3 to 4 minutes or until translucent. Add tomatoes, anchovies, and basil. Lower heat slightly, stir well, and simmer uncovered for 8 minutes, mixing occasionally.

Put fish in a lightly oiled baking dish just large enough to hold the fish in a single layer. Spoon tomatoes evenly over the top and bake for 7 minutes. Sprinkle with remaining bread crumbs and bake for 6 to 8 minutes, or until fish is cooked through but moist and bread crumbs are golden.

Remove to a warm serving platter and serve immediately.

Serves 4

Pesce Spada al Forno
Baked Swordfish with White Wine

Swordfish and tuna recipes are often interchangeable, as in this dish. Fresh swordfish should have no yellow tint and tuna no brown tint—signs that they are old. In Italy, swordfish and tuna are available in outdoor markets, plump and moist, ready for the skilled cook to transform into irresistible entrées.

1	pound fresh swordfish, cut into 4 pieces
¼	cup all-purpose flour
½	teaspoon salt
¼	teaspoon freshly ground black pepper
2	tablespoons extra-virgin olive oil
½	small sweet onion, finely chopped
3	cloves garlic, finely minced
½	cup dry white wine
1	medium lemon, freshly juiced
2	tablespoons fresh Italian parsley, finely chopped
1	lemon cut into wedges, for garnish
	fresh Italian parsley leaves for garnish

Preheat oven to 350° F.

Wash swordfish under cold running water. Drain on paper towels and pat dry. On a flat plate, put flour, salt, and pepper; mix well. Dredge fish lightly in flour and set aside.

In a large, heavy, oven-proof skillet or roasting pan, add olive oil over medium heat. Add onion and sauté for 3 to 4 minutes until translucent. Add garlic and sauté for 1 to 2 minutes or until light golden brown. Remove both and reserve. Sauté fish for 3 to 5 minutes or until lightly browned, turning once.

Return onion and garlic to the skillet, drizzle contents with wine and lemon juice, and sprinkle with parsley. Cover skillet loosely with foil, tent-style. Put in the middle of the oven. Bake for 12 to 14 minutes or until fish is cooked through and golden.

Remove to a serving platter and garnish with lemon wedges and parsley leaves. Serve immediately.

Serves 4

Tonno Fresca alla Marinara
Mariner's Style Tuna

A fresh, flavorful approach to tuna is to gently coat it with a savory tomato mixture and bake. While it is cooking, prepare a large mixed green salad and maybe a seasonal vegetable. Serve with plenty of crusty Italian bread for a gratifying dinner that's ready in less than 30 minutes.

> 1 pound tuna, cut into 4 pieces
> 2 tablespoons olive oil
> ½ onion, finely chopped
> 3 cloves garlic, finely chopped
> 2 anchovy fillets, coarsely chopped
> 1 cup fresh or canned Italian plum tomatoes, coarsely chopped
> 1 tablespoon fresh Italian parsley, finely chopped
> ½ teaspoon crushed red pepper
> ¼ teaspoon salt

Preheat oven to 375° F.

Wash tuna under cold running water. Drain on paper towels and pat dry.

Heat olive oil in a large, heavy skillet over medium heat. Add onion and sauté for 3 to 4 minutes or until translucent. Add garlic and anchovies and sauté 1 to 2 minutes or until garlic is light golden brown. Add tomatoes, parsley, crushed red pepper, and salt. Simmer for 10 minutes.

Place tuna in an oiled 8-inch square casserole, and dot here and there with sauce. Bake for 14 to 17 minutes or until fish is cooked through and no pink remains.

Serves 4

Tonno con Vino Bianco alla Contadina
Peasant Style Tuna with White Wine

Tuna has played a major role in the province of Calabria since about 1000 B.C. Salted tuna was an important export for centuries, and festivals still celebrate its importance. This dish is easy to prepare, yet elegant enough to serve guests.

> 1 pound fresh tuna, cut into 4 serving pieces
> 2 tablespoons olive oil

1 small onion, thinly sliced
¼ cup dry white wine or white wine vinegar
3 tablespoons fresh Italian parsley, finely chopped, divided
1 bay leaf
¼ teaspoon crushed red pepper
¼ teaspoon salt
2 tablespoons capers for garnish
1 lemon, quartered, for garnish

Wash tuna and pat dry.

In a large, heavy skillet, heat olive oil over medium heat. Sauté onion for 3 to 4 minutes or until translucent. Remove with a slotted spoon and reserve.

Add tuna to the skillet and sauté for 4 to 5 minutes, turning once, until lightly browned. Reduce heat, return onion to the skillet, and stir in wine or vinegar, 2 tablespoons parsley, bay leaf, crushed red pepper, and salt.

Cook for 10 to 12 minutes, until fish is cooked through and no pink remains, turning once.

Transfer the fish to a serving platter. Garnish with remaining parsley, capers, and lemon wedges.

Serve immediately.

Serves 4

Cozze con Pomodori e Basilico
Mussels with Tomatoes and Basil

This zesty mussel dish can be served over spaghetti or linguine as a first course. As a second course, serve it with vegetables or a mixed salad. Either way, present it with crusty Italian bread to soak up the savory pan juices.

2½ pounds mussels
2 tablespoons olive oil
3 cloves garlic, finely minced
1 pound fresh Italian plum tomatoes or 1 16-ounce can, coarsely chopped
2 tablespoons fresh basil, coarsely chopped
¼ teaspoon salt
¼ teaspoon crushed red pepper

Scrub mussels thoroughly and rinse several times in salted water to remove sand or grit.

Drain and set aside on paper towels.

In a large, heavy skillet add olive oil over medium heat. Add garlic and sauté for 1 to 2 minutes or until light golden brown. Lower heat and add tomatoes, basil, salt, and crushed red pepper. Simmer for 15 minutes. Add the mussels and stir well. Simmer for 10 to 12 minutes. If any have not opened by this time, remove and discard them. Serve immediately.

Serves 4

Fritto Misto di Pesce
Mixed Fish Fry

Every mother and grandmother in Calabrian fishing towns makes this dish. The usual combination is squid, shrimp, and smelts, but you can substitute any other small fish if one isn't available. If possible, always opt for fresh fish. This dish is sometimes called *soffrito*, a broad term that encompasses fried meat, fish, or vegetables. Of course, frying each of these fish alone is fine, but Calabrians will tell you that it's more interesting to eat a grouping for contrast in texture and taste. Even if you don't fry foods often, this recipe is a worthwhile treat.

½ pound squid
½ pound medium shrimp
½ pound smelts
½ cup all-purpose flour
½ teaspoon salt
¼ teaspoon freshly ground black pepper
⅓ cup olive oil, divided
1 lemon, cut into wedges for garnish
2 tablespoons of parsley, finely chopped, for garnish

Cut tentacles from head of squid just below the eyes and discard the mouth, which is hidden in the tentacles. Peel off the outer skin, squeeze out the insides, and pull out the center bone. Wash thoroughly under cold running water. Drain on paper towels and pat dry. Cut tentacles in half, and with scissors or a knife, cut bodies into rings.

Shell the raw shrimp and devein, but leave tails on. Wash under cold running water. Drain on paper towels and pat dry.

Cut off heads of smelts, slit down one side, and remove the backbone. Wash under cold running water. Drain on paper towels and pat dry.

On a flat plate, combine the flour, salt, and pepper. Dredge the fish in the flour mixture and set aside, in a single layer, on a large dish until all are dredged.

In a medium skillet, heat half the olive oil over medium-high heat. Fry each fish separately, without crowding, turning frequently until golden brown. Fry squid for 2 to 3 minutes, shrimp for 3 to 4 minutes, and smelts 3 to 4 minutes. Add remaining olive oil as needed.

Using a slotted spoon, remove fried fish from the skillet and drain on paper towels. Keep warm until all are fried. Arrange fish neatly on a large serving dish, surround with lemon wedges, and sprinkle with parsley. Serve immediately.

Serves 6 to 8

Insalata di Calamari e Gamberi
Squid and Shrimp Salad

Squid and shrimp are compatibly paired in this delightful salad. If you have not been exposed to squid, you are in for a pleasant treat. It has a unique nutty taste that you must experience for yourself. Many markets sell it precleaned, but don't be discouraged if you have to clean it yourself. It is easier to do than to describe and is well worth the trouble. This impressive dish will add pizzazz to an antipasti table or summer luncheon. For a small dinner party, serve it well chilled as a single appetizer.

¾	pound squid
¾	pound medium shrimp
1	large lemon, freshly juiced
4	tablespoons extra-virgin olive oil
1	small clove garlic, finely sliced
¼	teaspoon freshly ground black pepper
¼	teaspoon crushed red pepper
½	small red onion, thinly sliced
¼	cup black olives, brine-cured, pitted and halved
½	teaspoon salt
½	lemon, thinly sliced and halved, for garnish
2	tablespoons fresh Italian parsley, finely chopped, for garnish

Cut tentacles from head of squid just below the eyes and discard the mouth, which is hidden in the tentacles. Peel off the outer skin, squeeze out the insides, and pull out the center bone. Wash all parts under cold running water. Drain on paper towels.

Wash shrimp under cold running water. Drain on paper towels.

In a 3-quart saucepan of softly boiling water, add squid and shrimp. Simmer over moderate heat for 1 to 1½ minutes, or until shrimp begins to turn pink. Add cold water to stop cooking and drain. Cut squid tentacles in half and with scissors or a knife; cut bodies into small rings. Shell shrimp, devein, and rinse.

In a small bowl, prepare the marinade. Blend the lemon juice, olive oil, garlic, pepper, and crushed red pepper. Mix thoroughly.

Put the squid, shrimp, onion, and olives in a shallow glass baking dish. Pour marinade over the mixture and stir. Let marinate in refrigerator for at least 2 hours but not more than 24, as fish continues to "cook" in the marinade. Just before serving, remove from refrigerator, sprinkle with salt, and mix thoroughly. Arrange fish on a serving platter, pour marinade over top, surround with lemon slices, and sprinkle with parsley.

Serves 6 to 8 as a main dish, or up to 16 as an antipasto

Calamari Ripieni
Stuffed Squid

The people of Italy and other Mediterranean countries, China, and Japan have long raved about the unique taste of squid, considering it a delicacy. Americans are only recently coming to appreciate it. In this version, the flavor-laden stuffing permeates the squid as it simmers in white wine, and the result is mouthwatering.

    8   medium squid, fresh or frozen, about 1 pound
    2   tablespoons olive oil
    ½   cup fresh bread crumbs, coarsely chopped
    3   anchovy fillets, finely chopped
    2   tablespoons grated pecorino or Parmesan cheese
    2   tablespoons fresh Italian parsley, finely chopped
    2   cloves garlic, finely minced
    1   egg, lightly beaten
    ½   teaspoon salt

¼ teaspoon freshly ground black pepper
⅓ cup dry white wine
½ lemon, freshly juiced

Cut tentacles from head of squid just below the eyes and discard the eyes and mouth, which is hidden in the tentacles. Peel off the outer skin, squeeze out the insides, pull out the center bone, and cut off the tentacles. Wash all parts under cold running water and pat dry with paper towels.

Add olive oil to a large, heavy skillet over medium heat. Add tentacles and sauté for 2 minutes. Remove them using a slotted spoon, chop coarsely, and place in a medium mixing bowl. Set skillet aside.

To the mixing bowl, add the bread crumbs, anchovies, cheese, parsley, garlic, egg, salt, and pepper. Mix until well blended. If the stuffing seems a little dry, add a few teaspoons water. The amount of water needed depends on the dryness of the bread.

Hold squid body in one hand and use your thumb to stuff loosely, to about ⅔ full. Secure ends firmly with wooden toothpicks.

Return skillet to stove over medium heat. Add squid and sauté for 4 to 6 minutes, turning until browned on all sides. Lower heat, add the wine, cover, and simmer slowly for 10 to 12 minutes or until squid is white and firm, turning several times. If necessary, add a little water. Remove toothpicks, drizzle with lemon juice, and serve immediately.

Serves 4

TIP: Squid shrinks while cooking and bread crumbs expand. Do not overstuff, as it will cause the squid to burst.

VARIATIONS:
- One large, ripe tomato, coarsely chopped, can be added to skillet along with the wine.
- To bake, preheat oven to 375° F. Brush squid with olive oil and bake in a lightly oiled casserole for 12 to 15 minutes or until white and firm, basting occasionally. Remove toothpicks, drizzle with lemon juice, and serve immediately.

Frutti di Mare
Marinated Seafood Salad

Originally, this dish included whatever the catches of the day were. This wonderful melange of seafood, intermingled with tasty ingredients such as olives and capers, perfectly seasoned, is sensational. It is easier to make than it looks—the majority of ingredients are condiments or spices. It is best to use fresh fish, and substitutions of other fresh fish work well. In a pinch, substitute frozen or canned fish.

1½	pounds fresh mussels
1½	pounds fresh baby clams
¾	pound fresh squid
¾	pound fresh medium or large shrimp
2	lemons, freshly juiced
⅓	cup extra-virgin olive oil
1	clove garlic, finely minced
1	teaspoon fresh rosemary
1	bay leaf
¼	teaspoon freshly ground black pepper
1	small sweet white onion, finely sliced
½	cup black olives, brine-cured, pitted and halved or sliced
2	tablespoons capers
½	teaspoon salt
1	lemon, thinly sliced and halved, for garnish
1	tablespoon fresh Italian parsley, finely chopped, for garnish

Wash and scrub fresh mussels and clams thoroughly in cold, salted water. Pat dry with paper towels. In a covered 3-quart saucepan, bring water to a boil and add salt. Lower heat, cover, and steam mussels for 2 to 3 minutes or until they just open. With a slotted spoon, remove to a colander and drain. Do not discard water.

Meanwhile, raise heat again on saucepan.

Remove mussels from shells, rinse, and set aside. Discard any mussels that did not open. Add clams to boiling water. Lower heat, cover, and steam for 8 to 10 minutes or until clams open. Remove to a colander and drain, discarding any that did not open. Discard water or reserve for *Brodo di Pesce* (Fish Broth, page 69).

Cut tentacles from head of squid just below the eyes and discard the mouth, which is hidden in the tentacles. Peel off the outer skin, squeeze out the insides, and pull out the center bone. Wash under cold running water.

In a 3-quart saucepan of softly boiling salted water, add squid and shrimp. Lower heat to medium and cook for 1 to 1½ minutes or until shrimp begin to turn pink. Add cold water to stop cooking. Rinse and drain. Cut squid tentacles in half and with scissors or a knife, cut bodies into small rings. Shell shrimp, devein, and rinse. Set aside.

In a small bowl, prepare the marinade. Blend lemon juice, olive oil, garlic, rosemary, bay leaf, and pepper.

Put seafood in a large, shallow glass baking dish. Add onion, olives, and capers. Pour marinade over seafood and stir. Let marinate in refrigerator for at least 2 hours but not more than 24 hours, as fish continues to "cook" in the marinade. Just before serving, remove from refrigerator, discard bay leaf, sprinkle with salt, and mix thoroughly. Arrange fish on a serving platter, pour marinade over top, surround with lemon slices, and sprinkle with parsley.

Serves 6 to 8 as a main dish, or up to 20 as an antipasto

SCENES

VISITING CALABRIA
AND TASTING THE FOOD

Calabria offers much in beauty, diversity, and hospitality. The willingness of Calabrians, with little or no coaxing, to share the natural beauty of their province and their generous hospitality makes a visit tremendously rewarding. Calabria, the southernmost province of Italy, is rich in mountain splendor, unspoiled beaches, museums with world-renowned works of art, clever artisans, diverse and interesting architecture, delicious and exciting food, and as friendly a people as you will find anywhere.

Research for this book took me to Calabria twice, although I had been there and to other parts of Italy before. The search took me to major cities, small towns and villages in the countryside, in and around the major mountains, and up and down the Ionic and Tyrrhenian coasts. A seasoned traveler, reasonably conversant in Italian and brimming with questions about recipes and customs, I was well received everywhere in Calabria, and I enjoyed many delightful and rewarding experiences. I would like to share with you not only the recipes but also some of those experiences. Allow me to take you on an armchair tour of Calabria, home of my ancestors, and present you with a firsthand portrait of it.

Still relatively undiscovered by most American tourists, the province of Calabria, with its 2 million residents and 485 miles of wraparound coastline, is located at the toe and instep of Italy's boot. Because of the encircling Tyrrhenian and Ionian seas, mild weather prevails in Calabria for most of the year. As a result, Italians from all over Italy, particularly from the steamy north in summer, as well as nature and beach lovers, flock to Calabria to enjoy the beautiful beaches, magnificent mountains, and enticing food. I once read that even when Italians go away on holiday, they tend to flock. It's true! Their idea of getting away is getting together! For the past 40 years, new hotels, inns, and homes have sprung up along the coasts. I suspect that Americans who love to travel and who love southern Italian food will also want to visit beautiful Calabria and partake of its exciting food.

Driving is the best way to visit Calabria's hilltop villages and coastal towns, although one can travel comfortably and economically by train. The entire drive from Rome to Calabria is a pure delight, with endless sloping hillsides, lush horizons, spectacular mountain scenery, and dense forests. In the north, the dramatic Pollino Mountains rise to almost 7,500 feet, separating Calabria from the province of Basilicata. Along the rocky Tyrrhenian coast, one is treated to exquisite scenery, with sweeping, panoramic views of the magnificent mountains and luxuriant forests that look down on waves crashing against the rocky shores.

The Sila Massif in central Calabria is a truly magnificent area with mountains, forests, and rivers enjoyed by nature lovers year-round. Collectively called Italy's "Little Switzerland," the northernmost area is known as Sila *Greca* (Greek); the central area is known as Sila *Grande* (large); and the southernmost area is known as Sila *Piccola* (small). Sila's highest point, Botta Donata, reaches 6,332 feet and boasts dense and magnificent forests of multicolored trees. Sila, derived from the Latin *sylva* (forest), is rich with water, not an insignificant commodity in southern Italy. The many Sila rivers feed artificial jade-green lakes that bring electrical power to the area. On the Sila plateau, chestnuts and rare mushrooms abound.

Still sparsely populated, the area has scarcely changed since the days of ancient Rome. San Giovanni in Fiore, the capital of Sila, has preserved most of its traditions and customs. There you can find clever carpet weavers, lace makers' intricate works, and potters with a flair for color and pattern.

The sometimes wild and mountainous beauty of Calabria produces spectacular scenery, yet most areas yield little in the way of arable land. Even though little moisture reaches the Calabrian interior, farms are kept verdant by diligent labor and difficult irrigation. The constant struggle to tame this rugged geography has made every morsel of food count, and therefore has made it both appetizing and sustaining. Rich olive plantations, lemon groves, and Muscato grapevines coexist peacefully amid the grand mountains, forests, and coastline.

The nearby hills are dotted with quaint villages, some quite spectacular, that sit harmoniously side by side. Tranquil now, they were once fortified to fight off invaders, especially the Saracens. Some houses are made of stone, dramatic and perched on ledges. Other medieval stucco farmhouses with tile roofs jut out from the hills. Most village houses are small, with living quarters just slightly larger than the bedrooms. Bedrooms are used for sleeping only, giving the feeling that one's private life is considered secondary to one's public life. Outside each Calabrian house (as in all of Italy) rows of laundry flutter in the breeze like flags. The winding highways pass lovely bays, inviting beaches, and always, everywhere, vegetable and flower gardens.

Heading south, you will pass many picturesque seaside villages. Let's begin at Praia a Mare on the northwestern tip of Calabria. Praia a Mare and nearby

Scalea are tourist centers, where swimming and boating are popular. The Sanctuary of the Madonna della Grotta in Praia a Mare has a cave, still in some use, dating back to the Paleolithic era; Scalea has a fine Norman castle to view.

Cirella, situated on a rocky coast, offers the remains of Cirella Vecchia, a Sybarite colony, destroyed by Hannibal, again by the Saracens, and again by the French. Much-admired Diamonte has a lovely wide beach with clear water. Over the centuries, the cultivation of citron trees has been responsible for the town's prosperity. More recently, Diamonte has become known for its contemporary murals. Since 1981, more than 100 frescoes have been painted on walls of houses by Italian and international artists.

Sapore Calabria is the best place to buy provincial products. Enzo Monaco, resident *gastronomo*, owns a gourmet store filled with foods everyone wants to take home. He happily encourages people to taste all his products, from liqueurs to cheese.

Belvedere excels in Calabrian ceramics with Greek and Roman influences, which are great mementos of Calabria. Another pleasant beach town is Paola, best known for its sanctuary of San Francesco di Paola. On his feast day on May 5th, his statue is rowed out to sea in his honor. The church recently was restored to its late Renaissance splendor. The monastery houses *Ecce Homo* by the renowned writer Caracciolo. If films are your thing, you'll want to know about the summer film festivals in Paola.

For a glimpse back into the Middle Ages, stop at Guardia Piemontese. Historians will want to read the inscriptions on ancient doors labeled *Porta del Sangue* (Bloody Door) and *Porta dei Valdesi* (Door of the Waldensians) in memory of the Waldensians. A Protestant religious sect founded in Lyons, France, a group of Waldensians fled to Guardia during the Inquisition but were persecuted, declared heretics, and killed by the Spaniards in the mid-1500s.

Those in the know stop at Pizzo for their *gelato*, the best in the area. If you go inland to Serra San Bruno, you can visit the Aragonese castle where Joachim Murat, marshal of France and king of Naples, was executed in 1815 after failing to recover his Neapolitan kingdom.

You must stop at Soriano for their famous chocolate *mostaccioli* cookie. Then head for the Abbey di Santo Stefano del Bosco in the Serra San Bruno woods. Founded in the eleventh century by San Brunone, founder of the Carthusian order, it was restored in the sixteenth century. The classic restoration had such geometric beauty and grace that some experts believe the famous Renaissance architect Andrea Palladio contributed to its creation. His influence traveled the world—from England to Thomas Jefferson's Virginia home, Monticello.

Perched on Capo Vaticano is lovely, ancient Tropea, a fishing port, built into a cliff. Its beach of fine white sand and its picturesque setting are inviting. Visit the Chapel of St. Mary of the Isle built on a rocky islet and the Romanesque Norman cathedral. From Tropea to Reggio Calabria, the coast southward is known as the Violet Coast, so named because of its color at sunset.

Below Tropea, between the Marina di Gioia Tauro and Reggio Calabria, the Calabrian Riviera offers grand views of the Tyrrhenian coastline, the mountains, Sicily, and the Lipari Islands. On the lovely seaside, Gioia Tauro sits near ancient olive groves. Soon you come upon Palmi, with fantastic views of surrounding villages. It houses a folklore museum with a collection of traditional costumes, ancient musical instruments, and other fascinating folklore objects.

Farther down the Tyrrhenian coast are many archeological sites including ancient temples, theaters, churches, and palaces of Greek, Norman, and Arab influence. One can still see some fishermen in Bagnara Calabra and Scilla employing the same techniques of harpooning swordfish used by the Phoenicians and later the Greek colonists. Others in their little fishing boats, called *ontri* or *paranze*, catch fish the more conventional way.

Scilla is a charming little town with a beach resort. As I came upon the village fountain, in my best Italian, I asked directions from a young lady. In English she said she had moved to Scilla from the United States. The familiar village fountain is said to have first appeared in the fourteenth century, greeted joyfully by the people, who were grateful for water in the public place. Soon, the fountain began to play a dual role. Even though women had to walk a considerable distance to the nearest fountain and on their way back had to carry filled water jugs on their heads with balance and poise, the fountain became a meeting place where pleasantries and gossip could be exchanged. The fountain is still being used today!

The entire area is covered with lovely flowering shrubs, trees, and flowers. Flowers are everywhere—in fields, on balconies, in gardens, in pots, on steps. Fields of bergamot and jasmine flowers are cultivated here to make up the essences of perfume and tea. Capturing in oils the beauty of Scilla, the flowers, and the Calabrian coastline is the internationally famous Calabrian artist Giuseppe Marino, who was born in Scilla but now lives in Reggio Calabria.

The Aspromonte Mountains stand close to Reggio Calabria. They offer some of the most spectacular mountain scenery of pine, beach, and chestnut trees with panoramas of the Tyrrhenian Sea and the Straits of Messina. The Aspromontes peak at Montalto at more than 6,450 feet.

Sitting at the tip of the Italian boot is the province's largest city, Reggio Calabria, population approximately 175,000. Surrounded by the Tyrrhenian, Mediterranean, and Ionian seas, Reggio, as it is commonly called, with its subtropical climate, is ruggedly beautiful. Its origins go back at least to the seventh century B.C., when the Greeks landed there. Reggio had many rulers, among them the Romans, Byzantines, Turks, Aragonese, and later the Spanish Bourbons (the latter were removed by Garibaldi in the mid-1800s).

As you approach Reggio, you are greeted with sweeping views in all directions. Its backdrop are the lofty Aspromontes; its rugged coastline is lovely. A stone's throw away are the Straits of Messina. The surrounding waters are beautiful, changing in appearance from deep indigo to purple to jade nearest the sand. This well-known phenomenon has earned it the name of "The Rainbow of Italy." Yet another phenomenon awaits you. In calm morning weather, the town of Messina in Sicily is sometimes reflected on the surface from across the Straits. This phenomenon is known as *Fata Morgana*, Fairy Morgana, or "the miracle of the fairy Morgana."

Reggio Calabria has a superb promenade along the sea called *Lungomare Matteotti* with lovely views of the city and of Messina—all against the backdrop of some of the most architecturally beautiful buildings in the city. Writer Gabriele D'Annunzio once called it the "most beautiful kilometer in Italy." I loved walking that kilometer, different to behold by day and by night. At night, the lights of Sicily beckon from across the Straits.

Reggio has recovered from several devastating earthquakes and from widespread damage in the 1943 wartime bombardment. In 1783, a major earthquake caused much destruction. The sea seemed almost to boil at times, with a fierce whirlpool swallowing up everything in its path. Another major earthquake in 1908 destroyed much of the city, including many historic treasures and magnificent buildings. As a result, some of the city was rebuilt in a somewhat more modern style.

Many buildings that grace the city are extraordinarily beautiful. The beautiful cathedral, reconstructed in 1920 in Neo-Romanesque style, contains an exquisite Baroque chapel. Reggio also has many other fine churches, lovely *piazzas*, castles, historic monuments, and parks. The elegant main street, Corso Garibaldi, is brimming with smart designer shops displaying their wares. There are also an abundance of fine *ristoranti, trattorie, pasticcerie,* and *gelaterie.* It is on Corso Garibaldi where a nightly, lively *passegiata,* or promenade, takes place.

Reggio is also well known for its three-story National Museum, which houses the outstanding and famous fifth century B.C. sculptures discovered in 1972 in the nearby town of Riace. It also contains many impressive archeological and prehistoric collections, a vast collection of antiques, bronze statues, sculptures, and paintings by great masters such as Antonella da Messina and Mattia Preti. And Reggio Calabria has its own airport and a busy port.

Traveling up the Ionic coast, noted for its lovely white sandy beaches, Melito di Porto Salvo is situated about 20 miles east of Reggio. It was made famous because Garibaldi, leader of the uprising, landed there on his way from Sicily to Naples, where he would begin the war that would ultimately make Italy independent of foreign domination. It was in Melito that Garibaldi first ate pasta with a tomato sauce. He was so enamored of it that he brought the recipe back with him to his home in the north.

An interesting stop about five miles inland is Pentedattilo, meaning five fingers in Greek, so named because the huge rock formation erupts upward into five peaks in front of a mountain. Farther along the coast are villages where Greeks who still speak their Greek dialect live. Among them are Bova Marina and Bova Superiore, home of my ancestors. Many residents still live on small farms where ancient customs prevail. Bova Superiore is one of the oldest settled small country towns in Calabria. Situated on a rocky mount, the panoramic view is superb. Continuing on the Ionian coast, you will come upon tiny towns like Bianco and Bovalino Marina, among others, en route to the lovely seaside resort of Locri.

Ruins of Greek temples and theaters are especially fine at Locri, one of the earliest Greek settlements in Italy. Built about the seventh century B.C., it is an important center of archeological discoveries, many of which are housed in the fine museum there. Do not overlook the sanctuary in honor of Persephone, who in Greek mythology was goddess of fertility and queen of the underworld.

Visit Punta Stilo for its ancient Roman promontorium. Continue inland to Stilo on the Ionic shore to visit the birthplace of the noted philosopher Tommaso Campanella (1568–1639). Campanella led an uprising, but local resistance was quickly wiped out by the Spanish and he was imprisoned. The thirteenth-century *duomo* contains the well-known painting of St. Francis of Assisi by renowned artist Mattia Preti.

Next are the dramatic, odd rock formations at Campanello and Squillace. Both towns were of Greek origin, although Roman relics were uncovered nearby. Restaurateurs in Squillace still prepare foods according to the ancient writings of Cassiodoros. Just outside Catanzaro, the large Byzantine basilica Roccelletta del Vescovo di Squillace is difficult to miss. It dates back to 1000 A.D.

Catanzaro sits on a hill with a view of the sea. Founded in the tenth century by the Byzantines, it was famous for its silk and velvet. The more interesting part of this city is its old part. A remarkable church, St. Dominic's, houses an altarpiece that contains fifteen panels relating to scenes in the life of Mary and Jesus. One depicts them giving a rosary to St. Dominic. The altarpiece is remarkable for its harmony and delicate coloration.

Two other churches of interest are St. Omobono, a Norman church with Byzantine decor, and the Immacolata, rebuilt after the earthquake of 1783 and again in 1960 after wartime bombings. Further on, visit the Renaissance church Rosario, which was rebuilt after the 1832 earthquake. The Museum Provincale contains prehistoric collections and contemporary paintings. Painter Mattia Preti was born in the nearby town of Taverna.

Farther up, Capo Colonna awaits you with its rocky masses. A Doric temple gives evidence of Greek life, and remnants of Roman life also are evident. Crotone, founded in 710 B.C., was once an important city of Magna Graecia. Celebrated in antiquity for its riches, lovely homes of the aristocracy graced the city. Relics of its grand past can be viewed in the local museum. Crotone was also known for its beautiful women and strong athletes, most notably Milo of Crotone. Today it is a prosperous town and holiday resort.

Before arriving at Sibari, stop off for a tasting at Ciro, where Calabria's most famous wine is made. Enchanted with Sibari's past, I stayed there overnight, allowing myself ample time to wander about the town looking for evidence of its past glory. Settled about the eighth century B.C., it was once a grand town and one of the country's richest until it succumbed to a flood that took its grandeur and riches with it. The words *sybarite* and *sybaritic* are derived from the once luxurious Sibari (Sybaris). Evidence of Greek heritage is still visible but no evidence of grandeur remains.

The drive from Sibari to Castrovillari is lovely, the Pollino Mountains glorious. The archeological museum contains paleological relics and works by the painter Andrea Alfano (1879–1967). The lovely church of Santa Maria del Castello was built by the Normans about 1090 but has since been restored. I liked the busy little town. My determined plan to dine at the Ristorante Alia materialized. Highly acclaimed as one of the best in Calabria, it more than fulfilled my expectations. I spoke with the chef and his brother, also owners, who described various recipes, including their version of fusilli or *maccarruni*.

Mormanno, which has roots going back to the Lombards, invites you to partake of its cool breezes when summer is scorching. Morano Calabro, with its impressive Baroque church Collegiata della Maddelena, the San Bernadino monastery, and a fine Norman castle, rates a stop.

Another day, take the inland route from Cosenza to Catanzaro through the Ascione Pass, where you are treated to glorious views of the Tyrrhenian Sea, serene lakes, and inviting beaches. Dominated by a Norman castle, Cosenza, with its medieval quarters, is the site of the University of Calabria. The cathedral was begun in the late 1100s in the Romanesque style and was completed with a Gothic facade. The castle and cathedral have remarkable histories worth exploring.

As I traveled along twisting roads in and out of the inviting, charmed towns and villages, I stepped back in time, eager to learn of Calabrian history and tradition. Peering through tiny doors into shops carved out of mountains centuries ago, walking down old cobbled streets, noting the friendly scale of buildings—most no more than two or three stories high—admiring quaint period houses where I could hear quick, passionate conversation echoing down the alleys, chatting with passersby, all was an adventure. In the cities, I admired the varied architecture with its Lombard, Saracen, and Norman influences. I savored the contrasts of the past alongside the present and was enormously grateful for such a rich treasury of memories.

As I returned to the spectacular rocky coastline, I realized I had been witness to a lifestyle I admired, even envied. I saw repeated evidence of impassioned family- and community-oriented communities. I saw steadfast commitment and devotion to spouses, children, grandparents, parents, grandchildren, relatives, and friends. I saw *piazzas*, town squares, where people of all ages congregate and where continuous, lively festivals take place. And next to family, I saw the important role the church played in their lives. Visiting many held special meaning for me. I thought of the many generations who had prayed there, fervently believing their prayers would be answered. I hoped that they were. Summing up those realizations, I felt a bond, a connection, and a part of Calabria, as indeed I am.

The People

First and foremost, the Calabrian people are lovers of family. Family is supportive, family is dependable, family is everything. It has nurtured and sustained them over the years, providing the strength to withstand centuries of exploitation. There exists within the family fierce loyalty and deep, devoted caring for one another. Families form a close-knit community, sharing the best and the worst of times. It is often stated that Italian patriotism is first loyalty to the family. The breakdown of families is sometimes attributed to poverty. But in southern Italy, where poverty cut deep and long, poverty was the force that made the family strong.

Calabrian people are kind. They intuitively understand the need for kindness, having endured the harshness of many invaders. And it extends beyond family to all who cross their path, including the tourist. Somewhere I read, "If you ask these people a question, they do a dance for you." They are tenacious and hard-working. And they are survivors. During adversities, they learned to *arrangiarsi,* to make the best of things, to make do, or to find a way out.

The exuberance of Italian life and the spectacular extravagance of it has been enchanting visitors for centuries. They enjoy the vitality of the gregarious, mellifluous, lusty people and applaud their determination to experience everything deeply and live life to the fullest. Visitors find Italians vigorous, engaging, affectionate, versatile, histrionic, courteous, spontaneous, generous, and friendly. Italians also love to party. It is said that they are still gloriously pagan in their unsurpassed love for *la dolce vita,* the sweet life. While life may be frugal for some, Calabrians and southern Italians are extroverts known for their cheerfulness and gaiety despite invasions, wars, volcanic eruptions, and earthquakes. No doubt the wonderful sunny climate contributes to their sunny disposition.

When you visit Italy be sure to note the flair Italians have for the dramatic. Less reserved and even more demonstrative are southern Italians, unafraid to show genuine, undisguised emotion—they sing, laugh, cry, curse, love, kiss one another on both cheeks, and irresistibly though gently pinch the round, rosy cheeks of infants. Facial expressions speak volumes. Often you need only to watch the changing expressions to understand the topic. Observe the use of hands to accentuate speech, see wrists fly, watch graphic facial expressions and eyes that roll to the sky. Notice the young on their *Vespas* (motor scooters) displaying bravado, defying gravity as they round corners, challenging trucks and buses, calling to friends as they buzz by. Enjoy all the thoroughly charming, utterly amusing histrionics.

As in other parts of Italy, Calabrians have a dialect of their own, although it appears to be disappearing. Calabrians visiting their native province who perhaps haven't heard the dialect since childhood (like me) are sure to conjure happy memories upon hearing it. They will be witness to a people who fill their lives not only with love of family and friends, but also with fine food, the arts, and love itself. They marvel at all of life. Their joy of living and animated lifestyle is at the same time spontaneous and splendid, yet simple and relaxed. Southern Italians are unpretentious; they believe that association with but one type of people is the equivalent of reading but one book. I leave it to you to decide if Calabrians have a *testa dura* (hard head). More of a certainty is that Calabria is still seductive even though Homer's sirens have long disappeared!

If you are lucky enough to have relatives living in Italy, visiting them will enrich your life. Even a remote cousin will lavish you with attention and affection. On my two trips to research this book, my cousins taught me new lessons on love. On my first visit, they threw a *festa* (party) for forty of my cousins who live within fifty miles, served many delicious dishes, and sent me off with gifts for my mother, sons, sister, and myself. The warm hospitality, closeness of family, and genuine contentment with their splendid but sometimes simple lifestyle made me proud of them and my ancestry.

On my return visit, I brought the recipes and, with the help of some of my cousins in the kitchen, treated *them* to dinner. I brought each of them gifts and as before, received many from them as well. More photographs and another night to remember. Undoubtedly, like countless others whose parents emigrated, I wondered what it would have been like had I been born and stayed there. But no answer was (or could be) forthcoming

Even if you don't have relatives in Calabria, or anywhere in Italy, I urge you to visit. You will be amply rewarded with unforgettable memories. Such a visit may later cause you, as it did me, to reflect upon the American way of life and its more hectic ways and how, unlike our Italian brethren, we sometimes forget, postpone, or even neglect the most important priorities in life so evident to them—family and love.

A trip to any part of Italy is unlike any other journey. It is more than sea and scape, more than charm and climate, and more than exceptionally good food. It is a land rich in natural and manmade beauty, a land of festivals and processions, a land that encourages spiritual contact with a people rich in the way they live life. It is a feast for the senses! For me, all of Italy, but especially Calabria, is everything I imagined or anticipated. Like Stendhal, I find it difficult to put in strong enough terms. He aptly said, "I find a charm in this country that I cannot quite grasp. It is like love . . . I cannot say what I mean—everything I use to depict it is too weak."

I urge you to consider including Calabria and southern Italy in your next Italian trip. But if you can't make that trip just now, relax, light the candles, pour the wine, leaf through the pages of this book, and imagine you are there. *Buon viaggio* and *buon appetito*!

VOVA

EGGS

Eggs have always played an important role in rites of spring and religious festivities throughout the world. Traditionally they evoked fertility and good luck and were eaten to ensure eternal life. Eggs also symbolized renewal of life, new beginnings, and Christ's Resurrection. In ancient Rome, eggs were brought to the temple to honor Ceres, goddess of grains who taught men to till the soil, to sow and to reap, and to bake. German peasants smeared their plows with a mixture of eggs and flour, hoping to improve their harvest. In France, a seventeenth-century bride cracked an egg on her new home's doorstep before her first entry to ensure a big family. In the nineteenth century in Bombay, India, builders put an egg mixed with milk into the foundation of a new building to protect it from harm. The Chinese congratulated new parents with a red hard-boiled egg. The charming custom of exchanging eggs each spring is attributed to the Egyptians, coloring them to the Persians. However, Polish legend has it that the Virgin Mary painted boiled eggs to please the infant Jesus. German immigrants introduced the Easter bunny to us to deliver colored eggs to the children.

Roasted eggs are still one of the symbolic foods served at the Passover Seder around the world, representing fertility in the spring and mourning for the destruction of the Temple. In Italy, eggs are still a part of Easter dinner in one or more forms, continuing the deep-rooted heritage.

Today, we eat eggs mostly because we like them. They are rich in protein, vitamins, and minerals. Happily, eggs may not be quite the dietary killer about which we have been hearing for some time. In 1995 the Research Clinic of the University of Washington reported that most people, even those with elevated cholesterol levels, can safely eat several eggs per week as long as they follow a low-fat diet. Because of salmonella, it is still wise not to eat raw eggs or to leave them unrefrigerated.

In Italy, eggs are rarely eaten for breakfast; most Italians eat a very light breakfast. Instead, the egg enjoys a more prominent and lofty status in a wholesome and delicious entrée, the *frittata*. *Frittate* were cooked even back in ancient times. According to Apicius, the first-century Roman gastronome and food writer, *frittate* were an excellent way to use leftover vegetables.

The Italian *frittata* is quite different from the American omelet. *Frittate* are laden, almost overflowing, with a wide variety of vegetables, cheese, or meat. *Frittate* are not rolled or folded but rather are served in wedges, like pizza. While omelet is not the exact translation of *frittata,* it is the closest one I know of and is therefore the one I use throughout. Included here are several diverse, plump, and great-tasting *frittata* recipes that provide a speedy but satisfying dish for lunch or dinner. Also included is an altogether different and festive omelet made with spinach, cheese, and prosciutto called an *omeletta.*

Want to hard boil an egg perfectly? Though boiling eggs sounds simple, done incorrectly or overcooked, they can come out rubbery and hard to peel, with green yolks. Follow this easy method and they will be moist and white, with a golden yellow yolk in the center where you want it. Carefully place eggs in a small saucepan. Cover by 1 inch with lukewarm tap water. Bring to a boil. Remove from heat. Cover and let eggs stand for 20 minutes. Remove from pan and let cool before slicing or serving.

Want to test an egg for freshness? Put the egg in a pan of cold water. If it sinks to the bottom it is fresh, if it floats, it is old and should be discarded.

Frittata di Asparagi
Asparagus Omelet

Renowned in Imperial Rome and older than Egypt itself, asparagus is a regal vegetable. First-century gourmand Apicius referred to asparagus *frittata* in his writings. If you wish you can add 3 tablespoons of raw red pepper, cut into ¼-inch pieces, along with the asparagus.

> 1 **pound fresh asparagus**
> 2 **tablespoons olive oil**
> 5 **large eggs**
> 2 **tablespoons freshly grated pecorino cheese**
> ¼ **teaspoon salt**
> ¼ **teaspoon freshly ground black pepper**

Cut off hard stems of asparagus. If the remaining stems are not pencil-thin, slit bottom of stems up 2 inches so they will be cooked at the same time the tips are. Rinse well and tie loosely in a bundle. Using a steamer or a tall asparagus pan, add water and bring to a boil. Add asparagus, tip side up. Lower heat and cook for 6 to 10 minutes depending on thickness, or until just tender when pierced with a knife. Remove and drain on paper towels. Cut into 1-inch pieces and set aside.

In a 10-inch nonstick skillet, add olive oil over medium heat. Add asparagus and toss to coat. Sauté for 3 to 4 minutes or until lightly browned.

In a large mixing bowl, add eggs, cheese, salt, and pepper. Beat until frothy. Lower heat and pour egg mixture over asparagus. Do not stir. As eggs begin to set, lift edges to let remaining liquid flow underneath. Cook for 4 to 6 minutes or until bottom is a light golden brown and little liquid remains on top.

Shake pan to loosen omelet. Cover skillet with a flat plate (or baking sheet) larger than the skillet and invert the omelet onto it. The uncooked side of the omelet will be on the bottom of the plate. Slide it back into the skillet. Cook for 2 to 3 minutes or until set.

Slide omelet onto a round serving dish. Cut into wedges and serve hot or at room temperature.

Serves 4

Frittata di Funghi
Mushroom Omelet

Variations on eggs were created to provide a light entrée for the noontime or evening meal. At one time, Roman Catholics abstained from eating meat on Fridays, and *frittate* were often served then. Although that restriction has been repealed, omelets are still in favor.

> 2 tablespoons olive oil
> 1 medium onion, thinly sliced
> 8 ounces button mushrooms, thinly sliced
> 5 large eggs
> 1 tablespoon fresh Italian parsley, finely chopped
> ¼ teaspoon salt
> ¼ teaspoon crushed red pepper

In a 10-inch nonstick skillet, add olive oil over medium heat. Add onion and toss to coat. Sauté for 8 to 10 minutes or until lightly browned. Add mushrooms and sauté for 2 or 3 minutes, stirring frequently.

In a large mixing bowl, add eggs, parsley, salt, and crushed red pepper. Beat until frothy. Lower heat and pour egg mixture over onions and mushrooms. Do not stir. As eggs begin to set, lift edges to let remaining liquid flow underneath. Cook 4 to 6 minutes or until bottom is a light golden brown and little liquid remains on top.

Shake pan to loosen omelet. Cover skillet with a flat plate (or baking sheet) larger than the skillet, and invert the omelet onto it. The uncooked side of the omelet will be on the bottom of the plate. Slide it back into the skillet. Cook for 2 to 3 minutes or until set.

Slide omelet onto a round serving dish. Cut into wedges and serve either hot or at room temperature.

Serves 4

Frittata di Cipolle e Pancetta
Onion and Pancetta Omelet

A melange of eggs, onion, and pancetta, unsmoked Italian bacon, makes this omelet especially appetizing. If you wish, two ounces of bacon or prosciutto can be substituted for the pancetta.

2 **ounces pancetta, coarsely chopped**
2 **tablespoons olive oil**
2 **medium onions, thinly sliced**
5 **large eggs**
¼ **teaspoon salt**
¼ **teaspoon freshly ground black pepper**

In a 10-inch nonstick skillet add pancetta over medium-high heat. Sauté for 3 to 5 minutes or until crisp. Remove and drain on paper towels. Remove fat from skillet and discard. Wipe skillet almost clean, but do not wash. Lower heat to medium, add olive oil and onion, and toss to coat. Sauté for 8 to 10 minutes, or until lightly browned. Return pancetta to skillet.

In a large mixing bowl, add eggs, salt, and pepper. Beat until frothy. Lower heat and pour egg mixture over pancetta and onion. Do not stir. As eggs begin to set, lift edges to let remaining liquid flow underneath. Cook 4 to 6 minutes or until bottom is a light golden brown and little liquid remains on top.

Shake pan to loosen omelet. Cover skillet with a flat plate (or baking sheet) larger than the skillet,and invert the omelet onto it. The uncooked side of the omelet will be on the bottom of the plate. Slide it back into the skillet. Cook for 2 to 3 minutes or until set.

Slide omelet onto a round serving dish. Cut into wedges and serve hot or at room temperature.

Serves 4

Frittata di Peperoni, Patate, e Cipolle
Pepper, Potato, and Onion Omelet

Many Calabrians rate this the queen of *frittate* and with good reason. Delightfully delicious, this gratifying and colorful medley of pepper, potato, and onion encased in the eggs creates a hearty dish. If you wish, you can add a couple of heaping tablespoons cooked, crumbled sausage along with the eggs.

1 large potato
1 large onion
1 large green or red bell pepper
3 tablespoons olive oil, divided
5 large eggs
½ teaspoon salt
¼ teaspoon freshly ground black pepper

Peel potato, cut into ½-inch cubes, and set aside. Peel onion, cut into ½-inch cubes, and set aside. Wash and dry bell pepper, cut into ½-inch pieces, and set aside. Do not mix the vegetables together.

In a 10-inch nonstick skillet, add 2 tablespoons olive oil over medium heat. Add the potatoes and onions and toss to coat. Sauté for 12 to 15 minutes, stirring occasionally, until tender and a light golden brown. Remove both with a slotted spoon and set aside.

Add remaining tablespoon olive oil. Add peppers, toss to coat, and sauté for 10 to 12 minutes, or until tender and a light golden brown, stirring occasionally. Return onions and potatoes to skillet and mix thoroughly.

In a large mixing bowl, add eggs, salt, and pepper. Beat until frothy. Lower heat and pour egg mixture over vegetables. Do not stir. As eggs begin to set, lift edges to let remaining liquid flow underneath. Cook for 4 to 6 minutes or until bottom is a light golden brown and little liquid remains on top.

Shake pan to loosen omelet. Cover skillet with a flat plate (or baking sheet) larger than the skillet, and invert the omelet onto it. The uncooked side of the omelet will be on the bottom of the plate. Slide it back into the skillet. Cook for 2 to 3 minutes or until set.

Slide omelet onto a round serving dish. Cut into wedges and serve hot or at room temperature.

Serves 4

Omeletta con Spinaci, Formaggio, e Prosciutto

Omelet Roll with Spinach, Cheese, and Prosciutto

Most Italian omelets are thick, hearty, and pan-sized. A delightful contrast of flavor and color, this *omeletta* is delicate and rolled. While in Italy, I was invited to lunch at the home of my first cousin Giovanna (Gana) Minniti of Reggio Calabria. Her daughter Angela and grandson John were also present. Among other things, Gana introduced me to this elegant omelet.

4	ounces fresh spinach, thoroughly washed
5	large eggs
3	tablespoons freshly grated pecorino cheese
¼	teaspoon freshly ground black pepper
1½	tablespoons olive oil
2	ounces prosciutto, thinly sliced
2	ounces provolone cheese, thinly sliced
	fresh Italian parsley leaves for garnish

Preheat oven to 350° F.

In a steamer, heat a small amount of water. Add spinach and steam for 2 to 3 minutes or until wilted. Remove, drain, and squeeze out as much moisture as possible. Chop coarsely and set aside.

In a large mixing bowl, add the eggs, grated cheese, and pepper. With a whisk, beat until frothy.

In a cast iron skillet, add olive oil over low to medium heat. Pour egg mixture into skillet. As eggs begin to set, lift edges to let remaining liquid flow underneath. Cook for 4 to 6 minutes or until the bottom is a light golden brown and little liquid remains on top. Remove skillet from burner.

Spread cooked spinach over center third of the omelet. Cover spinach with the prosciutto and provolone. Fold the omelet into thirds, turning it seam side down. Bake for 4 to 6 minutes or until a slit in the omelet with a knife indicates eggs are cooked through and cheese has melted.

With the aid of a spatula, slide omelet onto a serving platter and cut into 1½-to 2-inch slices. Garnish with parsley leaves and serve immediately or at room temperature.

Serves 4

Frittata di Zucchini
Zucchini Omelet

This recipe will be a regular part of your repertoire, especially when zucchini is in season. A favorite Calabrian vegetable, zucchini can stand alone or can successfully find its way into many different dishes such as this nourishing omelet. The addition of a little cheese and parsley and a touch of fiery red pepper gives it a bit of zip.

> 1 medium zucchini, about 1 pound
> 2 tablespoons olive oil
> ½ small onion, coarsely chopped
> 5 large eggs
> 2 tablespoons freshly grated pecorino cheese
> 1 tablespoon fresh Italian parsley, coarsely chopped
> ¼ teaspoon salt
> ¼ teaspoon crushed red pepper

Wash zucchini and pat dry with paper towels. Cut in half lengthwise and then into thin slices.

In a 10-inch nonstick skillet, add olive oil over medium heat. Add onion and toss to coat. Sauté for 4 to 6 minutes or until lightly browned. Add zucchini and sauté for 8 to 10 minutes or until tender and a light golden brown.

In a large mixing bowl, add eggs, cheese, parsley, salt, and crushed red pepper. Beat until frothy. Lower heat and pour egg mixture over vegetables. As eggs begin to set, lift edges to let remaining liquid flow underneath. Cook 4 to 6 minutes or until bottom is a light golden brown and little liquid remains on top.

Shake pan to loosen omelet. Cover skillet with a flat plate (or baking sheet) larger than the skillet and invert the omelet onto it. The uncooked side of the omelet will be on the bottom of the plate. Slide it back into the skillet. Cook for 2 to 3 minutes, or until set.

Slide omelet onto a round serving dish. Cut into wedges and serve hot or at room temperature.

Serves 4

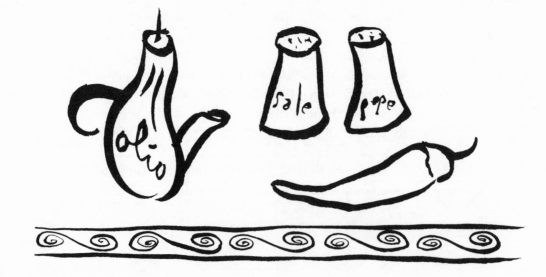

LE VERDURE E INSALATE

VEGETABLES AND SALADS

Chi zappa buono miegliu ricogli.

He who tills well reaps well.
<small>CALABRIAN PROVERB</small>

Italians deal with vegetables better than anyone else in the Western world. Agricultural know-how in Italy predates the Romans, going back to the Etruscans. The latter were so devoted to farming that the idea of owning and working the land was part of their religion. The Romans were well informed about harvesting many vegetables and alternating crops as well as irrigation, drainage, and fertilization. Some of their favorites were squash, beets, carrots, asparagus, cucumbers, radishes, onions, shallots, leeks, and a wide range of greens.

So highly esteemed were vegetables in the ancient world that many early Romans were named after vegetables: Cato, Fabius, and Cicero after cabbages, beans, and peas. Italy continues this delightful custom by bestowing high honors to notables through special dishes containing vegetables. In 1889, Queen Margherita was honored by the creation of a special pizza in her name (*Pizza Margherita*, page 263). On December 26, 1831, Vincenzo Bellini's operatic masterpiece, *Norma*, was honored by a special sauce in her name, *Salsa alla Norma* (Sauce Norma with Tomatoes and Eggplant, page 123).

No surprise then that Calabrians and southern Italians also have an affinity with the land and a deep love for cultivating the soil. Their very soul is tied to the land. They consider it sinful not to cultivate every available bit of land. They give loving care to the art of planting and harvesting a vegetable garden, a love that continues to assume an almost religious devotion and one that rewards them with their beloved fresh vegetables and herbs. For the most part, Italian immigrants continued that tradition in the United States.

It is impossible to know when man first began to dig for food in addition to gathering plants. It is thought that in prehistoric times, onions, turnips, and radishes were in use. Cabbages, mushrooms, various forms of beans, chickpeas, peas, and lentils were also known to have existed in very ancient times. Lentils, said to be one of the world's first cultivated foods in the Middle East as far back as 6000 B.C., occupy a secure role in Calabrian soups and side dishes.

It is believed that the cooking of food first occurred quite by accident, sometime between 1,400,000 B.C. to 500,000 B.C. Thus the first deliberate use of fire was implemented and cooking was discovered. Applied primarily to roasting meat at first, the next step was the invention of pots in which vegetables could be cooked.

My father had a backyard garden of which 85 percent was vegetables and 15 percent fruit trees, grape and rose arbors, and flowers. The only lawn in the back of the house was the path between the two halves of his long and productive garden. In addition to the tomato, to which was delegated the largest area, Dad grew green beans, pole beans, zucchini, cucumbers, escarole, garlic, lettuce, onions, potatoes, broccoli, and many herbs, particularly basil and parsley.

My mother was adept at serving nicely seasoned vegetables, which appealed to my sister and me even as little children. We remember our parents telling us how tasty and large the fruits and vegetables were in Italy. I thought they had exaggerated until I went to Italy and saw for myself. All were huge, had intense color, and when cooked were tastier than any I had ever had before.

Because anyone could grow vegetables on a bit of land, many poor Italians depended on gardens as their greatest food source. If they had little or no land of their own, Calabrians willingly did truck farming, tier farming, and tenant farming, even on rugged hillsides. Those with no access to land could buy vegetables. Since ancient times, street markets brimming with seasonal fruits and vegetables have flourished. They are an ideal place to learn about Italian food and Italian character. Vendors eagerly talk about how to plant vegetables, care for them, and cook them; how their grandmothers cooked them; and more. If you want to eat a purchased tomato or apple, they will cheerfully rinse it for you on the spot.

The tomato holds a special place in the hearts of all southern Italians. Succulent and savory, sensual and seductive, tomatoes are one of life's joys. It is hard to imagine southern Italian cuisine without the tomato, so fundamental is it to the diet. Yet it did not arrive in Europe until the sixteenth century. Brought by South Americans who ate it unadorned, Europe was slow to discover its charms. Some considered it poisonous, lacking nutritional value, magical, or medicinal; others claimed it was the evil apple of the Garden of Eden; the French called it *pomme d' amour*, love apple.

It wasn't until it arrived in Italy that the tomato reached its zenith and fulfilled its destiny. Calabrians and southern Italians were the first Europeans to recognize its culinary potential, first to find its greatest use—tomato sauces—and first to proclaim its diversity in other spectacular dishes as well. They called it *pomidoro*, the golden apple, because the first were yellow. It was love at first bite, and from then on, tomatoes never left their side. They crowned tomato king, and kings rate festivals. In September, parts of southern Italy hold a festival in the tomato's honor and serve various tomato sauces over several varieties of pastas. Tomatoes were not restricted to sauces, however. Soon Calabrians and southern Italians were skillfully combining tomatoes with vegetables, meats, soups, and salads.

For centuries Italians have preserved what they grow in a variety of ways, for times when a particular favorite, like the tomato, is not in season. Some are air dried, others are canned. Sun-dried tomatoes are a huge hit in the United States. As little girls, my sister and I helped preserve tomatoes in a family affair that lasted several days. There was always enough to give to friends and neighbors, often along with a bottle of homemade wine or homemade cookies. My mother made her own tomato paste, called *stratto* or *conserva di pomodoro*, but few do this today. A long and arduous task, it takes 15 or 16 pounds of tomatoes to make a pound of paste.

Eggplant, a highly versatile vegetable, is considered to be the queen of Calabrian vegetables. Originally from the East Indies, eggplant arrived in Calabria and Sicily in the eleventh century. It had a tough history to overcome. People thought it could poison you at worst and could lead to insanity at best. Like the tomato, however, southern Italians soon adopted it as their own, devising numerous ways in which to serve it. Meaty and luscious, deep purple eggplant can be paired with other vegetables and added to soups and sauces. The necessity of sprinkling it with salt and to weigh it down to draw out bitter juices is disputed by many. Because it is so porous, broiling eggplant slices lightly brushed with oil instead of sautéing them considerably reduces the amount of fat.

Peppers are a more recent find. Columbus was credited with discovering them in Haiti and bringing the seeds to Spain. The Spanish later brought them to Calabria. Shiny, firm, and heavy, they are fried, stuffed, roasted, and added to soups, sauces, and frittatas. Peppers come in a rainbow of colors: red, green, yellow, orange, and purple. When using all in one recipe, the dish bursts with color and flavor. Red peppers are vine-ripened green peppers that have become luscious and sweet. Calabrians also grow a delicate and tender pepper known as *friarelli* in some villages. Long, yellow-green, and sweet, they can be simply sautéed in a fine olive oil and sprinkled with crushed red pepper or stuffed with a rich, flavorful bread dressing.

The best porcini mushrooms are found in three regions of Italy, one of which is Sila Massif in Calabria. An expensive but highly prized delicacy, they are hunted by thousands of men, women, and children from late May to July and again from September to November. Because their flavor intensifies when dried, a little goes a long way. As little as ½ to 1 ounce is all that is needed to impart their powerful flavor to other ingredients. Add them to pasta and rice dishes, or sauté them along with white mushrooms or other vegetables, greatly enhancing each dish.

Salads in Italy have been around for a long time. A mixed green salad of sorts was served at meals by the ancient Romans. Over time, salads evolved into more than just greens. The harmonious, hearty ingredients of some salads work equally well as a meal in one dish or as an antipasto. Other salads are cool and refreshing, perfect on a hot summer night. Some are elegant enough for a special luncheon. Most take little time to prepare. Greens should be washed quickly and well dried, as oil does not adhere well to damp lettuce. Dressing should be added just before serving.

A good guide to salad preparation is to use whatever is fresh and in season. Sensational springtime salads combine two or three different greens that appear in the early growing season. Shimmering brightly, combined with other colorful vegetables such as juicy tomatoes, crisp green peppers, fresh mushrooms, and herbs, mixed salads please all the senses. In the fall, hearty ingredients such as broccoli and cauliflower can be added. The dressing most Calabrians use consists of a top-quality extra-virgin oil, most often red wine vinegar (sometimes lemon juice), salt, and pepper.

Many of the vegetable recipes in this book were handed down to me by my mother, Jennie Marino Amabile, an excellent cook. Others came from Calabrian cousins, friends, restaurateurs, and other sources. They have all been adapted to work with our ingredients. Calabrians have perfected the art of cooking vegetables in skillful and zesty combinations with just the right fresh herbs and seasonings in imaginative ways, with as much reverence as though creating a work of art. I am confident that you will agree with me when I say that in these pages are some of the tastiest vegetable dishes you will have ever eaten. I hope that you, like me, will be further rewarded by finding that your children will enjoy them, too.

Asparagi al Sesamo e Limone
Asparagus with Sesame Seeds and Lemon

Romans and Egyptians both relished asparagus. Roman gourmand Apicius applauded it in his cookbook *De re Coquinaria*. Low in calories and high in vitamins A and C and fiber, when in season, I could eat it every day. Select asparagus of uniform size for good presentation and even cooking time. Asparagus lovers use a tall pan specifically designed to steam asparagus but a large pot with a steamer insert will do.

1	pound fresh asparagus
2	tablespoons extra-virgin olive oil
2	cloves garlic, finely minced
1	lemon, freshly juiced
½	teaspoon grated lemon peel
1½	tablespoons sesame seeds
1	tablespoon fresh Italian parsley, finely chopped
¼	teaspoon salt

Cut off hard stems of asparagus. If the remaining stems are not pencil-thin, slit bottom of stems up 2 inches so they will be cooked at the same time the tips are. Rinse well and tie loosely into a bundle. Using a steamer or a tall asparagus pan, add water and bring to a boil. Add asparagus, tip side up. Lower heat and cook for 10 to 12 minutes, depending on thickness, or until tender.

Meanwhile, in a small skillet, add olive oil over medium heat. Add garlic and sauté for 1 to 2 minutes or until light golden brown. Add lemon juice, grated lemon peel, sesame seeds, parsley, and salt. Heat and mix well.

Carefully remove asparagus with tongs and arrange the asparagus tips to point outward at opposite edges of an oblong platter. If using a round plate, arrange spears neatly in a circle, tips pointing inward. Pour dressing evenly over the asparagus and serve immediately.

Serves 4

Broccoli con Formaggio, Aglio, e Limone
Broccoli with Cheese, Garlic, and Lemon

A favorite of the ancient Romans, broccoli has been in existence for over 2,000 years. Nutritionists consider it a perfect food. Calabrians seem to have known this for some time. In this dish, the cheese, garlic, and lemon add zip. It is best to make this dish at least 1 to 2 hours before serving to allow the flavors to mingle. If made early in the day and refrigerated, remove it 1 hour prior to serving, reheat if desired, but do not add parsley until the last minute.

- 1 large bunch broccoli, about 2 pounds (3 cups)
- 3 cloves garlic, thickly sliced
- 4 tablespoons grated pecorino or Parmesan cheese
- ½ teaspoon salt
- ¼ teaspoon freshly ground black pepper
- 2 tablespoons extra-virgin olive oil
- 2 tablespoons freshly squeezed lemon juice
- 2 tablespoons fresh Italian parsley, finely chopped

Rinse broccoli well and separate into long stalks. Cut into 4-inch stems and separate florets. Peel remaining bottom stems and cut into ¼-inch slices. In a double boiler, steam the broccoli for 5 to 7 minutes or until it is cooked but still crisp. Remove and set aside.

Put broccoli in a large mixing bowl. Distribute the garlic throughout. Sprinkle with cheese, salt, and pepper. Drizzle olive oil and lemon juice evenly over broccoli and toss gently.

Just before serving, remove garlic slices, mix again gently, and arrange on a serving dish. Sprinkle with parsley. Serve at room temperature.

Serves 4 to 6

Broccoli Piccanti
Piquant Broccoli

Melted anchovies and lemon combine to produce a distinctive taste, enhancing without overpowering the broccoli. The bread crumbs add crunch. Even if you are not fond of broccoli or are unaccustomed to using anchovies as a seasoning, you may become a convert after the first bite.

1 large bunch broccoli, about 2 pounds (3 cups)

2 tablespoons, plus 2 teaspoons olive oil, divided

1 medium onion, finely chopped

3 or 4 anchovy fillets, mashed

2 cloves garlic, finely minced

1 large lemon, freshly juiced

¼ cup dry white wine

½ teaspoon salt

¼ teaspoon freshly ground black pepper

¼ cup dried bread crumbs

Rinse broccoli well and separate into long stalks. Cut into 4-inch stems and separate into florets. Peel remaining bottom stems and cut into ¼-inch slices. In a double boiler, steam the broccoli for 5 to 7 minutes or until it is cooked but still crisp. Remove and set aside.

In a large, heavy skillet add 2 tablespoons olive oil over medium heat. Sauté onion for 3 to 4 minutes, or until translucent. Add anchovies and garlic, and sauté for 1 to 2 minutes, or until the garlic is light golden brown. Add lemon juice, wine, salt, and pepper. Stir well. Add broccoli, then lower heat, cover, and simmer for 2 to 4 minutes or until just tender.

In a small skillet, add remaining 2 teaspoons olive oil over medium heat. Add bread crumbs and sauté for 2 minutes, turning constantly. Put broccoli on serving platter and pour pan juices over all. Sprinkle with toasted bread crumbs and serve immediately.

Serves 4 to 6

Cavolo con Pomodori
Sautéed Cabbage with Tomatoes

Cabbage has been around since prehistoric times. Homer referred to it in *The Odyssey*. The Romans relished it. Cooking cabbage at a high temperature and for too long causes a strong odor. High in vitamin C, some people love cabbage, recognize its nutritional value, and enjoy it cooked or raw. Others don't or think they don't. When I served this nicely herbed dish to my family, my son John said the best thing about it was that it didn't taste like cabbage. He meant it as a compliment.

2   tablespoons olive oil
1   large onion, coarsely chopped
2   cloves garlic, finely minced
1   16-ounce can Italian plum tomatoes, coarsely chopped
½   head cabbage, coarsely chopped
2   tablespoons fresh Italian parsley, finely chopped
½   teaspoon salt
½   teaspoon crushed red pepper
¼   teaspoon dried oregano (optional)

In a large, heavy skillet add olive oil over medium heat. Add onion and sauté for 3 to 4 minutes or until translucent. Add garlic and sauté 1 to 2 minutes, or until light golden brown. Lower heat, add tomatoes, and sauté for 5 minutes.

Add remaining ingredients and stir well. Lower heat and simmer for 30 to 40 minutes or until cabbage is tender. Serve immediately.

Serves 6 to 8

Melanzane Ripiene
Stuffed Eggplant with Prosciutto and Provolone

Eggplants originated in India and were brought to the Mediterranean by the Arabs. When they arrived in southern Italy, Calabrians adopted them as their own and have been perfecting ways in which to serve them ever since. This fine creation with its sensational stuffing was contributed by my cousins. I tasted a similar version at a fine restaurant in Benevento, Campania. Vegetarians can omit the prosciutto and still enjoy this great dish.

2   small to medium eggplants, about 1 pound each
1½   cups day-old, coarse Italian bread crumbs
6   slices prosciutto, coarsely chopped
⅓   cup provolone, coarsely chopped, divided
1   large egg, lightly beaten
¼   cup water
2   cloves garlic, finely minced
2   tablespoons fresh basil, coarsely chopped
½   teaspoon salt
¼   teaspoon freshly ground black pepper
1   tablespoon olive oil

Preheat oven to 350° F.

Wash eggplant and pat dry with paper towels. Put whole in a lightly greased 12-inch square baking dish. Bake for 10 minutes, then remove from oven and cut each in half lengthwise. Leave oven on.

Scoop out center of eggplant halves, leaving a ½-inch thick shell. In a large bowl, add scooped eggplant, bread crumbs, prosciutto, half the provolone cheese, egg, water, garlic, basil, salt, and pepper. Mix thoroughly. If mixture does not stick together, add more water gradually. The exact amount of water depends on how dry the bread crumbs are. Stuff eggplants, sprinkle with the remaining provolone cheese, and drizzle each with olive oil.

Put stuffed eggplants in an oiled 12-inch square baking dish. Return to oven and bake for 35 to 40 minutes, or until eggplant is tender and cooked through. Transfer to a serving platter and serve at once.

Serves 4 to 8

Ciambotta
Eggplant with Mixed Vegetables

This well-known hearty and chunky vegetable dish is prepared throughout Calabria. It always includes onion, eggplant, peppers, potatoes, and tomatoes. Other vegetables are often added depending on the season or the cook's favorites. If one of your favorites is not included in the options, try adding a small amount at first to be certain it does not overpower the others.

4 to 5	tablespoons olive oil, divided
1	large onion, coarsely sliced
2	cloves garlic, finely minced
1	large eggplant, about 1 pound, unpeeled and cut into 1-inch cubes
3	green, red, or yellow bell peppers, seeded and cut into 1-inch cubes
3	medium potatoes, Idaho or Russet, peeled and thinly sliced
1	pound fresh tomatoes or 1 16-ounce can Italian plum tomatoes, coarsely chopped
½	teaspoon salt
¼	teaspoon oregano
¼	teaspoon crushed red pepper

Heat 1 tablespoon olive oil in a large, nonstick skillet over medium heat. Add onion and sauté for 3 to 4 minutes or until translucent. Add garlic and sauté for 1 to 2 minutes or until light golden brown. Add 1 tablespoon olive oil and the eggplant. Lower heat slightly and sauté gently for 10 to 12 minutes or until lightly browned, turning frequently. Remove all to a large bowl and set aside.

To the skillet, add 1 tablespoon olive oil and the peppers. Sauté for 12 to 15 minutes, turning frequently until lightly browned and tender. Remove and put in the bowl with the onion, garlic, and eggplant. Add 1 tablespoon olive oil to skillet and, when hot, add potatoes. Add remaining tablespoon olive oil, if needed. Sauté for 12 to 15 minutes or until lightly browned and just tender. Remove and put in the bowl with the other vegetables. Add tomatoes, salt, oregano, and crushed red pepper to the skillet. Sauté for 15 minutes.

Return all vegetables to the skillet and mix well. Sauté for 5 to 7 minutes or until all vegetables are cooked through.

Serves 6 to 8

Fagiolini con Peperoni, Formaggio, e Limone
Green Beans with Peppers, Cheese, and Lemon

Green beans prepared this quick way are especially zesty. A dash of red from a pepper, a sprinkling of green from Italian parsley, and a dusting of pale gold cheese and this dish becomes as colorful as it is palatable. You can use ½ pound green beans and ½ pound yellow beans for even more color. You also can substitute strips of *Peperoni Arrostiti* (Roasted Peppers, page 52) for the raw red pepper.

> 1 **pound green beans**
> 1 **red bell pepper, seeded and cut lengthwise into ¼-inch strips**
> 3 **tablespoons extra-virgin olive oil**
> 3 **cloves garlic, coarsely sliced**
> 3 **tablespoons freshly grated pecorino or Parmesan cheese**
> ¼ **teaspoon salt**
> ¼ **teaspoon freshly ground black pepper**
> 2 **tablespoons freshly squeezed lemon juice**
> 2 **tablespoons fresh Italian parsley, finely chopped, for garnish**

Wash and trim green beans. In a steamer, cook beans for 5 to 10 minutes or until just tender. The exact cooking time depends on the age and size of the beans.

Put beans in a large mixing bowl. Add red pepper strips. While the beans are still warm, drizzle with olive oil and toss until each bean is coated. Add the garlic and sprinkle evenly with cheese, salt, pepper, and lemon juice. Toss gently. Let stand for at least 10 minutes to allow flavors to blend. Just before serving, remove garlic slices, put on serving dish, and sprinkle with parsley. Serve hot or at room temperature.

Serves 4

Fagiolini con Pomodori
Green Beans with Tomatoes

Calabrians combine crisp green beans with fresh tomatoes and sweet onion for a succulent side dish. This easy dish in a skillet is a fine contrast in taste and color.

> 1 pound green beans
> 1 cup coarsely chopped very ripe fresh tomatoes
> 1 tablespoon olive oil
> ½ medium onion, coarsely chopped
> 1 small clove garlic, finely minced
> ¼ teaspoon salt
> ¼ teaspoon freshly ground black pepper
> 1 tablespoon fresh basil, finely slivered

Wash and trim green beans. Set aside. Plunge tomatoes into boiling water for 10 to 15 seconds. Remove peel and chop coarsely, then set aside.

In a large, heavy skillet, add olive oil over medium heat. Sauté onions for 3 to 4 minutes or until translucent. Add garlic and sauté for 1 to 2 minutes or until light golden brown.

Add green beans, tomatoes, salt, and pepper. Mix well. Lower heat and simmer for 5 to 10 minutes, or until beans are just tender. The exact cooking time will depend on the size and age of the beans.

Just before serving, add the basil and stir. Serve in small individual bowls, hot or at room temperature.

Serves 4

Minestra al Forno
Greens Baked with a Crusty Topping

A vegetarian delight! This wonderful, textured mixture of different vegetables coated with bread crumbs is baked to a crisp, golden brown. *Minestra* more generally describes a soup, but in some parts of southern Italy, it is also used to describe a dish consisting primarily of greens.

1	pound broccoli florets, about 1 ½ cups
½	pound shredded cabbage, about 2 cups
½	head coarsely chopped escarole, about 2 cups
½	teaspoon salt
2	tablespoons fresh Italian parsley, finely chopped
2	tablespoons olive oil
2	cloves garlic, finely minced
½	cup dried, fine bread crumbs
½	teaspoon crushed red pepper

Preheat oven to 400° F.

In a large saucepan, bring a quart of water to a boil. Add the broccoli, cabbage, escarole, and salt. Cook for 4 to 5 minutes. Remove vegetables and plunge into cold water to stop the cooking process and to retain color. Drain and set aside. Reserve water for use in *Brodo di Verdure* (Vegetable Broth, page 69).

Put vegetables in a lightly greased 8-by-10-inch casserole and sprinkle with parsley. Bake for 10 minutes.

Meanwhile, in a small skillet add olive oil over medium heat. Sauté garlic for 1 to 2 minutes or until light golden brown. Add bread crumbs and crushed red pepper. Stir constantly for 1 minute or until bread crumbs are just lightly toasted.

Remove casserole and distribute toasted bread crumbs evenly over top of vegetables. Return to oven and bake for an additional 2 to 3 minutes, or until top is crusty and golden brown.

Serves 4 to 6

Insalata di Lattuga con Sugo di Arancia
Lettuce Salad with Orange Juice Dressing

Oranges are abundant in Calabria. This delightfully different use of sweet, succulent oranges is an interesting find—a salad to remember. Normally served at the end of a meal, this particularly refreshing salad also can be served between courses to cleanse the palate.

½	head romaine lettuce
1	medium orange, peeled and thinly sliced
¼	small sweet white onion, very thinly sliced
10	green olives, brine-cured, pitted and halved (optional)
1	medium orange, freshly juiced
2	tablespoons extra-virgin olive oil
⅛	teaspoon salt
⅛	teaspoon freshly ground black pepper

Wash lettuce. Pat dry with paper towels or put through salad spinner. Tear into 1½-inch pieces. Add the orange and onion slices. Add the olives if using.

In a small bowl, combine the orange juice, olive oil, salt, and pepper. Pour over lettuce and toss well. Serve immediately.

Serves 4

Lenticchie, Scarola, Peperoni, e Cipolle
Lentils, Escarole, Peppers, and Onions

This traditional Calabrian New Year's Eve dish is supposed to bring good luck. Whether or not that works, the recipe does. Lentils were one of the first foods cultivated and were brought to Europe from Asia. My Aunt Catherine (Teta) Dieni learned to make this dish from her mother, Domenica Nucera Marino, and taught her daughter, Mimma, to make it. I'll wager Mimma has taught her daughter, Antonella, to make it as well. They said that at one time in Bova Superiore, a wild green called *segara* was used, but escarole or spinach has since replaced it.

1	pound dried lentils, rinsed
3	tablespoons olive oil, divided

2   medium onions, thinly sliced
2   red and/or yellow bell peppers, cut into 1-inch pieces
¼   head escarole, or 2 cups fresh spinach
2   tablespoons fresh Italian parsley, coarsely chopped
½   teaspoon salt
¼   teaspoon freshly ground black pepper

In a large saucepan, add washed lentils and cook for about 1 hour, or until tender. Drain and cool.

In a large, heavy skillet, add 1 tablespoon olive oil over medium heat. Add onion and sauté for 3 to 4 minutes or until translucent. Remove and set aside. Add remaining 2 tablespoons olive oil and sauté peppers for 5 to 6 minutes or until lightly browned, stirring frequently. Lower heat and cook slowly for 8 to 10 minutes more, or until peppers are tender.

Meanwhile, in a small steamer, steam escarole for 5 to 7 minutes or until just cooked. Cool and chop coarsely.

Add cooked lentils, onion, escarole, parsley, salt, and pepper to skillet with peppers. Mix well. Simmer for 2 minutes or until all ingredients are heated through. Serve hot or at room temperature.

Serves 6 to 8

Peperoni, Patate, e Uova
Peppers, Potatoes, and Eggs

This short-order dish is simple yet satisfying. Different from a *frittata,* these eggs are scrambled. Served with soup or a mixed salad and country-style Italian bread, dinner goes from refrigerator to table in about 30 minutes.

2   large bell peppers, 1 red and 1 green
2   large Idaho or Russet potatoes
3   tablespoons olive oil, divided
4   large eggs
½   teaspoon salt
¼   teaspoon freshly ground black pepper

Cut peppers into 1-inch pieces Set aside. Peel potatoes, quarter them, and cut into ¼-inch slices. Set aside.

In a large, heavy skillet over medium heat, add half the oil. Add the peppers and toss to coat. Lower heat, cover, and cook for 10 minutes, stirring frequently. Add the remaining olive oil and the potatoes; turn to coat. Cover and cook for 10 minutes, stirring frequently.

Remove the cover and sauté slowly for 10 minutes more, or until the potatoes are light golden brown and the peppers are tender.

Meanwhile, in a medium bowl, beat the eggs, salt, and pepper until frothy. Pour egg mixture evenly over vegetables. Stir frequently over medium heat until the eggs are cooked and not runny. Serve immediately.

Serves 4

Bocconotti
Potato Croquettes

With this recipe, Calabrians make the ordinary potato extraordinary. So widely known and loved is this potato croquette that it has many names: *crocchette* or *crocchettine di patate, fritelle di patate, pansorta*, and there are probably other names for it as well. *Bocconotti* is what my mother called them. I have enjoyed eating them ever since I was a child. A friend, Bob Grillo Lane, gave me his grandmother's version, which includes mozzarella cheese. It produces a pleasant surprise when you cut into the croquette and melted cheese oozes forth. I have listed the cheese as optional. For a change, tuck a bit of salami into each croquette.

> 1 **pound potatoes, about 4 medium, unpeeled**
> 2 **large eggs, divided**
> 2 **tablespoons freshly grated Parmesan or pecorino cheese**
> 1 **tablespoons fresh Italian parsley, finely chopped**
> ½ **teaspoon salt**
> ¼ **teaspoon freshly ground black pepper**
> ⅛ **pound mozzarella, cut into ¼-inch cubes (optional)**
> ⅛ **pound Italian salami, cut into ¼-inch cubes (optional)**
> ½ **cup all-purpose flour**
> ½ **cup very fine bread crumbs**
> 3 **tablespoons olive oil, divided**

Wash potatoes and put in a large saucepan of boiling water sufficient to cover them. Lower heat and simmer for 20 to 30 minutes, or until a potato is easily pierced with a fork. Drain, cool slightly, peel, and mash.

In a small bowl, beat 1 egg lightly. Stir in the grated cheese, parsley, salt, and pepper. Add to potatoes, mix thoroughly, and shape into 8 rounded oblong patties. If including mozzarella or salami, divide it equally into 8 portions and insert in the middle of each potato croquette.

On a flat dish, add flour. In a small bowl, add 1 egg and beat lightly. In another flat dish, add bread crumbs. Roll croquette first in a little flour, then with a spatula roll it in the egg, and finally roll it in the bread crumbs. Repeat until all are coated.

In a large, heavy skillet, add 2 tablespoons olive oil over medium-high heat. Carefully add croquettes. Do not crowd. Sauté for 6 to 8 minutes, turn once only, and cook until golden brown. Add more olive oil as needed. Remove and drain on paper towels. Arrange croquettes on a serving platter and serve piping hot.

Makes 8 croquettes

Insalata Di Patate alla Calabrese con Pomodori e Cipolle Rosse
Calabrian Style Potato Salad with Tomatoes and Red Onion

An aromatic salad, this is an excellent choice for a summer buffet. Ripe tomatoes are a must, and the parsley and oregano add the distinctive Calabrian touch. It is important to add the olive oil dressing while the potatoes are still warm so the potatoes will absorb it; there is a vast difference in the taste if the dressing is mixed into cold potatoes. Mom picked the tomatoes from Dad's garden, then prepared this dish about 1 hour before serving, eliminating the need for refrigeration. From my own experimentation, I learned that Mom knew instinctively that this dish is best served at room temperature without previous refrigeration to best allow the flavors to come through.

- 4 medium Idaho or Russet potatoes, unpeeled
- 2 medium ripe tomatoes
- 1 medium red onion
- 5 tablespoons extra-virgin olive oil
- 3 tablespoons red wine vinegar
- 1 teaspoon salt
- ½ teaspoon freshly ground black pepper
- 3 tablespoons fresh Italian parsley, finely chopped
- 2 teaspoons dried oregano

In a large pot of water put the washed, unpeeled potatoes over high heat. Cover the pot. When water comes to a boil, lower heat and simmer for 20 to 30 minutes, or until potatoes are tender when tested by a fork. Remove cooked potatoes and rinse under cold water only until cool enough to handle.

Meanwhile, halve the tomatoes, cut each into ½-inch wedges, and set aside. Cut onion into very thin slices and set aside. In a small bowl, combine the olive oil, vinegar, salt, and pepper.

While potatoes are still warm, peel, halve, and cut into ¼-inch slices. Place in a large mixing bowl, drizzling some dressing and mixing gently after each potato is sliced. Continue until last potato is sliced and all dressing is used. Carefully fold in the tomatoes and onions; sprinkle with parsley and oregano. Mix gently. Serve at room temperature.

Serves 4 to 6

Patate al Forno
Golden Roasted Potatoes

Potatoes are delicious when cooked in a very hot oven long enough so they become crispy and golden brown on the outside and soft and moist on the inside. They go well with almost any meat or fish dish. So popular is this method of cooking them that often recipes for any roasted meat dish call for these potatoes to be added to the roasting pan.

- 4 large Idaho or Russet potatoes
- 2 tablespoons olive oil
- ½ teaspoon salt
- ¼ teaspoon freshly ground black pepper

Preheat oven to 400° F.

Wash and peel potatoes. Drain on paper towels and pat dry. Cut each potato into 6 wedges. Put in a bowl, add oil, and mix well until all sides are coated. Scatter potatoes in one layer in a large roasting plan. Do not crowd. Roast uncovered for 1 hour, turning occasionally with a sturdy spatula, until golden brown but tender. Halfway through, season with salt and pepper.

Serves 4

Patate Fritti con Peperoni
Fried Potatoes with Peppers

Pairing potatoes and peppers is ideal. Toss in an onion and you've got a great-tasting side dish to complement nearly any entrée. Although the recipe calls for green bell peppers, you can use any combination of green, red, or yellow for a more colorful presentation and a slightly sweeter taste.

- 1 pound Idaho or Russet potatoes (3 or 4 medium)
- 4 large green bell peppers
- 4 tablespoons olive oil, divided
- 1 medium onion, coarsely sliced
- ½ teaspoon salt
- ¼ teaspoon freshly ground black pepper or crushed red pepper

Wash, peel, and thinly slice potatoes. Wash, dry, and cut peppers into 1-inch pieces.

In a large, heavy skillet over medium heat, add 2 tablespoons olive oil. Add onion and sauté for 3 to 4 minutes or until onions are translucent. Remove with a slotted spoon and set aside. Add potatoes and stir to coat. Sauté for 8 to 10 minutes, or until potatoes are lightly browned, stirring occasionally. Remove and set aside.

Add remaining 2 tablespoons olive oil and the peppers and stir to coat. Sauté for 8 to 10 minutes, or until peppers are lightly browned, stirring occasionally.

Return onions and potatoes to skillet. Add salt and pepper and mix thoroughly. Lower heat, cover, and cook for 10 to 12 minutes or until vegetables are tender, stirring occasionally. Serve immediately.

Serves 4 to 6

Patate Ragante
Radiant Potatoes

Ragante means radiant. That describes the finished product well. It is also easy to prepare. Ideal for a party, it can be assembled before the guests arrive and popped into the oven to bake along with an entrée while you're having an aperitif and an antipasto or two.

- 2 pounds Idaho or Russet potatoes (6 or 8 medium)
- 3 medium red onions, coarsely sliced

2 tablespoons olive oil
1½ ripe tomatoes
  ½ teaspoon dried oregano
  1 teaspoon salt
  ½ teaspoon freshly ground black pepper
  5 teaspoons finely grated dried bread crumbs
  5 tablespoons grated pecorino or ricotta salata cheese

Preheat oven to 375° F.

Wash, peel, and cut potatoes into ⅓-inch slices. In a medium mixing bowl, add sliced potatoes, onions, and the olive oil. Toss to coat.

Plunge tomatoes into boiling water for 10 to 15 seconds. Remove skins and cut tomatoes into ¼-inch slices.

Lightly oil an 8-by-12-inch baking dish. Add about ⅓ of the potatoes and onions. Sprinkle evenly with the oregano, salt, and pepper. Add ½ of the tomatoes. Continue layering and seasoning until all ingredients are used, ending with a layer of potatoes.

Sprinkle bread crumbs and cheese evenly over the top layer of potatoes. Bake covered for 1 hour, then uncover and continue baking for another 15 to 20 minutes, or until topping is a golden, radiant color.

Serves 6 to 8

Patate Ru Cannarutu
Fried Potatoes and Red Onions

Combining potatoes and red onions yields simple but savory results. *Cannaratu* means epicurean in dialect, and you'll understand where the name comes from when you taste this aromatic dish.

  1 pound Idaho or Russet potatoes (3 or 4 medium)
  2 tablespoons olive oil
  2 medium red onions, thickly sliced
  ½ teaspoon salt
  ¼ teaspoon freshly ground black pepper

Wash, peel, and cut potatoes into ¼-inch slices.

In a large, heavy skillet add oil over medium-high heat. Sauté the potatoes for 4 to 5 minutes. Lower heat, add onion, and mix with the potatoes. Do not cover pan. Continue to sauté for 15 to 17 minutes, turning frequently, until potatoes are golden brown and cooked through. Sprinkle with salt and pepper and serve immediately.

Serves 4 to 6

Insalata Mista Varie
Mixed Salad

Nothing pleases more than a mixed salad, brimming with a host of greens and seasonal vegetables and glistening with extra-virgin olive oil. Unlike Americans, however, who usually eat their salad first, Italians serve it at the end of dinner in the belief it settles the stomach. Whatever your choice, select from a large variety of fresh greens, then add whatever vegetables are in season and any other suggestions listed below.

SALAD:
- ½ head romaine
- ½ pound spinach
- ½ small sweet onion, thinly sliced
- 1 red or green bell pepper, seeded and cut in thin strips
- 1 fresh, ripe tomato, cut into small wedges
- 12 black or green olives, brine-cured, pitted and halved
- 2 tablespoons Gorgonzola cheese, crumbled

DRESSING:
- 3 tablespoons extra-virgin olive oil
- 2 tablespoons red wine vinegar, or to taste
- ¼ teaspoon salt
- ¼ teaspoon freshly ground black pepper

Wash greens and pat dry with paper towels or dry in salad spinner. Tear into 2-inch pieces and put into a large salad bowl. Add onion, pepper, tomato, olives, and cheese.

In a small bowl or jar, combine ingredients for the dressing. Drizzle dressing over salad and toss thoroughly.

Serves 4 to 8

VARIATIONS: ADD ANY OF THE FOLLOWING.

Greens:	*Other:*
arugula	3 or 4 anchovy fillets, mashed
Boston lettuce	2 tablespoons capers, drained
chicory	1 stalk celery, thinly sliced
dandelion greens	2 tablespoons freshly grated ricotta salata cheese
escarole, center portion	2 tablespoons freshly grated pecorino or
oak leaf lettuce	Parmesan cheese
radicchio	4 ounces fresh mushrooms, thinly sliced
	½ cucumber, thinly sliced
	½ red onion, thinly sliced
	2 scallions, cut in thin rounds

Spinaci Aglio e Olio
Spinach with Garlic and Oil

Nutritious and flavorful, this is a traditional recipe common to Calabria and all of southern Italy. You may also use escarole in place of spinach, sautéing it a bit longer. Freshly squeezed lemon juice splashed on top adds a nice tartness no matter which vegetable you use.

> 1½ **pounds fresh spinach**
> 2 **tablespoons extra-virgin olive oil**
> 2 **cloves garlic, finely minced**
> ¼ **teaspoon crushed red pepper**
> ½ **teaspoon salt**

Wash spinach thoroughly and remove heavy stems.

In a large steamer or double boiler, add spinach and steam for 5 minutes. Drain and chop coarsely.

In a large, heavy skillet add olive oil over medium heat. Sauté the garlic and crushed red pepper for 1 to 2 minutes or until garlic is light golden brown. Add spinach and stir to coat. Sauté for 2 to 4 minutes or until spinach is tender, mixing constantly. Add salt and mix well. Serve immediately.

Serves 4

Pomodori Secchi sott' Olio
Sun-dried Tomatoes in Oil

Sun-dried tomatoes have a concentrated tomato taste and add intense flavor and a chewy texture to sauces, vegetable dishes, and soups. Dried tomatoes are available in Italian specialty stores and most supermarkets, but drying your own is not difficult and far more economical. All you need is a lot of sun and ripe but firm tomatoes that are at their peak. You can also bake them ever so slowly. Southern Italians, lovers of tomatoes, were the first to devise this ingenious method for preserving many vegetables.

1   **pound plum or cherry tomatoes**
¼   **teaspoon salt**
1   **clove garlic, coarsely sliced**
1   **very small pinch crushed red pepper (optional)**
     olive oil, sufficient to fill jar

To air dry: Select perfect tomatoes, just ripened. Wash and cut in half lengthwise. Sprinkle lightly with salt. Place them cut side up on a perforated flat surface such as screening, cover them with cheesecloth, and let them dry in the sun for 4 to 7 days—until they are dry, begin to curl, and deepen in color. The exact length of time will depend on the intensity of the sun. Bring them in at night when the sun goes down. If the weather turns humid in the middle of the drying cycle, finish drying the tomatoes in a 200° F oven for 30 minutes or more, or until they are dry as described above; otherwise they will get moldy. Remove and cool at room temperature. Store either dry-packed or oil-packed.

To oven dry: Preheat oven to 200° F.

Select perfect tomatoes, just ripened. Wash and cut in half lengthwise. Sprinkle lightly with salt. Put them cut side up on a lightly oiled cookie sheet. Bake for 11 to 13 hours or until shriveled, wrinkled, and dry. Check after about 9 hours and every hour thereafter, as the exact cooking time will vary from oven to oven. Do not let tomatoes become brown. Remove and cool at room temperature. When completely dried, store either dry-packed or oil-packed.

To dry-pack: When tomatoes are completely dried, store in sterilized glass jars in the refrigerator.

To oil-pack: Place tomatoes in sterilized glass jars, pressing hard with spoon to allow little space. Add garlic and crushed red pepper, if using. Fill jars completely with olive oil and cover tightly. It is not necessary to boil jars after filling.

Store in a cool, dark place. Tomatoes will be ready to use in 3 to 4 weeks. Use the flavorful oil for salads, but remove and discard the garlic.

To reconstitute dry-packed tomatoes, put required amount in a small bowl and add boiling water to cover. Let stand until soft, 1 to 2 minutes. Drain and slice as desired.

Insalata di Pomodori, Cipolle Rosse, e Basilico
Tomato, Red Onion, and Basil Salad

Tomatoes, glorious tomatoes. Attempt this simple but savory jiffy salad only when tomatoes are in season. You need their juice to mingle with the dressing to create a heavenly dip for crusty Italian bread! For crunch and flavor, add one celery stalk, finely sliced; or one-half green pepper, thinly sliced. Have all ingredients cleaned and at room temperature but do not prepare until close to serving time—it takes only minutes.

4	large ripe tomatoes
1	medium red onion, finely sliced
2	tablespoons extra-virgin olive oil
1 to 2	teaspoons red wine vinegar
2	tablespoons fresh basil, thinly slivered
1	tablespoon capers
1 to 2	ounces Gorgonzola cheese (optional)
¼	teaspoon salt
¼	teaspoon freshly ground black pepper

Wash tomatoes and cut each into 6 or 8 wedges. Put into a large salad bowl and add onion. Drizzle with olive oil and toss gently. Sprinkle vinegar; add basil, capers, Gorgonzola cheese if using, salt, and pepper; and mix thoroughly. Serve at room temperature.

Serves 4 to 8

Zucchini con Pomodori
Zucchini with Tomatoes

Satisfying but simple home cooking stars in this savory dish that is easy to prepare, is ready in minutes, and is delicious. It is an especially tasty dish to serve in summer when zucchini and tomatoes are in season and at their peak.

 4 small zucchini, unpeeled, about 2 pounds
 2 tablespoons olive oil
 1 large onion, thinly sliced
 2 cloves garlic, finely minced
 1 pound fresh, ripe tomatoes, coarsely chopped
   or 1 16-ounce can Italian plum tomatoes, coarsely chopped
 2 tablespoons fresh basil, slivered; divided
 1 bay leaf
 ¼ teaspoon salt
 ¼ teaspoon freshly ground black pepper

Wash and dry zucchini and trim both ends. Cut in half lengthwise, and then into ⅛-inch slices.

In a large, heavy skillet, add olive oil over medium heat. Add onion and sauté for 3 to 4 minutes or until translucent. Add garlic and sauté for 1 to 2 minutes or until light golden brown.

Add zucchini, tomatoes, 1 tablespoon basil, bay leaf, salt, and pepper. Lower heat, cover, and simmer for 7 to 9 minutes or until zucchini is cooked but still firm. Remove bay leaf and add remaining basil. Mix and simmer for 1 minute. Transfer to a warm platter and serve hot.

Serves 4 to 6

MEMORIES

Chi e' ricco ha parenti.

He is rich who has relatives.

Vicinatu e' mienzu parenti.

A good neighbor is half-relative.

<small>CALABRIAN PROVERBS</small>

I have such loving memories of my mother making holiday dinner plans weeks in advance. She did it willingly, with love and patience, tending to every detail. Almost everything served was homemade. Wonderful aromas filled the house throughout the long hours of preparation, some of which began days in advance and lingered beyond the meal itself. The dining room table would be set with the finest linens and candles. Her final creation was home cooking at its best, delighting the eye as well as the palate.

Cooking for the family is an Italian mother's labor of love and proof of devotion. It has been said that she spends more time in the kitchen than in the living room. That was true of my mom who, it seemed, was always at the stove preparing some wonderful dish for us. Stovetops of old had other uses, too. Mom roasted red peppers or chestnuts on the wood-burning part and browned orange peels, creating a natural potpourri fragrance that drifted lazily throughout the house.

As is the custom throughout most of Italy, when little Italian-American girls are old enough, their mothers let them help in the kitchen. Such was the case with my sister and me. I remember Mom gently leading us by the hand into the kitchen and showing us how to cook and follow directions. Handing down recipes and cultural traditions began in the kitchen. In Italy, by the time girls are teenagers, they are skilled in many aspects of cooking, especially in making homemade *maccarruni.*

All meals are treated with reverence in the *Mezzogiorno,* for southern Italians are kindred souls with similar ties with regard to traditions, temperament, and some food. The family eats the evening meal and quite often the midday meal together daily. Meals are never rushed—the time is reserved to relax, talk to one another, instill values, and form a close, unbreakable, lifelong bond. This cozy, warm, and loving atmosphere provides a "blueprint" for the future. The same sentiments apply to the extended family; relatives gather on holidays, and no one ever eats alone. Those lessons were not lost on me, and I tried to impart them to my sons as well.

Italians here and abroad love to entertain and try to please their friends, as they do their families, with the best they can afford. If an unexpected extra guest arrives at the last minute or if someone drops in near mealtime, it is no problem—there is always enough food. In my childhood home, my sister and I could bring friends for dinner—they were always welcomed. My parents loved having "company," as we used to call guests. Hospitality came naturally to them; it was an old virtue. If the host made his own wine, as my dad did, his friends were given a bottle as they left; Mom, known for her wide assortment of delicious cookies, shared a plateful for guests to take home. A guest never left empty handed.

Feasts, Festivals, Holidays, and Special Occasions

Senza 'a festa, non si cridi alli santi.

Without the feast, one cannot believe in saints.
CALABRIAN PROVERB

Celebrating feasts, festivals, and holidays holds an exalted place in the hearts of Italians, as it has since ancient times. Many had their beginnings as pagan observances—some to honor gods, others to appease them. Ancient Romans celebrated about 200 different feast days.

When in the fourth century Catholicism became the state religion, the church recognized that such festivals were the people's main source of social activities and that abolishing them might hinder the conversion of many to Christianity. Pagan festivals were converted to Catholic ones, and many temples were converted into Catholic churches.

Most saint's day festivals follow ancient protocol. After the religious portion is concluded, the saint's statue is carried through the streets accompanied by a band and a procession. My Aunt "Teta" Dieni recounted how in Bova Superiore, young boys follow bands banging tambourines, ringing cowbells, and prancing gaily through the streets. Music fills the air, and dancing breaks out spontaneously. My dad played the mandolin on such occasions. Overflowing with people, the piazza and adjoining streets are plastered with color, decorated with garlands, and illuminated by Roman candles. Revelers celebrate well into the night, which ends dramatically with a torchlight procession and fireworks. Some cities return to the Middle Ages as thousands appear in period dress.

The most important feasts and holidays in Calabria are Christmas Eve and Christmas, Easter, the Feast of the Madonna, the Feast of St. Joseph, the Feast of

St. Anthony, New Year's Eve, and New Year's Day. Often, dishes are created especially for them. Sometimes an enormous *banchetto,* or banquet, is served in the *piazza,* sanctifying the event with an almost Dionysian abandon.

Throughout all of Italy on January 16, the eve of the Feast of St. Anthony the Abbot, a huge bonfire is lit in the town square of each village. In Calabria the feast is called *La Festa di la Tentazione di Sant Antonio,* the temptation of St. Anthony, since during his life he was beset by demons of desire. Traditional St. Anthony festival foods include *Maiale Arrosto con Patate* (Roast Herbed Pork with Golden Roasted Potatoes, page 159) and *Taralli col Pepe* (Bread Rings with Black Pepper and Fennel Seed, page 259). The Feast of St. Anthony of Padua on June 13 is more often observed in America, and in the North End of Boston is celebrated in August, when attendance is higher.

The Feast of St. Joseph, celebrated on March 19, honors the patron saint of the family (and of pastry chefs)! Prior to his feast, a large altar is built in the *piazza,* covered with flowers and a huge variety of breads from tiny to large, shaped into flowers, fruits, baskets, birds, suns, stars, and moons. A round bread is baked for Jesus, representing eternal life; Mary's is shaped like a date palm; and St. Joseph's is shaped like a staff. Candles are placed in front of his statue. At home, foods such as *Pasta con le Sarde e Finocchio* (Pasta with Sardines and Fresh Fennel, page 114) and *Sfinge di San Guiseppe* (St. Joseph's Feast Day Cream Puffs, page 283) are served.

The Feast of the Madonna, or Feast of the Assumption, is celebrated on August 15, the day Mary died and ascended to heaven. On a trip to Calabria, my cousin Maria's three sons sang hymns, and their five-year-old sister Maria Chiara learned the hymns from them and rattled them off for me one after the other, to their smiling approval. The family traditionally feasts on *Maiale Arrosto con Patate* (Roast Herbed Pork with Golden Roasted Potatoes, page 159). My late mother-in-law ate bread and watermelon on the eve of the Feast of the Madonna, a tradition she learned in her native village of Dugenta.

So deeply rooted and so important a part of their lives were such feasts that when Italian emigrated to this country, they brought many celebrations with them. While some festivals have been discarded, their integrity diminished due to significant changes in lifestyle, many are still enthusiastically celebrated.

Music and Dance

Italians are almost as passionate about music as they are about food. Calabrians use music both to entertain and to celebrate. It is an integral part of religious and other feasts, festivals, weddings, ceremonies, and informal gatherings. From opera to simple folk tunes, to romantic serenades accompanied by musical instruments, to brass bands, to contemporary music—music reflects the Italian character. Calabrian folk songs and ballads are charming, romantic, and amusing. My father played the mandolin and sang. He taught many songs to my sister and me and later taught his three grandsons as well. He loved opera and was especially fond of the incomparable Caruso. I remember how heartbroken he was when I sat on and broke a favorite Caruso record.

Italy has always been a mecca for music. When Mozart was a teenager, he came to Italy to learn about composition and opera. Later, he was knighted by the Pope in Rome. Italy's genius extends to all aspects of music, including the crafting of musical instruments. The world knows of the Stradivarius violin, but perhaps not everyone knows that Guido d'Orezzo established the musical staff, making music writing much easier; that Galileo's father, Vincent, wrote music for the lute 150 years before Bach; that in the 1600s, Italian poets and painters from all of Italy met with the hope of setting music to Greek drama, and instead the opera was born. Although La Scala, in Milan, is ranked the best opera house in the world, southern Italians need not travel far north to witness good, live opera. There are at least three opera houses—in Naples, Bari, and Palermo. Palermo possesses the largest opera house in Europe. Among its distinguished list of famed conductors was Toscanini. Construction began in 1776 and was completed two years later. Known for its perfect acoustics, it accommodates 2,000 people. Its museum overflows with theatrical mementos.

I recall an amusing opera incident in Rome some years ago. Inquiring of the concierge about the availability of tickets for *La Boheme,* I was told that hearing opera anywhere except at La Scala was "kid stuff." I'm sure there are some in New York who feel similarly about the Metropolitan Opera. Regardless, I enjoyed the Roman rendition.

Although bagpipes were most widely used in Ireland and Scotland, they were also favored by ancient Greeks and Romans. *Zampognari*, bagpipers, paraded through village streets during celebrations. Vivaldi included *zampogni*, bagpipes, in some of his major compositions. My late uncle, Joseph Dieni, learned how to make (out of pigskin) and play a bagpipe with its plaintive sound. He surprised me with a song on one of my research trips.

Recently, Boston hosted an Italian Festival in City Hall Square. Entertainers came from various provinces of Italy as well as from Massachusetts. The folk singers and dancers from Calabria were so well received, their hour ran beyond two. I captured their lively movement in photographs as they danced various charming folk dances. As they sang songs like "*Calabrasella*" ("Young Calabrian Girl") and "*Calabria mia . . . lo cianciu pi 'tia.*" ("My Calabria, I cry for you"), the crowd spontaneously joined in. The master of ceremonies dashed off the stage and pushed the microphone into any willing singer's face. They sang the bittersweet song with their lungs and their hearts. It was so moving, they became teary eyed, and to my surprise, so did I.

At religious festivals, street festivals, and weddings, dancing is enthusiastically engaged in by all. I love watching the people dance, sometimes in costume, at such festivals. The *tarantella*, a lively, festive folk dance, was originally danced to purge the body of poisons and evil spells. It is still danced in celebration at most weddings. I remember the many weddings at which I too danced the *tarantella*. A more reserved *tarantella* begins slowly, gradually quickens, and ends only when dancers are short of breath.

Storytelling

My journey into folklore led me to the delightful custom of storytelling. Long before books came into being, folk tales were passed down as a form of entertainment and escapism. Probing deeper into folk tales, one discovers inner moral lessons, self-awareness, and realism, to some degree. Many popular tales spread throughout Europe and Asia with slight variations. Each contained local lores, conventions, and customs. Besides varied versions of universal folk and fairy tales such as "The Three Little Pigs," "Snow White," "Cinderella," "The Frog Prince," and "Little Red Riding Hood," there were tales whose themes included love and loneliness, morality and fidelity, amorous longing and desires satisfied, romances and fantasies, adventures, kings and peasants, riddles and magic, spells, witches, and supernatural beings. Not all folk tales were for children only. Many themes were drawn from everyday experiences, others from ancient paganism.

In the seventeenth century, folk tales were being recorded. It is generally accepted that Italian folk and fairy tales were recorded in literary works long before those from any other country. People wrote down tales as told to them by their grandparents, parents, and village elders, usually women. Even after the advent of books, many southern Italians could not afford the luxury of buying them, but their fondness of storytelling continued from one generation to the next.

Italo Calvino, the well-known and highly praised Italian novelist, made a collection of about 200 folk tales from all regions of Italy. Published in 1980, his *Italian Folk Tales* received rave reviews. It is the Italian equivalent of *Grimm's Fairy Tales* or *The Arabian Nights*. In his introduction, Calvino states that Calabrian storytelling exhibits "a rich, colorful, and complex imagination." He also points out that Italian folk tales in general were less cruel than Grimm's tales. Many tales in Calvino's book deal with joy and sorrow, persecution of the innocent and their subsequent vindication, unemployment, deep poverty, and hunger. My mother told us folk tales at bedtime and even during the day. We also had one tiny book of folk tales, though it is now lost.

Games

Carta jettata e carta jocata.

A card thrown is a card played.

<small>CALABRIAN PROVERB</small>

In Italy, there are many different kinds of games, ancient and modern, providing welcomed relief from the hard labor of life. Among them are:

Card Games: In Italy, there is a different variety of playing card for every province. Card games were brought to Italy from Arab countries in the fourteenth century. Common Calabrian card games, *carta da giuoco*, are *Briscola, Scopa,* and *Tressette.* The latter is the most widely played in southern Italy and Mediterranean countries. A children's card game, *Ruba Mazzo,* is a simplified version of *Scopa.* My parents taught us these games as children and later introduced them to other members of our family. The dramatic flair with which a player snaps a card to be played on the table defies description. It is done with such gusto, exuberance, and aplomb. Occasionally, a misplay ends in a heated (but friendly?) argument. Mozart loved the card game *Mercante in Fiera* (Merchant at the Fair). The game of *Faro,* a descendant of the Venetian *Farona,* was once played on Mississippi steamboats and is still played in Nevada. *Tarocchi* (tarot cards), were invented in Italy in the fifteenth century. Italians still tell fortunes using *tarocchi* much the same as people in other countries, including America.

Backgammon: Backgammon dates back to early Roman days. Emperor Claudius was fond of it. Called *tabula* in his day, it was backgammon's predecessor.

Bingo: A kind of bingo game called *Tombola,* another Italian invention, is said to be the forerunner of lotteries. Among other things, my early memories of Christmas Eve include playing bingo.

Bocce: Bocce is a popular, spirited Italian game that traveled to the United States with the immigrants. My parents played it at festivals and at friends' homes. Children in attendance were taught to play it as well. Many with ample space have backyard picnics and also dish up a game of *bocce. Bocce* is still very much alive today; *bocce* courts can be found in parks and indoors in clubs. *Bocce* is similar to the game of horseshoes but without the ringer. The ringer is stationary in horseshoes, but the *palletta* or *boccino* (small ball taking the place of the ringer) in *bocce* is not. *Bocce* is played with two teams, with up to ten players each—with game at eleven or twenty-one points. Each team has different colored balls. The game begins when the team who won the coin toss tosses the *palletta* forward. The object is then to toss the *bocce* ball closest to the *pal-*

letta, or to hit the *palletta* away from the opponents' balls if their *bocce* balls are closer. The team with the most *bocce* balls near the *palletta* wins.

Some Italian games don't require balls, gadgets, or props of any kind. One such game, called *Moto,* reminds me of "Kick the Can," the inexpensive version of kick ball that I played as a child with boys and girls in the middle of the street. You didn't need a ball, any old can would do. No props are needed to play *Moto,* either, all you need is your right hand! Two players place their right hand behind their backs. On the count of three, each extends one to five fingers and simultaneously shouts out the number he or she thinks will be the total of the opponent's extended fingers. Call out the correct total and you win! If you are walking through an Italian neighborhood, you may chance upon two "old timers" sitting in a park, outside a coffee house, or on a front porch (back porches are too quiet and lonely) calling out numbers in the identical tonal sounds and facial expressions I remembered.

At Christmastime in Calabria, boys and girls make themselves a *cupo-cupo.* A crude instrument consisting of a tin can covered with stretched skin, it resembles a drum. A wooden stick strikes the can, producing a low-pitched sound, not very endearing. A few nights before Christmas, they parade through the part of town where the gentry live, singing simple verses personalizing and praising the residents. In return, they receive gifts of food or small change.

Soccer: I'm always amused when I hear that Italians have a passion for food or soccer. Italians have a passion for everything! But soccer is another thing. More than other countries, thanks to regional loyalties, soccer is attended, watched, and written about with true passion.

Superstitions

> *Dammi fortuna, e jettami a mare, e tornu a chiamare.*
>
> Give me good fortune, throw me in the ocean, and I will rise to the surface.

> *Occhio, malocchio, mi ti nescinu e' occhi.*
>
> Eye, evil eye, may your eyes come out."
> CALABRIAN PROVERBS

Many Italians believe in good fortune or good luck, if only lightly. One often hears them proclaim "*buona fortuna.*" Naples has the dubious reputation of being the most superstitious city in Europe, but that distinction can probably be challenged by many others. Italians, and most of the world, for example believed in the power of witches well into the eighteenth century. European witchcraft was the remnant of ancient pagan cults often referred to as the "old religion." It survived long after Christianity was adopted, defying Christendom's attempts to assimilate medieval paganism.

Belief in the *malocchio,* "evil eye," is not just an Italian phenomenon. The superstition dates back to about 1000 B.C. and was believed in by much of the world. Jews believed that acknowledging good fortune would attract an evil eye, a *kineahora.* The evil eye was a supposed power some had of harming others out of jealousy, envy, or hostility through different means, or by merely looking at them. It supposedly could immediately manifest itself in the form of a severe headache. To ensure not being suspected of giving someone the evil eye, a compliment was followed with an affirmative like "What a beautiful child—God bless him" or even more to the point, "*fuori malocchio,*" no evil eye intended. To discern if one was inflicted by the evil eye and to rid him or her of it, a bowl half-filled with water was placed over the head of the victim. Several drops of oil were added, and special sayings or prayers were said. As I remember it, if the oil sank, the person had the evil eye.

People also wore amulets or charms or nailed horseshoes over their doors to protect themselves and their homes from the evil eye. Even today, some men and women still wear charms in the shape of a small hot red pepper on gold chains, even if only by tradition. One can spot such charms in strange places both in Italy and in the United States. Recently, I detected one over the kitchen door of an Italian restaurant in East Boston.

Several sources refer to the famous walnut tree in Benevento in southern Italy as one of the three meeting places in Europe of self-proclaimed witches. (Others were near the River Jordan in Israel and somewhere in Germany.) En route to Rome when returning home from one of my research trips, I stopped in Benevento for lunch. I visited its famous museum and purchased an incredible book entitled *Streghe, Diavole e Morte* (*Witches, Devils and Death*), produced by members of the Museum and town administrators. I read that the walnut tree had long been cut down by the townspeople to discourage witches from continuing to meet there. A city map in the book cited the tree's location—quite near the Catholic church. A native Italian, Ramona Pascucci, told me of a saying widely repeated throughout southern Italy: "*La strega di Benevento con uno minuto vada e venni.*" (The witch of Benevento in one minute goes and comes.)

Many witch-finders and fanatics sought to eliminate self-proclaimed or accused witches worldwide, including the United States. Although estimates as to the numbers of "witches" put to death throughout the world ranged from 200,000 to 400,000, Italy and the United States ranked among those countries with the fewest.

Proverbs

Proverbs were a form of education in Calabria and other parts of Italy, often providing important moral lessons. Often rhyming, sometimes amusing, several are sprinkled throughout this book. Perhaps the one most often quoted in my home fits a variety of situations and is widely known: "*Cu spudda in cielo, cade in facci.*" (Who spits at heaven, it falls on his face.) That literal translation requires an explanation: It means, for example, don't be critical of your neighbor's children's behavior—someday you may have children, they too may misbehave, and your criticism will backfire.

Others with which my sister and I were raised include: "*Dimmi cu cu vai, e ti digo chi fai.*" (Tell me who you go with, and I'll tell you what you do, or who you are.) "*Quando educate homo, educate una persona; quando educate femina, educate la famiglia.*" (When you educate a man, you educate a person; when you educate a woman, you educate a family.) "*La vecchia e na carogna, ma si non ci riva, e piu vergonia.*" (Old age is hard, but not to reach it is even more of a shame.) "*Fai bene e scordide; fai male e ricordide.*" (Do good and forget it, do bad and remember it.) A lot harder than the reverse.

A contribution by Joseph Pascucci, a native of Abruzzi: "*Chi cambia, sa quello che lascia, non sa quello che trova.*" (Who changes partners knows what he left but doesn't know what he will find.) Finally, here is one from my late mother-in-law, Stella Palmer Palleschi, originally from Dugenta, Campania: "*Chi tieni e non sabba tene, volese tene ma nu poi avei.*" (He who does not appreciate what he has, will one day want it back but won't be able to have it.)

Memories

Finally, I remember family holidays—the aromas, the hugs, and the love. Those memories will live forever. My father's contributions were great—the fresh vegetables from his oversized garden, the homemade wine and liqueurs. And he provided the money to make the celebrations possible and memorable. Sometimes he, and others like him, took second jobs to earn extra money for food and gifts. Dad was very active. He never sat still except to eat and read the paper. I'm sort of like that, too.

Most of all, however, I remember my mother's unselfish efforts in preparing food every day, on holidays and special occasions, and in bringing it all together with a smile on her face and love in her heart. Mom educated a family. My dear mother passed away a short time ago. Toward the end, when she forgot something, she would say, "I remember in my heart." To her, and to all mothers, living or departed, we are all eternally grateful. And we will forever remember them in our hearts.

I have tried to instill ethnic pride in my children and grandchildren through words and deeds. My granddaughter Jennifer wrote in her thank-you note after a large family reunion at my home one Christmas, "It was the nicest Christmas ever. And the food was so good—it was so Italian." Sons John, David and families, sister Margaret and family, and everyone else's thank-you notes extolled the adherence to a traditional Calabrian Christmas.

Granddaughter Katherine wrote in a school paper about a summer visit here when we had "pizza made from scratch." Grandson Spencer received an apron from me at age 3 and helps me make pies and pizza, spin lettuce dry, and stir sauces. And, of course, this book's collection of recipes and stories has been my labor of love, a gift from the heart to my loving family, to all who buy this book, and to posterity.

At a recent family celebration, my son David, an excellent cook, said "Mom, who will do these theme parties when you are gone?" It wasn't until he asked the question that I knew the answer. "You," I said. "It will be your turn to make new memories with your family, your brother and his family, and your cousin. Then, when you are gone, it will be your children and your brother's children's turn."

PANE E PIZZA

BREAD AND PIZZA

'U buon uomo e buono como 'u pane.

A good man is as good as bread.
<small>CALABRIAN PROVERB</small>

Bread is life in Italy. Its importance cannot be overestimated. Still a staple of the Calabrian and southern Italian diet, it is revered above all foods. At one time, Italians kissed the knife before cutting bread and then made the Sign of the Cross or traced it over the bread with the tip of the knife. If a piece of bread dropped to the floor, peasants quickly picked it up, kissed it, and returned it to the table.

Bread is the most constant of all foods and has been a part of every meal in Italy, in one way or another, of the rich and poor alike, since ancient times. Centuries back in Calabria and southern Italy, bread dough was made once or twice a week in a large wooden tub called a *madia*. After rising, it was slid into the oven on a long-handled wooden paddle. If no oven was available, people took the mixed ingredients to the local bakery, kneaded the dough, and left it there to rise. For a small fee it was baked for them. This practice continued into the twentieth century.

A crusty bread is the favorite in Italy, and there are many varieties, sizes, shapes, and textures in white or whole wheat (though white is preferred). Flatbreads are called *pizza di pane* in Calabria and are usually flavored with rosemary and other herbs. *Panini* are crusty sandwich rolls; *bruschetta* is a full-bodied, thick-crusted bread cut into ½-inch slices, rubbed with garlic, brushed with oil, and grilled or toasted; and *crostini* are thinly sliced pieces of toasted bread. Long, thin bread sticks are called *grissini*.

Food writer Serafino Amabile Guastella explained that in the seventeenth and eighteenth centuries, hunger was rampant in Sicily and southern Italy, and even bread was not available to the poor in abundance. Perhaps because of that, Italians don't waste food; none is ever thrown away. Chunks of dry bread are still added to soups, and bread crumbs still weave their way into and atop many dishes, not of necessity but of preference.

Some Calabrians still bake bread, though not necessarily every day. Many bake bread for holidays and special occasions. It has been said that there are between 250 and 300 excellent varieties of bread available in local *panetterias* (bakeries) throughout Italy. Thus, more and more Italians now buy much of their bread. During my trips to Calabria, I attended celebrations by my cousins Maria and Enzo Cuppari and by Mimma and Nino Favasuli. Many relatives were invited. The picture I have of Mimma baking 12 loaves of bread in the outdoor, dome shaped, masonry wood-burning oven built by her husband, Nino, is priceless. The oven was large enough to hold the entire meal with all its many courses. The bread was delicious! Her recipe was probably the same one used by my ancestors for hundreds of years.

There appears to be a resurgence of Americans baking bread. Bread machines may have helped. While it is easier to bake bread if you have a bread machine, food processor, or blender that either mixes, kneads, or bakes the bread, making it without a machine is not very difficult and is one of the most rewarding cooking tasks there is. I have a bread machine that kneads, lets rise, and bakes a variety of breads, and with no additives or preservatives. Most often, however, I remove the risen dough, shape it into a loaf or rolls, a flatbread or pizza dough, and bake them in my conventional oven. This allows me to cover the bread with herbs or seeds and also delivers a better crust.

I am aware that many bread experts recommend using a "starter" when making bread, claiming it enhances the flavor of bread. But for those who want to bake bread on the spur of the moment, there is such a recipe included. Remember that breads baked at lower temperatures are thicker and chewier; breads baked at higher temperatures have a thinner, crispier crust. Vary your choices for different textures. To serve, line the serving dish or basket first with foil and then with a cloth or doubled-up paper napkin to hold in the heat.

Recently an article caught my eye about the mating of Italian or French bread with Chinese food in the greater Boston area. The unlikely relationship began in 1918, when an Italian bought a bakery near Chinatown. Wishing to expand, he convinced Chinese restaurateurs that bread was an important part of the meal. According to the North American Chinese Restaurant Association, the habit took root here like in no other part of the country, though it is not uncommon in Europe. Many Chinese restaurants still serve it—customers say they like to dip bread in the sauces. But the *piece de resistance* in the article was a quote from a 1956 episode of the television series "The Honeymooners," in which Jackie Gleason pleads with a waiter for bread, exclaiming "How else am I going to push food on the fork?"

Pizza is also a national dish, next only to bread and pasta. It is Italy's version of fast food. Like bread, making pizza is easier than you might imagine. Knead the dough a mere 6 to 8 minutes if by hand, less with a bread machine or food processor. It rises without human assistance and in no time is ready to convert into crusty, crispy pizza.

Originating in Naples, pizza ovens were at work as early as 500 B.C., making pizza an even older tradition than pasta. To honor their creation, Neapolitans even wrote a rhymed pizza recipe poem! Baked in wood-fired ovens, hot flat-bread pies garnished with cheese, pizza's prototype, were being eaten in nearby Pompeii long before Mount Vesuvius erupted in 79 A.D. Later, the plentiful olive, seasonal vegetables, and fresh herbs were added. All this before tomatoes.

Unlike most other regional dishes, the allure of earthy pizza spread to every province of Italy. Each region, indeed each village, developed its own version. In 1889, a perky pizza was created to honor Queen Margherita. A classic, still popular throughout Italy, *Pizza Margherita* (page 263) contains colors of the Italian flag—red (tomatoes), green (basil), and white (mozzarella). With all its simplicity, when made with the freshest ingredients in restrained portions, it is extraordinarily beguiling. Americans tend to smother pizza with too much sauce and globs of cheese. Just a whisper of sauce and a gauzy veil of cheese creates pizza, Italian style.

In Calabria, one or more distinctive foods go into the building of a pizza, ascending into a masterly concoction: splashes of tomatoes, slivers of onions, bracelets of red or green peppers, joyful olives, tangy capers, assertive anchovies, princely proscuitto, spicy sausage, nuggets of tuna, or fresh, soft mozzarella. For more suggestions, see the list of more than 40 toppings or fillings following the recipe for *Pasta per Pizza* (Pizza Dough, page 260).

A Calabrian pizza with an entirely different spin, called *pitta*, has a top crust that protects selective delicate ingredients. Another top-crusted invention, *calzone*, cousin to pizza, was originally square, resembling a pant leg. Today, fillings are tucked securely inside a small circle of dough folded like a turnover and baked.

When southern Italians emigrated to America, they brought their pizza specialties with them. Mainly confined to the Italian community, however, pizza did not spread throughout America until after World War II when soldiers returning from Italy proclaimed the good word. Thereafter it caught on quickly, spreading from coast to coast. Today, it eclipses hamburgers as America's most consumed restaurant food. Ideal for lunch, dinner, or snacks, pizza is included in school lunches, sold at ball games, and is as essential a guest at festivals as sunshine. Its popularity has spread far beyond Italy's or America's frontiers. Pizza parlors with wood-fired brick ovens have cropped up all over the world. Travel almost anywhere and you will find people-pleaser pizza.

Thick or thin, the secret of good pizza is a crisp but light crust. To a majority, the second important ingredient is a good tomato sauce or fresh tomatoes. The concept of a pizza without tomatoes is incomprehensible to some Americans, but as more pizza houses include "white pizza" on their menu, that concept is fast changing.

In my family, from my mother to her great-grandchildren, pizza is a must! Mom made fabulous pizzas with a medium thick, crusty dough. Covering the dough with tomato sauce, she alternated toppings, making each pizza new and enticing. I also make "pizza from scratch," as my granddaughters Katherine and Jennifer described it when as little girls, standing on step stools, we made pizzas and memories. When grandson Spencer was three, I guessed it was "time to make the pizza." First, I gave him a toy pizza dough kit. A fast study, we went directly to the real thing. Solidly planked upon a step stool, together we created our own fresh "pizza with pizzazz."

It's worth investing in a baking stone or unglazed ceramic tiles if you get hooked on making pizza. The idea is to simulate the effects of a wood-fired masonry oven that produces crispy, crunchy crusts. However, you can make pretty darned good pizza using darkened cookie sheets or 15-inch round pizza pans, preferably perforated. Using a pizza cutting wheel with panache to cut your own gem is the final mark of a pizza connoisseur.

Prepared pizza freezes well. Eat one now and freeze the other for a day when time got away from you and won. Pizza dough alone can also be refrigerated or frozen. Even if you decide on pizza at the last minute, most supermarkets sell dough to go.

If you have never tried making it, go ahead, give pizza a chance. Create your own masterpiece. Choose dazzling combinations; the possibilities are endless. Have fun tinkering with it. It need not be complicated. Just think Italian and don't forget the wine!

Pane Crostoso
Crusty Bread

The aroma of homemade bread is almost reward enough, but the timeless appeal of serving warm bread enhances any meal and is worth the effort. Making bread is not as difficult or as time consuming as you may think. If you have a bread machine, it is even easier. Simply set your timer to alert you to remove the dough before it begins to bake. The exact time depends on your brand of machine. Remove dough and proceed with the last two paragraphs here.

1 package active dry yeast or 2 ½ teaspoons loose
1¼ cups warm water
3 cups unbleached or all-purpose flour
2 teaspoons sugar
1 teaspoon salt
1 tablespoon olive oil
cornmeal
1 egg yolk

In a small bowl, dissolve yeast with ¼ cup of the lukewarm water. Put flour, sugar, and salt onto a floured surface. Make a well in the center of the flour. Add dissolved yeast and remaining warm water, gradually pulling flour into the liquid. If the dough seems a little sticky, add a bit more flour. Flour absorbs less liquid in humid weather, but remember that using too much flour produces bread that is dry and dense. Knead for 6 to 8 minutes or until smooth and elastic. Put dough into an oiled bowl, turn to coat, cover with a thick towel, and let rise in a warm place, free from draft, until doubled in size, or about 1½ hours to 2 hours.

Preheat oven to 425° F.

Remove dough onto a floured surface. Punch down and shape into 2 oblong loaves about 12 inches long. If you own a baking stone or unglazed ceramic tiles, dust lightly with cornmeal and put into preheated oven. Put loaves on a peel (a large wooden spatula) also lightly dusted with cornmeal, or put them on a cookie sheet sprinkled with cornmeal. Let rise for 40 minutes.

In a small dish, add egg yolk and 1 tablespoon water. Slit tops of bread 3 or 4 times ¼-inch deep. With a brush, paint tops with egg wash. If on a peel, slide loaves onto stone or tile; otherwise put cookie sheet in oven. Bake for 10 minutes at 425° F. Lower heat to 400° F and bake for an additional 30 to 35 minutes or until golden and baked through. Tap bottom of bread; if it sounds hollow, it is done.

Makes 2 loaves

TIP: For crustier bread, put a shallow baking pan filled with boiling hot water on bottom shelf of oven.

VARIATION: To make rolls, preheat oven to 400° F. After dough rises, remove to floured surface. Punch down and shape into 12 to 14 rolls. Put on cookie sheet sprinkled with cornmeal. Let rise for 20 minutes. Slit each roll once and paint tops with egg wash. Bake for 18 to 22 minutes or until golden and baked through.

Pizza di Pane
Flatbread with Rosemary

An interesting alternative to bread is this versatile southern Italian flatbread. Often referred to as "pizza's cousin," it is also called *pizza bianca* and *schiacciata*. Glistening with olive oil, it is similar to the thinner northern version, *focaccia*, which means unleavened bread cooked with fire. Several sources report that a version of flatbread was the first type of bread ever baked in the world! Flatbreads are popular throughout Italy and have woven their way into the American scene as well. They can be sliced or cut into small wedges and toasted to complement a grouping of antipasti, served warm with dinner, or cut into large squares, halved, and used for sandwiches. Sprinkled with crystals of salt and herbs or dotted with bits of vegetables, this bread allows ample room for creativity.

1	package active dried yeast or 2½ teaspoons loose
1¼	cup plus 1 tablespoon warm water
3½	cups all-purpose flour
3	tablespoons olive oil
1	teaspoon salt
2	tablespoons extra-virgin olive oil, for brushing
1 or 2	tablespoons fresh herbs of your choice, finely chopped
1	teaspoon sea salt or coarse salt

In a small bowl, dissolve yeast with ¼ cup of the lukewarm water. Put flour and salt onto a floured surface. Make a well in center. Add dissolved yeast and remaining warm water, gradually pulling flour into the liquid. If the dough seems too sticky, add a bit more flour. Knead for 8 to 10 minutes or until smooth and elastic. Put dough into an oiled bowl, turn to coat, cover with a thick towel, and let rise in a warm place 1 to 1½ hours free from draft, until doubled in volume.

Preheat oven to 425° F.

Punch down and knead again briefly. Put on a lightly floured surface and roll or pat into 1 or 2 oblongs, about 1-inch thick. Dent dough here and there with your fingers. With a pastry brush, paint top with the olive oil. Put each on a cookie sheet or pizza pan sprinkled with cornmeal. Cover loosely with a sheet of foil and let rise for another 30 minutes. Sprinkle with sea salt, herbs, or your choice of toppings listed below. Put in lower part of oven and bake for 20 to 22 minutes or until golden brown. Cool slightly before serving.

Serves 8 to 10 for sandwiches or dinner, or makes up to 20 or more wedges for antipasti

VARIATIONS: Ideas for herbs and toppings include a sprinkling of rosemary, minced garlic, parsley, basil, sage, oregano, ground black pepper, or crushed red pepper; 12 sliced olives; ½ thinly sliced red onion; ½ red pepper, raw, fried, or roasted; thinly sliced or tiny bits of any kind of cheese; 10 sun-dried tomatoes; halved, cut side down; 1 or 2 plum tomatoes, thinly sliced and sprinkled with slivered fresh basil.

Taralli col Pepe
Bread Rings with Black Pepper and Fennel Seed

Crunchy *taralli* are often served with various antipasti instead of crackers. Pretzel-like rings flavored with black pepper and fennel seeds, they are spicy and tasty. They also make their appearance at outdoor festivals as street food, especially for the Feast of St. Anthony.

1	teaspoon active dry yeast or 2½ teaspoons loose
¾	cup warm water, divided
2	cups all-purpose flour
1	tablespoon freshly ground pepper
2	teaspoons fennel seeds
1	teaspoon salt
3	tablespoons olive oil
1	egg white, lightly beaten

In a small bowl, dissolve yeast with ¼ cup of the lukewarm water. Put flour, pepper, fennel seeds, and salt onto a floured surface. Make a well in center of the flour. Add dissolved yeast, remaining water, and oil, gradually pulling flour into the liquid. If dough seems a little sticky, add a bit more flour. Knead for 8 to 10 minutes until smooth and elastic. Put dough into an oiled bowl, turn to coat, and cover with a thick towel. Let rise in a warm place, free from draft, until doubled in size, about 2 hours.

Preheat oven to 375° F.

Remove dough from bowl and break off a small chunk. Roll into a strip about 6 inches long and the width of a pencil. Form each length into a ring, pinch ends together tightly, and put on a heavy-duty, ungreased cookie sheet. Cover with a towel and let rise until doubled, or about 1 hour.

Brush *taralli* tops with the egg white. Bake for 18 to 20 minutes or until light golden brown. Remove, cool on a rack, and store in tightly covered containers. They keep well for 1 month.

Makes 20 to 24 bread rings

Pasta per Pizza
Pizza Dough

This recipe makes enough dough for 2 pizzas on 10-by-15-inch cookie sheets or 15-inch round pizza pans. If you own a bread machine, let it knead your dough. Set the timer to alert you to remove dough before it begins to bake; the exact time depends on the brand of machine. Add ingredients in the machine in the order prescribed for bread. Remove dough and proceed with directions for any pizza recipe that follows.

        1   package active dry yeast or 2½ teaspoons loose
    1½   cups warm water, divided
        4   cups unbleached or all-purpose flour, divided
        1   teaspoon salt
        2   tablespoons olive oil

In a small bowl, dissolve yeast with ¼ cup of the warm water.

Put flour and salt onto a floured surface. Make a well in center of the flour. Add dissolved yeast, remaining water, and olive oil, gradually pulling flour into the liquid. If the dough seems a little sticky, add a bit more flour. Flour absorbs less liquid in humid weather, but remember that using too much will produce a dry, dense crust. Knead for 6 to 8 minutes, or until smooth and elastic. Shape the dough into a ball and put in an oiled bowl, roll to coat, and cover with a thick towel. Let rise in a warm place free from drafts for 1 to 1½ hours or until doubled in volume. Choose from the list of toppings below and proceed with the recipe of your choice, following preparation and baking instructions on page 263.

To freeze prepared pizza: Bake prepared pizza for 20 minutes, cool, wrap, and freeze. To serve, remove from freezer, put in preheated 400° F oven, and bake for 12 to 15 minutes or until heated through.

To freeze dough: Let rise, then wrap and freeze for up to 1 month. Thaw in refrigerator overnight. Remove, place in oiled bowl, turn to coat, and let rise in a warm place for 2 hours or more until doubled in size. Or thaw, draft-free, about 10 hours. Remove, put in oiled bowl and let rise as above.

To refrigerate dough: Let rise, then wrap and refrigerate for up to 2 days. Bring to room temperature for 1 hour or more before using.

Makes 2 pizzas

Choose from among these toppings for your pizza. For each pizza, use about ¾ to 1 cup of sauce, ½ cup vegetables, ¼ cup cheese or meat, and herbs of your choice, to taste.

Salsa Marinara Pronto! (Mariner's
    Style Tomato Sauce—Quick, Easy,
    and Perky, page 130)
anchovies
artichoke hearts
asparagus
basil
broccoli
capers
capicola
cauliflower
mild goat or Gorgonzola cheese
mozzarella cheese
pecorino or Parmesan cheese
provolone cheese
clams
eggplant
finely minced or roasted garlic
ham
mushrooms, all varieties
green or black olives
sweet, white, or red onions

oregano
parsley
pepperoni
raw, fried, or roasted peppers
pesto sauce
toasted pine nuts
prosciutto
crushed red pepper
ricotta
ricotta salata
salami
sardines
sausage (parcooked,
    cut into ½-inch slices)
scallions
seafood
sopressata
spinach
sun-dried tomatoes
plum or cherry tomatoes
tuna
zucchini

Calzone di Calabria
Calabrian Calzone

A cousin to pizza and another clever adaptation is the *calzone* (which means pants). It was originally made in the shape of a square, resembling a pant leg. Today, *calzone* take the shape of a small, round turnover, stuffed with a variety of ingredients and baked.

1	recipe *Pasta per Pizza* (Pizza Dough, page 260)
8	ounces ricotta, drained
3	ounces mozzarella, shredded
2	ounces sliced prosciutto or salami, cut into 1-inch squares
3	tablespoons fresh Italian parsley, finely chopped
1	tablespoon fresh basil, finely slivered
½	teaspoon salt
¼	teaspoon freshly ground black pepper
1	tablespoon olive oil for brushing tops

Preheat oven to 450° F.

Remove risen dough from bowl and put on floured surface. Divide into 8 pieces. Roll each piece into a round to desired thickness. For snacks or parties, make 16 about half that size.

In a large bowl, mix all ingredients except oil thoroughly. Divide mixture evenly between the circles of dough. Moisten edges of dough, fold over, and press to seal. Crimp as you would a pie with your fingers or a fork.

Lightly brush a large cookie sheet with olive oil, carefully put calzones on sheet, and brush tops with olive oil. Make 2 or 3 slits in each to let steam escape. Place on lowest oven rack. If making 8, bake for 20 to 25 minutes, if making 16, bake for 12 to 15 minutes or until golden brown.

Makes 8 or 16 calzone

Pizza Margherita

Pizza Margherita was created to honor Queen Margherita of Italy. The colors represent the Italian flag—green (basil), white (cheese), and red (tomatoes). Fresh mozzarella makes all the difference in this classic dish. Garlic was intentionally omitted in deference to the queen so that no odor would emanate from her breath. No longer a consideration, it is back where it belongs, in the sauce.

1 recipe *Pasta per Pizza* (Pizza Dough, page 260)
2 tablespoons olive oil, divided
1 recipe *Salsa Marinara, Pronto!* (Mariner's Style Tomato Sauce—Quick, Easy, and Perky, page 130)
8 ounces fresh mozzarella, shredded
¼ cup fresh basil, slivered

Preheat oven to 400° F.

Remove risen dough from bowl and put on floured surface. Divide in half for 2 pizzas. In a small dish, add 1 tablespoon olive oil. With a pastry brush, coat bottoms only of two 10-by-15-inch cookie sheets or two 15-inch round pizza pans. With a rolling pin, roll out each dough for each a little larger than the size of the sheet or pan. Make a thicker edge all around to prevent toppings from rolling off. Dent dough here and there with your fingers to hold toppings. Use remaining tablespoon olive oil to brush top of dough.

Meanwhile, assemble the toppings. In a medium saucepan, heat *Salsa Marinara, Pronto!* Spread sauce evenly over the 2 pizzas. Sprinkle the mozzarella and basil evenly over top. Bake on the lowest oven rack for 25 to 30 minutes or until top is brown and bubbling.

Makes 2 pizzas (16 slices)

TIP: If using a baking stone, dust lightly with cornmeal. Put free-form pizza on a peel (large wooden spatula) also lightly dusted with cornmeal. Add toppings and slide pizza directly onto the stone.

Pizza (Pitta) Ripiena
Stuffed, Top Crusted Pizza

Calabrian pizzas that have a top crust are called *pitta*. This prince of pittas contains a host of Calabrian favorite ingredients.

1	recipe *Pasta per Pizza* (Pizza Dough, page 260)
4	tablespoons olive oil, divided
½	onion, coarsely chopped
1	clove garlic, finely minced
1	pound fresh tomatoes or 1 16-ounce can of Italian plum tomatoes, coarsely chopped
2	tablespoons fresh Italian parsley, finely chopped
1	6-ounce can tuna, drained
¼	cup black olives, brine-cured, pitted and halved
3 or 4	anchovy fillets, cut into ½-inch pieces
1	tablespoon capers

Preheat oven to 400° F.

Remove risen dough from bowl and put on a floured surface. Divide dough in half with the bottom piece slightly larger than the top. In a small dish, add 1 tablespoon olive oil. With a pastry brush, coat the bottom only of a 10-by-15-inch cookie sheet or a 15-inch round pizza pan. With a rolling pin, roll out the bottom piece a little larger than the size of the sheet or pan.

In a medium skillet over medium heat, add 2 tablespoons olive oil. Add onion and sauté 3 to 4 minutes or until translucent. Add garlic and sauté until light golden brown. Add tomatoes and simmer 8 to 10 minutes. Add parsley and stir; set aside to cool slightly. Spread tomato mixture on the crust and cover with tuna, olives, anchovies, and capers.

Wet edges of bottom crust. Roll out the remaining dough and put atop the pizza. Pinch edges and crimp as you would a pie, with your fingers or a fork. Brush top with remaining tablespoon olive oil and make 3 or 4 large slits in the top to let steam escape. Bake on lowest oven rack for 35 to 40 minutes or until the dough is golden brown.

Makes 1 pizza

Pizza Bianca
White Pizza

Before southern Italians discovered the enormous potential of the simple but sublime tomato in the late sixteenth century, pizzas in Italy had a variety of toppings, but the tomato wasn't one of them. While Americans, and indeed the world, have adopted pizza as their own, white pizza, devoid of tomatoes, is rather new to many.

    1 recipe *Pasta per Pizza* (Pizza Dough, page 260)
    2 tablespoons olive oil, divided
    1 clove garlic, finely minced
    8 ounces ricotta
    8 ounces spinach, steamed for 2 to 3 minutes, slivered
    2 tablespoons Parmesan cheese, freshly grated
    ¼ teaspoon salt
    ¼ teaspoon freshly ground black pepper
    4 ounces sliced salami, rolled and cut in half

Preheat oven to 400° F.

Remove risen dough from bowl and put on floured surface. Divide in half for 2 pizzas. In a small dish, add 1 tablespoon olive oil. With a pastry brush, coat bottoms of two 10-by-15-inch cookie sheets or two 15-inch round pizza pans. With a rolling pin, roll out dough for each a little larger than the size of the sheet or pan. Make a thicker edge all around to prevent toppings from rolling off. Dent pizza here and there with your fingers to hold toppings. Add minced garlic and brush top of dough with the remaining 1 tablespoon olive oil.

Spread each pizza with the ricotta, followed by the spinach. Sprinkle with Parmesan cheese, salt, and pepper. Evenly distribute salami over each.

Bake on the lowest oven rack for 25 to 30 minutes or until crust is golden brown and top is brown and bubbling.

Makes 2 pizzas

DOLCI, FRUTTE, NOCE, E GRANITE

PASTRIES, FRUITS, NUTS, AND ICES

Serving a variety of desserts is an Italian tradition dating back to the ancient Romans, who loved sweets. One of their best-known inventions was a cheesecake called *savillum*. Sweetened with honey, the cheese they used is similar to today's ricotta. The Romans also ate a wide variety of fruits, among them apples, figs, peaches, apricots, cherries, dates, and melons.

Typically today in southern Italy, pastries are reserved for holidays and special occasions; fruit in season is the more common dessert. When pastries are served, however, there are many seductive ones to choose from. Because Italians do not rush through their meals, desserts appear some time after the meal, allowing the many previously eaten courses to settle. Occasionally, a small pastry is served with mid-afternoon coffee, and a *biscotti* or *cornetto* is served for breakfast.

A similarity exists between Sicilian and Calabrian desserts with their exotic Middle Eastern influences. Each, for example, has an exciting version of a triumphant sponge cake layered with a cream and/or chocolate filling, or a sponge cake filled with creamed ricotta, citron, nuts, shaved chocolate, and drizzled (or drenched is more like it) with rum or liqueurs.

Originally, honey was the sweetener used in pastries and cookies. It wasn't until the eleventh century that sugar appeared in Europe. The Crusaders discovered it in the area of Tripoli and brought the cane and refined sugar back with them. But it was still some time before the idea of using sugar to sweeten desserts took hold.

Rich, elaborate, and dazzling pastries are proudly displayed in every *pasticceria* (pastry shop) throughout all of Italy. Pastry chefs create artistic desserts that are both beautiful to behold and delicious to eat. Certain desserts are created for specific occasions, including holidays, feasts, and festivals; a cream puff was invented especially to honor St. Joseph on his feast day, for example. Many were essential to ancient rites and some possessed symbolic meaning; desserts with eggs always appear at Easter, symbolizing rebirth. The Romans fashioned certain desserts to resemble each other. Southern Italians continue that tradition with a slight variation; they painstakingly create artistic pastries that resemble fruits and vegetables.

Cookies also play an important role on holidays and at weddings along with the wedding cake. I recall attending traditional Calabrian weddings as a little girl in Schenectady, New York, where I was born. (Children of all ages were never excluded from weddings or any other family functions.) The bride and groom passed among the guests large silver trays with white paper doilies circling the edges and containing a variety of cookies mounded in pyramids, with *confetti*, white sugar-coated almonds (for good luck and fertility), and sometimes sparkling silver tinsel sprinkled over all. Two of the most popular cookies on the wedding tray were *Biscotti ai Pignoli* (Almond-Flavored Pine Nut Cookies, page 271) and *Amaretti* (Macaroons, page 280).

Biscotti, crunchy and delicious twice-baked biscuits (although the term is also used for cookies) designed for dunking, have entered our arena and can be found in cafés and restaurants, and in bakeries and supermarkets. Cookies and *biscotti* can be made in advance, a decided advantage when planning a large holiday dinner or a dinner party.

Fruits in Italy are abundant, sweet, and flavorful, and like vegetables are large. Italians in general consume more fruits than Americans do. And with outdoor markets open year-round in southern Italy, fresh fruit can be bought and eaten at any time of the day, making it easy to enjoy a snack as you stroll. Vendors smile obligingly as they rinse a pear, apple, or peach for you. At home, whole fruit is sometimes served in a bowl of cold water to chill it. Italians do not refrigerate fruit; they think it numbs the flavor.

Oranges are especially bountiful in southern Italy. They are sweet and juicy and often the size of American grapefruits. Oranges were brought to Italy by the Portuguese from China via India in the seventeenth century. Calabria has a large variety of other citrus fruits, including some unique to the area such as the *megalolo*, a lemon grafted onto a bitter orange tree; the *verdello*, a forced-growth, very soft, and aromatic orange used for perfumes; and the *bergamot*, a large, lemon-like fruit valued for its scented oil and used in perfume production.

Some fruits are cooked, such as *Mele al Forno* (Baked Apples with Chocolate and Raisins, page 289); some are fancily stuffed with almonds and dipped in chocolate, creating the appealing *Fichi al Cioccolata* (Figs Stuffed with Almonds and Dipped in Chocolate, page 292); some are turned into sauces, as in *Salsa di Fichi* (Fig Sauce, page 293); oranges, lemons, or grapefruits are made into marmalades; and lemons, in another role, are drizzled over fish and vegetables; and some fruits are combined with cookies, as in *Pesche agli Amaretti* (Stuffed Peaches with Macaroons, Almonds, and Sherry, page 293). What haven't they thought of?

Another favorite presentation combines fruit with wine. After dinner, my dad would sometimes slice fresh peaches or oranges and slip them into a glass of homemade red wine. He allowed it to steep for a minute or two, then ate the peaches and drank the wine.

Fruits play a significant role in the making of many *dolci, biscotti,* and *gelati.* Fruits are, in fact, an essential part of the Calabrian daily diet in one form or another and are also important to the economic well-being of the region. Cheese is sometimes served alongside fruit. Several cheeses, such as cacio-cavallo and incanestrato, pair well with fruits.

A bowl of mixed nuts and nutcrackers is never missing from the table beside fruit on holidays or any family gathering or special occasion. Among them are almonds, introduced to Italy during Arab conquests, and pistachio nuts, contributed by the Persians. The Persians also taught Arabs and Italians the trick of thickening foods with ground almonds, walnuts, and pistachios. Almonds and pine nuts are essential ingredients in many cookies and pastries. The ancient tradition of roasting chestnuts is always practiced at holidays, especially Christmas. In Italy, a festival is celebrated in their honor.

Gelato, the delightful Italian version of ice cream, comes in many incredible flavors. A form of *gelato* originated with the ancient Romans. They carried snow down from the mountaintops and flavored it with fruit juices. Travelers from the Near East were said to bring something similar to southern Italy, but the Italians pretty much perfected *gelato* by the seventeenth century. Therafter, it began to spread to France and other European countries. A little more dedicated tinkering and it became glorious and incomparable in the eighteenth century. *Gelato* is one of Italy's greatest contributions to gastronomy. Perfected with the just right amounts of cream, egg yolks, and sugar, it is richer and creamier than American ice cream or any other, for that matter. *Gelaterias,* sometimes a shiny, brassy modern ice-cream parlor, and sometimes a charming old *caffè,* display as large a variety of *gelati* as there are colors in the rainbow. They also provide the young and the not-so-young a meeting place to congregate and socialize.

Granita (ice) is refreshing and particularly favored in hot southern Italy. Eating cool and tart lemon ice at church festivals was a treat when I was a little girl. *Granita di Limone* (Lemon Ice) appears at religious festivals in the North End of Boston, to the delight of children and adults. Two other favorites are strawberry and mint. You will find recipes for these three *granite* in this chapter.

Biscotti alle Mandorle e all' Arancia
Almond and Orange Biscuits

Combining almonds with orange juice, candied orange peel, and zest yields a fabulously fragrant twice-baked biscuit. (Candied orange peel is available in most supermarkets.) This biscotti is my favorite. It pleases the palate, is perfect for dunking in coffee, is an appetizing accompaniment to wine, and lasts a long time when stored in an airtight container.

8 tablespoons butter or margarine, softened
1 cup sugar
1 large egg
½ cup freshly squeezed orange juice
2 cups unbleached all-purpose flour
1 teaspoon cinnamon
1 teaspoon baking soda
1 teaspoon baking powder
½ teaspoon salt
1 cup almonds, toasted and coarsely chopped
zest of 1 orange, grated
⅓ cup finely chopped candied orange peel

Preheat oven to 350° F.

In a medium mixing bowl, cream butter and sugar. Add egg and orange juice, and with a whisk, beat until blended. Gradually add remaining ingredients and mix well. With a spatula, spread the dough onto a cookie sheet, forming a 5-by-10-inch loaf.

Bake for 25 to 30 minutes or until dough is firm. Remove from oven and let cool for 5 minutes for ease in cutting. Cut crosswise diagonally into 1-inch thick slices.

Lower oven temperature to 300° F. Put biscotti on cookie sheet on their sides and bake for 10 minutes or until golden, turning once. Cool completely on a rack before storing.

Makes 30 to 34 biscotti

TIP: Grate orange zest before squeezing juice.

Biscotti ai Pignoli
Almond-Flavored Pine Nut Cookies

Southern Italians are enamored of this ever-popular cookie. It is almost always included on large trays filled with tempting Italian cookies that are passed at Calabrian weddings. So sensational and scrumptious are they that they are also served on many other special occasions. Most every Calabrian *pasticceria* I visited displayed this cookie. One fan of this recipe, Linde Piette of Andover, Massachusetts, told me that her 78-year-old father devoured 10 of them as soon as they came out of the oven!

1½	cups sugar
¼	teaspoon salt
4	large eggs
2	cups all-purpose flour
½	teaspoon baking powder
2	teaspoons almond extract
10	tablespoons pine nuts
	confectioner's sugar for sprinkling

Preheat oven to 375° F.

In the top of a large double boiler, over hot but not boiling water, put the sugar, salt, and eggs. You can also use a large mixing bowl over a pan of hot water. In either case, the heat must not be too high or the eggs will cook. With a whisk or an electric mixer, beat for 4 to 5 minutes, or until sugar is dissolved and batter is lemon colored. Mixture will resemble pancake batter.

Remove from heat and continue beating for another 4 to 5 minutes until eggs are foamy and the mixture is cool. Sift flour and baking powder and fold gently into the batter. Add almond extract and blend.

Line cookie sheets with parchment paper. Drop batter by teaspoonfuls 1½-inches apart. If the first 2 cookies spread and touch, add 1 or more tablespoons of flour to batter and blend. The size of the eggs affects the consistency of the batter. Cover tops with pine nuts and sprinkle with the confectioner's sugar. (If you have a container with small holes on top, it sifts and sprinkles at the same time.)

Bake in middle of oven for 12 to 14 minutes or until light golden brown. Cool thoroughly on a rack and store in an airtight container for up to a month.

Makes about 4 dozen

Biscotti d' Anice

Anise Biscuits

About the third century B.C., the Romans devised a way of baking a cookie that didn't require preserving: they baked it twice. Although *biscotti* is the generic word for cookies, it also refers to cookies that are twice baked. These twice-baked biscuits carried by sailors on extended voyages evolved from the hard, dry biscuits that originated with the Romans. Italians love to dunk, and if you do too, here is one of the most popular Calabrian "dunking" biscuits. My mother made these regularly, and I think we just took them for granted. They were always there to dunk in coffee for breakfast.

4   **large eggs, at room temperature for 15 minutes**
1¼ **cups sugar**
2½ **cups all-purpose flour**
2   **teaspoons anise seeds**
1   **teaspoon vanilla extract**

Preheat oven to 375° F.

In a large bowl, add eggs and with a whisk or an electric mixer at high speed, beat for 1 minute or until lemon-colored. Gradually add sugar and continue beating for 1 to 2 minutes or until sugar is dissolved. Add flour, anise seeds, and vanilla. Mix until well blended.

In two greased and floured 9-by-4-by-2-inch loaf pans, divide the batter equally in half. Bake in middle of oven for 18 to 20 minutes or until dough is firm and a light golden color. Remove from pan and let cool for about 10 minutes.

Lower oven temperature to 325° F. Cut each loaf into 1-inch crosswise slices. Lay slices on their side on a greased cookie sheet.

Bake for 8 to 10 minutes or until lightly browned, turning once to toast both sides. Cool thoroughly on a rack and store in an airtight container.

Makes about 3 dozen

Mostaccioli Calabrese
Chocolate Calabrian Cookie

There are several versions and as many names for this ancient, crunchy, delectable cookie. Of Arabic origin, different Calabrian regions call it *zulli, mostazzoli, nzuddi,* or *nsulli.* The Romans were particularly fond of it. It almost invariably appears on cookie trays on Christmas, at weddings, on the feast of St. Anthony the Abbot, and other special occasions. Originally the cookies were hand cut in the shape of animals or caricatures, a time-consuming process. With today's variety of cookie cutters, cutting time is considerably shortened. The cookies, which can be made in advance, are hard when first baked and soften with time. Either way they are delicious. If you wish to frost them, the recipe follows.

1⅓	cups almonds, divided into thirds
½	cup honey
1	cup cocoa
⅔	cup sugar
¼	cup candied orange peel, cut into tiny pieces
½	teaspoon grated orange zest
½	teaspoon cinnamon
¼	teaspoon cloves
¼	teaspoon grated nutmeg
5	tablespoons brewed American coffee
1	cup all-purpose flour
	confectioner's sugar for sprinkling (optional)

Preheat oven to 375° F.

If almonds have skins, remove by placing them in a small pan half-filled with boiling water for about 1 minute. Drain and pat dry with paper towels. Rub off skins and dry again with fresh towels.

By hand or with a food processor, grind about ⅓ of the almonds at a time as fine as possible. Put in a medium mixing bowl. Add honey, cocoa, sugar, candied orange, orange zest, cinnamon, cloves, and nutmeg. With a fork, mix until blended.

Gradually add coffee and flour, and with a pastry blender, mix until blended and dough can be formed into a ball. The dough will be stiff. Remove onto a floured surface and knead for 2 to 3 minutes or until dough is smooth, dusting surface with flour as needed.

Scrape surface clean and flour again. Divide dough into fourths for ease in rolling. With a rolling pin, roll each piece to about ⅓-inch thickness.

Line cookie sheet with parchment paper or butter lightly and sprinkle with flour. Using various shaped cookie cutters of about 2- or 3-inches in diameter, cut cookies and put them on the cookie sheet.

Bake in middle of oven for 9 to 11 minutes or until cooked through. Cool on a rack and store in an airtight container for up to 2 months. If using confectioner's sugar, sprinkle lightly before serving, or frost as desired.

Makes about 2½ dozen depending on cookie cutter sizes

TIP: Dip cookie cutters in flour occasionally to keep dough from sticking.

VARIATION: To frost, sift 1 cup confectioner's sugar into a small bowl. Add 3 teaspoons water and ½ teaspoon lemon extract. Mix until smooth. If stiff, add a few drops of lemon juice. Frost entire cookie or just dab the center.

Cuzzupe di Pasqua
Easter Ring or Basket with Colored Eggs

This Easter pastry is a Calabrian tradition. My mother made it every Easter. Also known as *ciambelle dolci,* the recipe combines deep-rooted ancient and religious meanings. At Easter, eggs always appear in one form or another. Symbolic of a beginning, a new life that springs forth at springtime, they also invoke fertility and good luck and are eaten to ensure eternal life. The pastry is shaped into a plain or braided ring and colored eggs are embedded throughout with strips of dough criss-crossed over them. If the dough is used to make individual baskets for children, an egg is placed into each basket. Whether you bake a ring or baskets, each child gets a colored egg. When my sister and I were little, Mom made a ring for the family and Easter guests and a basket for us while Dad busily made baskets for everyone out of the palm we had each received on Palm Sunday.

    4   tablespoons butter or margarine, softened
    ½   cup sugar
    ¼   teaspoon salt
    1   large egg
    ½   cup milk

1 teaspoon lemon extract
1¾ cups all-purpose or unbleached flour
1 teaspoon baking powder
8 eggs, hard boiled and colored

Preheat oven to 375° F.

In a large mixing bowl, add butter, sugar, and salt. Cream until well blended. Gradually add egg, milk, and lemon extract. Mix well. Stir in the flour and baking powder and mix until smooth.

For a ring: Remove dough from bowl to a floured surface. Cut away ¼ of the dough and set aside. Shape remaining dough into a ring large enough to accommodate the 8 eggs. Pinch edges together. For a braided ring, divide dough evenly into 3 pieces. Roll each piece, plait, and shape into a ring large enough to accommodate the 8 eggs. Pinch edges together. Place ring on a lightly greased cookie sheet. Press eggs gently into dough in evenly-spaced intervals. Roll out reserved dough and cut into 16 narrow strips. Criss-cross strips over each egg to form a cross, pressing edges into bottom dough. Brush strips with melted butter.

Bake for 17 to 20 minutes or until ring is a medium golden brown and is cooked through.

For baskets: Remove dough to a floured surface and cut into 8 pieces. Mold ⅔ of each piece into a small round with an impression in the middle. Roll remaining ⅓ to form a handle. Put an egg in the basket and lay handle over egg. Press edges securely to the basket. Place baskets on a lightly greased cookie sheet. Brush handles with melted butter.

Bake 13 to 15 minutes or until baskets are a light golden brown.

Makes 1 ring or 8 baskets

TIP: Fellow Calabrian and home economist Virginia Cunzola Evans said her mother used a glaze over the finished bread or rings: Mix ½ cup confectioner's sugar with 1 to 1½ teaspoons water. Add the water a few drops at a time until the glaze is thin enough to spread.

Petrali
Fig, Raisin, and Nut-Filled Cookies

My mom made a trayful of these rustic, crunchy concoctions, also called *cucidate*, every Easter, Christmas, and New Year's. She used a variety of cookie cutters befitting the occasion—some in the shape of animals, others in the shape of stars, Easter bunnies, and so on. I always knew they were important and special but never so much as during my last visit to Calabria. My cousin Mimma and I were in a jewelry store in Bova Marina. She told the owner I was writing a Calabrian cookbook. The owner looked at me quizzically and in Italian asked Mimma, "But can she make *petrali*?"

PASTRY:

4½ cups all-purpose flour
3   teaspoons baking powder
⅔   cup sugar
¾   teaspoon salt
1   tablespoon freshly grated orange zest
1¼ cups butter or margarine, softened
1⅓ cups cold water

FILLING:

1¼ cups dry figs, stems removed
1¼ cups seedless raisins
¾   cup almonds
¾   cup walnuts
¼   cup honey or sugar
2   tablespoons orange juice
2   tablespoons freshly grated orange zest
1   teaspoon cinnamon
    confectioner's sugar for sprinkling

In a large mixing bowl, add most of the flour, baking powder, sugar, salt, and orange zest. With a pastry blender, cut in butter. Add water gradually and mix until ingredients hold together. If sticky, add remaining flour. Put on a lightly floured surface and knead for 4 to 5 minutes or until the dough is smooth. Put in a lightly greased bowl, turn to coat, cover, and refrigerate while preparing the filling.

In a food processor with a metal blade, add figs, raisins, almonds, and walnuts. Pulse until contents are chopped into ¼-inch pieces. Otherwise, chop by hand. Transfer to a mixing bowl and add honey or sugar, orange juice, orange zest, and cinnamon. Mix thoroughly.

Preheat oven to 400° F.

Divide dough into 4 parts. On a floured surface, roll each piece of dough into a rectangle ⅛-inch thick. Using various cookie cutters or a fluted pastry wheel, cut into shapes or 3-inch rounds or squares. Put a heaping tablespoon of filling in center but do not cover cookies until all filling is used. Distribute any remaining filling evenly among cookies.

Fill a small bowl with water, dip in fingers, and moisten edges of dough. Put identically shaped cutouts on their mates, press lightly, and flute edges with a fork. Prick tops in interesting patterns and place on an ungreased cookie sheet.

Bake in top portion of oven for 25 to 30 minutes or until lightly browned. Cool on a rack and store in an airtight container for up to a month. Before serving, sprinkle lightly with confectioner's sugar.

Makes about 2½ dozen depending on the size of cookie cutters used

TIP: When fluting edges of pastry, dip fork in flour to prevent sticking.

VARIATION: A less labor-intensive method is to roll out the dough into 2 long rectangles, about ⅛-inch thick and about 9-inches wide. Divide filling between each rectangle and fill center. Fold dough over, seal tightly, and bake. When cool, cut into 1-inch slices, about the size of a *biscotti.*

Guanti o Wandi (Gloves)
Fluffy Fried Pastry Strips

This delightful delicacy wins the prize for the pastry with the most names. They include: *bugie* (lies), *cenci* (rags and tatters), *chiacchierata* (tittle tattle), *crostoli* (crusts), *linque delle suocere* (mothers-in-law tongues), *nastri delle suore* (nuns' ribbons), and *nastrini* (tiny ribbons). If those names weren't enough, this pastry is also known in English as bow-knots, egg twists, flat candles, fried ribbons, and love knots! No holiday is complete without them. I have called them *Guanti,* which is the name my mother used. She made extra platefuls for friends and neighbors. (They can be made days in advance.) Whichever name you choose, you will enjoy this light, irresistible classic.

3	tablespoons melted butter or margarine
¼	cup sugar
3	large eggs, well beaten
½	teaspoon vanilla extract
2	cups all-purpose flour
1	teaspoon baking powder
⅛	teaspoon salt
	zest of 1 small lemon
1 to 2	teaspoons milk
½ to 1	cup vegetable oil
	confectioner's sugar for sprinkling

In a large mixing bowl, cream butter and sugar. Add eggs and vanilla; mix thoroughly. Gradually add the flour, baking powder, salt, and lemon zest. Mix well. Place mixture on a lightly floured surface and knead for 6 to 8 minutes or until no more blisters form and the dough is smooth, soft, and elastic. If dough seems a little hard, add 1 to 2 teaspoons milk.

Form dough into a ball, place in greased bowl, and turn to coat. Cover with a towel and let stand for 10 minutes.

Roll out into 2 sheets, ⅛-inch thick each. With a fluted pastry wheel, cut one sheet into 3-by-5-inch pieces. Make 4 lengthwise cuts 4 inches long; when cooked they will resemble gloves. Cut the other sheet into ½-by-6-inch pieces. Form into bows or knots, or put a 1-inch slit in center and twist slightly. When all are cut, begin frying the first ones that have been allowed to "set."

In a medium pot, add ½ cup or more of the vegetable oil over medium-high heat. Fry strips, uncrowded, for 1 to 2 minutes or until puffed and golden brown. Do not leave unattended. Remove with tongs and drain on paper towels. Cool slightly and sprinkle with confectioner's sugar. Store in a cool place. Sprinkle again with confectioner's sugar just before serving.

Makes about 3 dozen

Struffoli (o Pignolata) alla Calabrese
Calabrian Style Honey Clusters

Struffoli are a popular dessert choice throughout Calabria and many, if not most, parts of southern Italy. Unknown to some people in Calabria was the name *struffoli*, and unknown to others was *pignolata*. It's a dilemma! Also known as *pitta 'mpigliata* in dialect (and by a few souls as *cicerata)*, this delightful dessert, always served at Christmas, is also customary at carnival time, just prior to Lent. The tiny pieces of fried dough are dipped in honey and piled into a conical mound. An attractive dessert that can double as a centerpiece, it can be made ahead, a blessing when planning a holiday meal. When Mom made it, she topped it off with colored sprinkles. As a little girl, I recall thinking how colorful and appropriate it was for Christmas.

3	cups all-purpose flour
⅛	teaspoon salt
1	tablespoon freshly grated orange zest
1	tablespoon freshly grated lemon zest
4	large eggs, lightly beaten
½	cup vegetable oil, or more if needed
¾	cup honey
¼	cup sugar
	colored sprinkles (optional)

In a large mixing bowl, add flour, salt, and orange and lemon zest. Add eggs gradually, mixing well. Remove dough and place on a floured surface. Knead for 3 to 4 minutes or until smooth. Cover with plastic wrap and let stand for 30 minutes to 1 hour.

Break off pieces of dough and roll into strips about ¼-inch in diameter. With a very sharp knife, cut into ¼-inch pieces and place on a floured surface.

In a large, heavy skillet heat vegetable oil over medium heat. Add pieces of dough to skillet. Do not overcrowd. Fry for 2 to 3 minutes or until they are light golden brown. Drain on paper towels.

In a small skillet, add honey and sugar over medium heat. Simmer for 1 to 2 minutes or until sugar is melted. Remove from burner and gently place bits of fried dough into warmed honey. Stir to coat. Remove with slotted spoon and place on a colorful serving dish. Let cool for barely 1 minute.

Wet your hands with cold water to keep cookies from sticking to your fingers and quickly begin layering, making each subsequent layer smaller so it ends up looking like a wide upside-down ice cream cone. If desired, sprinkle immediately with colored sprinkles. Cool thoroughly. Cover tightly with foil or plastic wrap. Keeps well for several days.

Serves 12 to 16

Amaretti

Macaroons

This cookie brings back fond childhood memories. I remember going to weddings where *amaretti* and other assorted cookies were mounded, pyramid style, on large silver trays encircled by white paper doilies. Made almost entirely of almonds, they are light, airy, and wonderfully chewy. It seems all of Italy wants to take credit for this wonderful creation—Calabrians, southern Italians, and northern Italians. The Sardinians have their own version. I don't know which part of Italy should get credit for the original, but no matter, it belongs to everyone.

> 1½ cups almonds, divided into thirds
> 1 cup sugar
> 2 egg whites, left out at room temperature for 15 minutes
> ⅛ teaspoon salt
> 2 teaspoons almond extract
> ½ teaspoon vanilla extract
> granulated sugar for sprinkling (optional)

Preheat oven to 300° F.

If almonds have skins, remove by placing them in a small pan half-filled with boiling water for about 1 minute. Drain and pat dry with paper towels. Rub off skins and dry again with fresh towels.

By hand or with a food processor, grind ½ cup of the almonds as fine as possible. Put in a medium mixing bowl. Continue grinding almonds in ½-cup increments. Put into the mixing bowl, add sugar, mix with a fork, and set aside.

With an electric mixer or a whisk, beat egg whites for 5 minutes or until stiff, adding the salt halfway through. With a rubber spatula, fold in the nut and sugar mixture and the almond and vanilla extracts. Line cookie sheet with parchment paper. Drop dough by teaspoonful 1½ inches apart. Set aside for at least 15 minutes. Sprinkle lightly with granulated sugar, if desired.

Bake in middle of oven for 15 to 20 minutes or until light brown. Do not remove from parchment until partially cooled; otherwise, they will break. Cool thoroughly on a rack and store in an airtight container for up to a month.

Makes about 3½ dozen

TIP: Grinding almonds in large amounts can cause overheating, turning them into nut butter. It is best to grind ½ cup at a time.

VARIATION: Dried red cherries are primarily added to cookies for weddings, but I like to add them year-round. To garnish, gently press halved cherries in center of cookie just before baking.

Sospiri di Monaca
Nun's Sighs

Don't you just love the name of this dessert? These cake-like cookies made with honey and almonds are popular in Calabria, Sicily, and Sardinia. Almost always served at Easter, they can be dusted with confectioner's sugar or dipped halfway into melted chocolate, or you can do half with sugar, half with chocolate.

2½	cups all-purpose flour
2	tablespoons baking powder
½	teaspoon salt
¼	teaspoon baking soda
½	cup almonds
½	cup butter or margarine, softened
⅓	cup sugar
1	egg, lightly beaten
½	cup honey
1	tablespoon lemon zest
3	ounces semisweet chocolate (3 squares)
	confectioner's sugar for sprinkling

In a large mixing bowl, add flour, baking powder, salt, and baking soda. Mix well. In a food processor, process almonds until finely chopped, then add to flour mixture. In a medium bowl, cream together butter, sugar, egg, honey, and lemon zest. Add to flour mixture and mix thoroughly. Knead into a ball, wrap in plastic wrap, and chill for 2 hours.

Preheat oven to 350° F.

Remove dough from refrigerator and form into 2 oblong rolls, about 1¾-inches in diameter. With a sharp knife, cut into ¼-inch slices. Place on a buttered cookie sheet and bake for 10 minutes or until lightly browned.

Meanwhile, add chocolate to a double boiler over medium heat. Stir 2 or 3 minutes or until melted. (Or microwave chocolate in a deep dish at medium-high for 2 to 3 minutes, or until melted.) Stir to blend.

Remove cookies from oven and when cool enough to handle, sprinkle with confectioner's sugar or dip halfway in melted chocolate. Put on waxed paper over a cookie sheet to cool. Store in an airtight container and refrigerate. Remove 1 hour before serving.

Makes 2 to 2½ dozen

Biscotti di Regina
The Queen's Sesame Seed Cookies

This delightful cookie whose name unmistakably informs us all that it is considered fit for a queen is served on Christmas Day in Saracena (a village in Cosenza), according to Domenica and Maddalena Barletta of Saracena. It is also one of the cookies included on the traditional cookie tray passed to guests at weddings by the bride and groom.

2¼	cups all-purpose flour
⅓	cup sugar
1½	teaspoons baking powder
¼	teaspoon salt
6	tablespoons butter or vegetable shortening
1	large egg, lightly beaten
¼	cup milk
2	teaspoons orange or vanilla extract
¾	cup sesame seeds, untoasted

Preheat oven to 375° F.

In a large bowl, sift flour, sugar, baking powder, and salt. With a pastry blender, blend in butter or shortening until mixture resembles coarse crumbs.

In a small bowl, combine egg, milk, and extract; add gradually to cookie mixture. If dough is too sticky, add an additional tablespoon of flour. Remove dough to a lightly floured surface and knead just until smooth.

Spread sesame seeds on a large, flat plate. Break off a piece of dough the size of a walnut and roll between palms of hands until about the size and shape of a finger. Roll each cookie in sesame seeds until fully coated. Flatten slightly and put cookies 1-inch apart on a cookie sheet lined with parchment paper.

Bake on middle rack for 20 to 25 minutes or until a light golden brown. Cool thoroughly on a rack and store in an airtight container for up to a month.

Makes about 2½ dozen

Sfinge di San Giuseppe
St. Joseph's Feast Day Cream Puffs

Much of southern Italy serves these cream puffs (also called *sfince* or *bigne*) on March 19th, the Feast of St. Joseph, father of the Holy Family, patron saint of the family, the Universal Church, and pastry chefs! But they are such a favorite, that they appear on dessert tables and in pastry shops frequently. Originally puffs were fried. Over time some people began baking them instead. I am among those who prefer baking them in the interest of reducing the fat content and because I think they taste better. There are two equally delicious fillings to choose from—ricotta or custard cream. The puffs, unfilled, can be frozen. To serve, remove from freezer, prepare filling, fill, and chill.

CREAM PUFF:

- 1 cup water
- ½ cup butter or margarine
- 1 cup all-purpose flour
- ⅛ teaspoon salt
- 4 large eggs, left at room temperature for 15 minutes
  confectioner's sugar for sprinkling

RICOTTA FILLING:

- 1¼ pounds ricotta, sieved
- ¼ cup sugar
- 2 tablespoons candied fruit, finely chopped
- 1 teaspoon vanilla extract

CUSTARD CREAM FILLING:

- 2 cups milk
- 6 tablespoons all-purpose flour
- ½ cup sugar
- ½ teaspoon salt
- 2 large eggs
- 2 teaspoons vanilla extract

Preheat oven to 400° F.

In a medium saucepan, add water and butter and bring to a boil over medium-high heat. Lower heat and add flour and salt all at once, stirring constantly with a wooden spoon until mixture is smooth, leaves sides of pan, and forms a ball. Remove pan from heat. Cool slightly. Gradually stir in eggs, 1 at a time, beating well after each addition until pastry is smooth and velvety.

Drop the puff mixture by rounded teaspoonfuls onto a lightly greased and floured cookie sheet, 2 inches apart. Bake for 25 to 30 minutes or until puffy, dry, and a light golden brown. Remove from oven and reduce oven temperature to 375° F.

Working quickly, make a 1-inch slit in one side of each puff to let steam escape and return to oven for 8 minutes more. Puffs will almost double in size. Cool on wire racks to allow air to circulate under the puffs, away from drafts.

Just before filling, with a sharp knife cut off top of each puff and set aside. Push aside soft interior with fingers. Fill each puff with the cooled filling mixture. Return the top at an angle; refrigerate. Just before serving, sprinkle with confectioner's sugar.

To make the ricotta filling: Put ricotta in a food processor and whirl until smooth. Remove and put in a mixing bowl. Add sugar and whip with an electric mixer until light and fluffy. Stir in candied fruit and vanilla extract. Cover and refrigerate until ready to fill puffs. Serve cold.

To make the custard cream filling: Add milk and flour to a medium saucepan over medium heat. Whisk until smooth and free from lumps. Add sugar and salt, stirring constantly until mixture thickens and comes to a boil. Remove from heat. In a small bowl, beat eggs lightly. Add a little of the creamed mixture to the bowl and mix. Return cream mixture to stove. Dribble egg mixture into pan while stirring constantly. Add vanilla extract and beat vigorously for 1 minute. Let cool slightly before filling. Serve cold.

Makes 24 puffs

Torta di Ricotta di Pasqua
Easter Ricotta Pie

Some traditions never die. This delicious Easter pie, the Calabrian version of cheesecake, has survived countless centuries, I was told. There are several variations: One, called *pastiera di Pasqua,* has more of a pie crust base. This base is a little richer, and I think it enhances the taste of this creamy pie. Despite its name, this pie is not reserved for Easter only; rather, it is shared with family and friends at family occasions.

PASTRY:
2 cups all-purpose flour
4 tablespoons sugar

¼	teaspoon salt
½	cup butter or margarine, softened
1	large egg, lightly beaten
3	tablespoons cold water

FILLING:

4	large eggs, left at room temperature for 15 minutes, separated
1½	pounds ricotta
½	cup sugar
4	tablespoons candied orange or lemon peel
1	tablespoon grated orange zest
1	teaspoon lemon extract
¼	teaspoon cream of tartar
⅛	teaspoon salt

In a large mixing bowl, mix flour, sugar, and salt. Cut in butter and mix until crumbly. Add egg and water and mix only long enough to blend. Put in a lightly greased bowl, turn to coat, and cover. Refrigerate for 1 hour.

Meanwhile, prepare filling. In a medium bowl, add egg yolks, ricotta, sugar, candied orange or lemon peel, orange zest, and lemon extract; beat until smooth.

In a large bowl, beat the egg whites, on low speed at first to prevent them from flying out of the bowl and gradually increasing to high speed. Beat until foamy. Add cream of tartar and salt and continue to beat until egg whites have very stiff peaks, about 5 minutes. Do not underbeat.

Preheat oven to 375° F.

Remove pastry from refrigerator. Cut off ¼ of the pastry and set aside. Roll remaining dough between 2 pieces of waxed paper to fit bottom and sides of a greased and floured 10- or 11-inch cake pan. Roll remaining pastry to about ⅛-inch thickness and cut into ¾-inch strips with a fluted pastry wheel. Set aside.

Gently and gradually fold the ricotta mixture into the beaten egg whites. Pour into the cake pan. Weave cut strips of dough over top of ricotta mixture, pressing edges against side dough.

Bake for 45 minutes, or until filling is set and pastry top is golden. Cool. Just before serving, sprinkle lightly with confectioner's sugar.

Serves up to 12

Torta Crema Chjina
Sponge Cake Layered with Ricotta Filling

This majestic sponge cake is an excellent choice for a party. It serves 10 to 12 comfortably and even more if you wish. Similar to Sicilian *cassata*, it is traditionally served at Christmas, Easter, weddings, and special occasions. There are two frostings from which to choose—almond or chocolate. The cake, without filling and frosting, can be made in advance and frozen. Defrost early in the day, fill, and frost.

SPONGE CAKE:

- 6 large eggs, left at room temperature 15 minutes, separated
- 1 cup sugar
- 1 tablespoon grated lemon zest
- 1 teaspoon lemon extract
- 1 cup all-purpose sifted flour
- ¼ cup water
- ½ teaspoon salt
- ½ teaspoon cream of tartar

FILLING:

- 1 pound ricotta
- ⅓ cup sugar
- 2 tablespoons milk
- 3 tablespoons candied lemon and/or orange peel
- 2 squares bitter or semisweet chocolate, coarsely chopped
- 2 tablespoons pine nuts or pistachios, finely chopped
- 1 tablespoon almond extract
- 1 tablespoon orange-flavored liqueur or orange extract

ALMOND FROSTING:

- 1 cup sifted confectioner's sugar
- 1 tablespoon almond extract
- 2 teaspoons milk or water
    maraschino cherries cut in half, for garnish
    mint leaves, for garnish

CHOCOLATE FROSTING:

- 2 squares semisweet chocolate
- 2 tablespoons butter or margarine

1   cup sifted confectioner's sugar
1   teaspoon vanilla extract
⅛   teaspoon salt

Preheat oven to 350° F.

Put egg yolks in a medium bowl and with an electric mixer at medium speed, beat for 5 minutes or until thick and lemon-colored. Gradually add sugar, lemon zest, and lemon extract, beating constantly. Fold in flour slowly, alternating with water until well blended.

In a large bowl, beat egg whites (about ¾ cup) on low speed at first, to prevent them from flying out of the bowl, gradually increasing to high speed. Beat until foamy. Add salt and cream of tartar. Beat until whites have very stiff peaks, about 5 minutes. Do not underbeat.

Line the bottom of a 9-inch ungreased tube pan with waxed paper, cut to fit.

With a spatula, gently and gradually fold yolk and flour mixture into the egg white mixture. Pour batter into the tube pan. Gently pull knife through batter in a wide circle to break air bubbles.

Bake for 1 hour or until cake tester or toothpick comes out clean. Immediately invert pan on a rack and let cake hang until cooled. Loosen cake with spatula, place serving dish on top of tube pan, invert pan, and tap bottom lightly until cake is released. Remove waxed paper and discard.

Meanwhile, make the filling. Beat ricotta, sugar, and milk with electric mixer at medium speed until smooth. Add candied lemon or orange peel, chocolate, nuts, almond extract, and liqueur. Mix thoroughly by hand. Place in refrigerator.

Mark cake with toothpicks and cut horizontally into three uniform layers. Spread half of the ricotta filling on bottom layer. Add second layer and press gently. Spread remaining ricotta filling on second layer. Add top layer and press gently. The layers may seem wobbly but will firm as the cake chills. Refrigerate for at least 2 hours before frosting.

To make almond frosting: In a small bowl add sugar, almond extract, and milk or water. Stir until well blended. If too thick, add a drop or two of milk or water. Frost top of cake, letting some frosting drip down sides. Swirl decoratively and garnish with cherries and mint leaves. Cover cake loosely with foil and refrigerate.

To make chocolate frosting: In a double boiler over medium heat, add chocolate and butter. Heat until mixture is melted, stirring occasionally. (In a microwave oven, in a small bowl add chocolate and butter and set on medium high for 2 minutes. Remove and stir. If chocolate is not melted, return to microwave for another 30 seconds.) Stir until smooth and pour into a medium bowl. Gradually add sugar, vanilla, and salt; beat until smooth and glossy. Frost top of cake, letting some frosting drip down sides. Swirl decoratively and garnish with cherries and mint leaves. Cover cake loosely with foil and refrigerate.

Serves 10 to 12, or can be cut into 20 party-size portions

TIPS:

- Bowl and beaters must be free of grease when beating egg whites.
- Make sure no yolk gets into the whites, or the whites will not beat properly.
- Do not hit beaters, spoon, or spatula on side of mixing bowl; it deflates the whites.

Torta Crema al Rum
Sponge Cake with Custard Cream Filling, Drizzled with Rum

This phenomenal cake has vanilla and chocolate cream fillings and is laced with sensuous rum. As if those heavenly combinations aren't dramatic enough, you can tuck fresh strawberries or other fruit between the layers or on top, adding extra elegance. Then either frost or sprinkle with confectioner's sugar. We are talking major center-stage dessert here! Like the other *torta,* this special cake is served on Christmas, Easter, weddings, and special occasions. When my sons were little, they often chose it as their birthday cake.

SPONGE CAKE:

Follow directions for *Torta Crema Chjina* (Sponge Cake Layered with Ricotta Filling, page 286)

CUSTARD CREAM FILLING (VANILLA AND CHOCOLATE):

- 2 cups milk
- 6 tablespoons all-purpose flour
- ½ cup sugar
- ½ teaspoon salt
- 2 large eggs, left at room temperature 15 minutes
- 2 teaspoons vanilla extract
- ½ cup chocolate chips or 2 squares semisweet chocolate
- ⅓ cup rum
  garnishes: whole or sliced strawberries, raspberries, sliced peaches, maraschino cherries, blueberries, and mint leaves

1   cup sifted confectioner's sugar
2   tablespoons fresh lemon or orange juice
1   tablespoon grated lemon or orange zest
1 to 2   teaspoons water

In a medium saucepan, add milk and flour over medium heat. Whisk until smooth and free from lumps. Add sugar and salt, stirring constantly until mixture just starts to thicken and comes to a boil, about 2 to 4 minutes. Remove from heat. In a small bowl, beat eggs lightly. Add a little of the mixture to the bowl and mix well. Return pan to stove and slowly dribble egg mixture into the pan, stirring constantly until mixture comes to a boil. Remove, add vanilla, and beat vigorously for another minute.

Remove half of the vanilla cream to a medium bowl. In a small bowl, add chocolate. Melt in microwave for 1 to 2 minutes, add to cream, and mix thoroughly.

Mark cake with toothpicks and cut horizontally into three uniform layers. Drizzle half the rum evenly over bottom layer. Spread the chocolate filling on top. If adding fruit, place on top of cream filling. Add second layer and press gently. Drizzle with remaining rum. Spread vanilla filling on second layer, and more fruit, if desired. Add top layer and press gently. The layers may seem wobbly but will firm up as the cake chills. Refrigerate for at least 2 hours before frosting.

If using frosting, in a small bowl add sugar, juice, and zest. Stir until well blended. If too thick, add water as needed. Frost top of cake, letting some frosting drip down sides. Swirl top decoratively and garnish with fruit and mint leaves, if desired. If not frosting, sprinkle generously with confectioner's sugar before garnishing. Cover cake loosely with foil and refrigerate.

Serves 10 to 12, or can be cut into 20 party-size portions

TIP: Bring custard to a boil only after eggs are added to ensure it remains thick.

Mele al Forno
Baked Apples with Chocolate and Raisins

Here is a divine way to serve baked apples. I make them in the fall when they're in their prime. Time this so the apples are done at end of dinner and you can serve them piping hot. However, they are equally good cold. Double the recipe and refrigerate the extras. Children love them and like to help prepare them. Nuts were not mentioned in the baked apple recipes I researched, but I have always added them. I like the crunch. And some recipes don't include chocolate chips. Their addition may be more recent, but they're such a delightful one, I have left them in.

> 4 firm apples such as Delicious, Rome, or Granny Smith
> 3 tablespoons raisins
> 2 tablespoons semisweet chocolate chips
> 2 tablespoons walnuts, coarsely chopped (optional)
> ½ cup water
> ⅓ cup sugar
> ¼ teaspoon freshly grated lemon zest
> ⅛ teaspoon salt

Preheat oven to 350° F.

Wash and core apples almost to the bottom. Peel an inch circle around top.

In a small bowl, mix the raisins, chocolate, and walnuts. Fill cavity of each apple with the mixture. Put apples upright in an 8-inch square baking pan.

In a small pan over medium-high heat, add water, sugar, lemon zest, and salt. Bring to a boil, remove from heat, stir, and pour over apples.

Bake covered with foil for 30 to 35 minutes, or until apples are tender and easily pierced with the tip of a knife but still retain their shape. Remove apples from oven, spoon syrup over them, and serve immediately.

Serves 4

Castagne Arrosto
Roasted Chestnuts

Sweet roasted chestnuts are a holiday tradition, especially on Christmas, always appearing after dinner in Italy and the United States accompanied by nuts, fruits, and desserts. Your chances of finding a street vendor selling them anywhere in Italy are quite good. At one time, chestnuts were dried and ground into flour and used to make desserts. The most traditional cooking method is to roast them on an open fire; however, oven roasting works well. They can also be sautéed or boiled. Boiled chestnuts are most often used in recipes calling for pureed or mashed chestnuts. All methods are easy to prepare. In my parents' home, chestnuts were placed on the wood-burning part of the kitchen stove and turned over and over until the skins were almost charred. A delightful aroma permeated the house.

TO ROAST IN OVEN:

1 pound of chestnuts
1 tablespoon oil

Preheat oven to 425° F.

With a sharp, pointed knife, slit each chestnut across top. Grease a heavy baking pan large enough to accommodate the chestnuts without crowding. Add chestnuts and roast for 25 to 35 minutes, until skins loosen and chestnuts pop open, or until tender when probed by the tip of a knife. Shake pan occasionally so they will brown evenly. Remove, peel, and serve at once.

TO SAUTÉ IN OIL:

1 pound chestnuts
2 tablespoons oil

With a sharp, pointed knife, slit each chestnut across top or side. In a large, heavy skillet, add oil over medium heat. Add chestnuts, lower heat, cover, and simmer for 30 to 40 minutes, or until skins loosen or the chestnuts pop open. Shake skillet occasionally so they will brown evenly. Remove, peel, and serve at once.

TO BOIL:

1 pound chestnuts

With a sharp pointed knife, slit each chestnut across top or side. In a saucepan over medium-high heat, add chestnuts and cover with cold water. When water comes to a boil, lower heat and simmer gently for 25 to 35 minutes until skins loosen and chestnuts pop open, or until tender when probed by the tip of a knife. To puree or mash, remove from heat, cool, and remove shells and skins.

TIP: To determine if chestnuts are fresh, feel them to check that the nut seems firm and has not drawn away from the shell. Chestnuts should be plump, shiny, and fragrant.

Fichi al Cioccolata
Figs Stuffed with Almonds and Dipped in Chocolate

Calabrians love figs, fresh or dried, and prepare them in many wonderful ways, but these figs are so special they are served on Christmas and New Year's Day. For an elegant touch, I like to serve them on a silver tray, alternating figs with a homemade white cookie such as amaretti. The contrast of dark and light is lovely. Then pile fresh raspberries or strawberries in the center atop mint leaves. Or, do what Paul King, chef at Davio's Restaurant in Cambridge, Massachusetts, did with this recipe. He placed a fresh fig totally immersed in chocolate on one side of a dessert plate, added three small white amaretti, scattered a few raspberries alongside, and zigzagged raspberry puree across the plate.

> 24 fresh or dried figs (about 1 pound)
> ¼ cup slivered almonds
> ¼ cup candied orange and/or lemon peel
> ½ teaspoon ground cloves
> 4 squares semisweet chocolate (4 ounces)

Preheat oven to 350° F.

Slice figs slightly more than halfway through.

In a small bowl, mix almonds, diced orange or lemon peel, and cloves. Stuff each fig with the mixture. Press closed and place on an ungreased cookie sheet, stems up. If figs are fresh, bake for 6 to 8 minutes; if dried, bake 3 to 5 minutes. Figs will be slightly darkened.

Meanwhile, in a double boiler over low to medium heat, add chocolate. Heat for 2 to 3 minutes or until chocolate is just melted, stirring constantly. (In a microwave oven, add chocolate in a deep bowl. Set on medium-high for 2 minutes. Remove and stir immediately. If not fully melted, return to microwave for an additional 10 to 15 seconds. Remove and stir thoroughly.)

Cover a cookie sheet with waxed paper. Remove figs from oven. Hold fig by the stem, dip into the warm chocolate, put on waxed paper, and let cool. Place in a covered container and refrigerate. Remove from refrigerator about 1 hour before serving.

Makes 24 stuffed figs

Salsa di Fichi
Fig Sauce

Served hot over ice cream or cake (it goes especially well with sponge cake), this fig sauce is sure to make a hit with family and friends. It is easy to make and can be made ahead and reheated just before serving.

- 1 cup dried figs, coarsely chopped
- 1 cup water
- ½ cup sugar (or less)
- 2 tablespoons freshly grated lemon or orange zest
- 1 cinnamon stick, 3 to 4 inches long
- 1 tablespoon brandy or rum

In a small saucepan over low heat, combine the first five ingredients. Simmer 20 minutes or until the figs are tender. Remove from heat. Remove the cinnamon stick and discard. Add brandy or rum and mix well. Serve immediately.

Serves 4 to 8

Pesche agli Amaretti
Peaches Stuffed with Macaroons, Almonds, and Sherry

When peaches are in season, I inevitably remember to serve this charming dessert. The scrumptious stuffing enhances the natural flavor of the fruit. Easy to assemble, prepare these just before dinner is served and bake them while you are eating. Serve with one of the homemade cookie recipes for a double treat.

- 4 large ripe peaches, unpeeled
- 2 tablespoons almonds
- 2 ounces *Amaretti* (Macaroons, page 280) or macaroon cookies, about ½ cup
- ¼ cup medium dry or sweet sherry, or white wine
- 2 tablespoons sugar
- 2 tablespoons unsalted butter, at room temperature
- 1 teaspoon grated orange zest
  mint leaves for garnish

Preheat oven to 350° F.

Wash peaches, cut in half, and remove pits. Scoop 1 tablespoon of pulp from each peach with a spoon to make a larger cavity. Reserve pulp. Put peach halves in a lightly buttered 8-by-12-inch baking dish.

Put almonds and cookies in a blender or food processor and process into coarse crumbs.

In a medium bowl, add reserved peach pulp, almond and cookie crumbs, sherry, sugar, butter, and orange zest. Mix thoroughly. Fill the peach cavities with the mixture. Bake for 25 to 30 minutes or until peaches are tender but still hold their shape.

Garnish with mint leaves and serve hot or at room temperature.

Serves 4 to 8

TIP: To loosen peach halves from the pit, twist gently back and forth in opposite directions.

Granite di Limone, Fragola, e Menta
Lemon, Strawberry, and Mint Ices

If you make all three ices, you will have the three colors of the Italian flag. Refreshing and thirst-quenching lemon ice is the most common and always appears as street food at religious feasts, both in Italy and in the United States. Ices are easy to make and are a welcomed accompaniment to cake or cookies, especially during the summer. For a deeper hue in lemon and mint ices, add one drop food coloring.

LEMON ICE:

2 cups water
¾ cup sugar
¾ cup fresh lemon juice
1 drop yellow food coloring (optional)
  mint leaves for garnish

STRAWBERRY ICE:

½ cup water
2 tablespoons sugar

10 ounces frozen strawberries, thawed and pureed; or 1 pound
    fresh, pureed
 2 tablespoons lemon juice
    mint leaves for garnish

 MINT ICE:
 2 cups water
 ½ cup sugar
 1 tablespoon mint liqueur
 ½ cup less 1 tablespoon juice
 4 mint leaves
 1 drop green food coloring (optional)
    mint leaves for garnish

Lemon Ice

Put the water and sugar in a 2-quart saucepan and simmer over low heat for 5 minutes. Cool to room temperature.

Add lemon juice and stir.

Strain, pour into a metal ice cube freezing tray without the divider or a small metal baking pan, and freeze. After 1 hour, remove and stir well. Return to freezer. After another hour, stir again until mixture is smooth and has a fine, snowy texture. Refreeze in a covered container until ready to use. Serve one or two scoops garnished with mint leaves.

Strawberry Ice

Put the water and sugar in a 2-quart saucepan and simmer over low heat for 5 minutes. Cool to room temperature.

Add the strawberries and lemon juice and stir.

Follow directions in last paragraph under Lemon Ice, except do not strain.

Mint Ice

Put the water, sugar, and mint leaves in a 2-quart saucepan and simmer over low heat for 5 minutes. Cool to room temperature.

Remove mint leaves. Add the mint liqueur and lemon juice and stir.

Follow directions in last paragraph under Lemon Ice, except do not strain.

Each ice serves 6 to 8

BEVANDI

BEVERAGES

'U mangiari senza bivere e come tronari senza chiovari.

Eating without drinking is like thunder without rain.

<small>CALABRIAN PROVERB</small>

Wines and Liqueurs

'U vino buono si reconoscie dal calore, gradezione e dal sapore.

Good wine is recognizable by its color, grading and taste.

<small>CALABRIAN PROVERB</small>

From earliest times *vino* has been favored for the way it lifts the spirit. Nowhere is this more so than in Italy, where it is the favored drink. Enjoyed in ancient Mediterranean civilizations, its heritage dates back some 4,000 years to when prehistoric people pressed wild grapes into juice that magically fermented into wine. It was mentioned in the *Book of Genesis*; the ancient Greeks who settled in southern Italy in the seventh century B.C. dubbed the colonies *Oenotria*, the land of wine; and the Etruscans and Romans enjoyed its charm. The Romans propagated the cult of Bacchus throughout their empire, and under their rule, grape cultivation quickly spread.

Today, Italy produces and exports more wine than any other country and offers the greatest variety. Serving wine with meals was and is a natural mealtime habit; is an integral part of the Italian family's culture and heritage. Wine, in fact, is viewed as food.

Southern Italy, whose perpetual sunshine and mountain air favor the making of wine, is known as the wine cellar of Europe. Many of their "sunshine wines" are worthy and distinguished and heretofore underestimated. Ciro, in the hills along the Ionian Coast between the ancient Greek cities of Sibari and Crotone, is among the oldest civilized regions of Italy. It is also the best-known wine-producing area of Calabria. Local legend has it that Ciro wine descended from Krimisa, a wine Calabrian athletes drank to celebrate victories in early Olympics, and that Ciro wines were served at festivals to honor Bacchus, Greek and Roman god of wine, vegetation, and fertility. Ciro wines were also praised in Imperial Rome in the first century by Pliny the Elder. Ciro is where the Librandi Brothers, among the finest wine producers in Calabria, produce wines now imported to the United States. In 1995 their Gravello, produced with Cabernet Sauvignon and Gaglioppo, the ancient grape brought to Calabria by the Greeks, received raves. They also produce two highly ranked, full bodied Ciro red wines, DOC Rosso Classico, with its bright fruitiness and soft tannins, and DOC Rosso Riserva, with its rich ruby red color and orange nuances, both created with the gaglioppo grape only. It was my pleasure to taste Rosso Riserva with a fine meal while dining at La Locanda di Alia, in Castrovillari, considered one of the best restaurants in Calabria. Both the meal and the wine were outstanding.

Several other well-known reds are Gragnano, Pollino, Lacrima di Castrovillari Pollino, and Savuto. Among the prized white wines are Greco di Bianco, considered the finest sweet wine in Calabria, and Ciro Bianco, also from the town of Bianco. In addition, these whites receive high praise: Rogliano, Zibibbo, Bianco di Squillace, and Bianco di Nicastro.

Vino di tavola (table wine) may lack a designer label, but most often lacks nothing in taste. Almost all of Italy produces regional wines, some of which fall into this category.

Vino di famiglia (homemade wine) can still be found throughout Italy and in some parts of the United States. My father made his own wine. He had a sturdy wine press that created zesty and potent red wine. He, and most southern Italians we knew, did not make white wine. Red was served with all foods. (Dad also made his own liqueurs, beer, and root beer!) When he was no longer able to make wine, he sold his press to a young Italian immigrant. Although it saddened him to sell it, he was consoled that the tradition of making homemade wine would continue after him, even though not in his immediate family.

Wine consumption, while high in European Mediterranean countries, has always been in moderation and most often, only during meals or at social gatherings. This is the way it was in our home and the way it is in Italy. It is customary for young children to be introduced to wine by adding a few drops of it to water. Gradually over the years, as the children get older, a little more wine and a little less water is added until the child is grown.

The popularity of Italian wines in the United States has increased over recent years. In fact, they have outsold all other imports combined. This is due to several factors. Foremost, it is because the quality of much of imported Italian wine has improved greatly over the years, considerably increasing its status; secondly, the most popular ethnic food in the world is Italian, and Italian food and wine belong together; thirdly, it is reasonably priced; and lastly, recent studies have shown that alcohol, particularly red wine, increases the level of HDL, or "good," cholesterol, good news for southern Italians who favor red wine.

The Italian Government successfully set out in the early 1960s to apply a nationwide control of rigid requirements over wines to ensure their worth. Only those of high reputation and produced under strict controls are labeled *Denominazione del Origine Controllata*, or DOC, as it is commonly called. The DOC designation applies to only about twelve percent of Italian wines. There are now about 240 such wines imported to the United States from 900 different sections of Italy. Calabrian wines from nine such areas have earned the DOC stamp. Some wines earn the even higher rating DOCG, the G for *garantita*, or guaranteed authenticity.

Calabria has several sweet or dessert wines worth mentioning: Greco di Gerace, Moscato di Calabria, Moscato di Cosenza, and Malvasia. On special occasions, champagne is served with desserts. Italy is also the largest producer of sparkling wines.

Like many other Europeans, the majority of Italians do not drink strong liquor or cocktails before dinner, contending that hard liquor kills the taste buds. Italians prefer an aperitif such as *Campari* (served with a splash of soda and orange juice, or plain), sweet vermouth (served with a twist of lemon), white or red wine, or sherry. Although *moscato* is generally classified as a dessert wine, it is sometimes served as an aperitif. The town of Bianco produces a sherry-like wine with hints of citrus and almond.

In Italy, there is no question that wine is the preferred drink, but beer is often chosen on hot summer nights over wine. That was when my dad served his own homemade beer. Italian beer is becoming more popular in the United States. Two brands are imported to New England, both of which are quite good. As in Italy, it is especially favored here in summer. Ice cold, refreshing beer pairs well with pizza and a salad.

Italians may also end their meal with an after-dinner drink. Typical after-dinner drinks served are amaretto, anisette, Frangelico, Galliano, grappa, sambuca, and Strega. Strega is a spicy liqueur made in Benevento and named after the witches who gathered there many years ago under an infamous walnut tree, since cut down.

While researching this book, I came upon a liqueur made in Calabria called Amaro Calabrisella. The packaging induced me to buy and try it. It is made with herbs and has no artificial additives, and I found it to be quite pleasant. As with wine, Calabrians and southern Italians also make homemade liqueur. The more common ones are anisette and lemon-flavored liqueurs. They are easy to make and store indefinitely.

Coffee

Coffee in Italy and most of Europe is served strong. Coffee originated in Ethiopia where it grew wild at high altitudes. In the fifteenth century, it was introduced to Europe by the Venetians. To an Italian, coffee means *espresso*. Cafés prepare it in a special *espresso* machine, which has become an emblem of Italy. It is best described as a short, rich drink, quickly made and intense in flavor. Surprisingly, *espresso* is lower in caffeine than drip coffee, because the water passes so quickly through the grinds.

In 1855, a Frenchman thought up the idea of making quick, flavorful coffee to be served aboard trains, for example. His method was not easily implemented; it took too long to make and produced overcooked coffee. The Italians took a different approach. They devised a way in which to make fresh coffee quicker. Their approach proved highly successful. In 1903, the Gaggia family in Milan improved upon the idea, making it even quicker and *espresso* was born.

In 1948, Giovanni Gaggia wrought a revolution. He perfected equipment that could produce hundreds of cups of fresh coffee quickly using steam pressure. In 1961, the Faema family, with the help of electromagnetics, produced an even slicker, efficient pump machine. In merely 20 to 30 seconds, an intense, delicious cup of coffee emerged. Today, even the smallest village has an *espresso* machine; in large cities, there are thousands. A large machine that operates from early morning to late at night can serve up to 10,000 cups per day.

Espresso machines immigrated to the United States with the Italians and are found in most Italian restaurants and cafés. Gradually, they are being introduced in international restaurants. *Espresso* coffee makers can be bought for home use, and Italian roasted and *espresso* coffee is readily available in Italian specialty stores and coffee shops. The coffee should be very finely ground. *Espresso* can be ordered in several ways:

Caffè	regular espresso
Caffè ristretto	short, dense, and stronger than *caffè*
Caffè lungo	diluted
Caffè macchiato	with a tiny bit of hot milk
Caffè latte	milky coffee without the foamy surface
Caffè senza schiuma	without foam
Caffè coretto	with a shot of brandy
Caffè amaro	bitter, without sugar
Caffè al vetro	in a glass cup
Caffè freddo	iced
Caffè decaffeinizzatto	decaffeinated

Espresso can also be served with sugar, a twist of lemon, a dash of anisette, grappa, whisky, cognac, or sambuca, and so on! Served this way, it often substitutes for fruit or dessert.

Heavenly cappuccino, made with steamed milk or cream, is also very popular in Italy and becoming more so in the United States. Most Italians drink cappuccino only in the morning, regarding it as a breakfast drink, but here it is ordered night and day.

Once consumed by children and occasionally by adults, tea, including herbal tea, has been gaining popularity in Italy, but has a long way to go to attain the status of the cherished coffee.

INDEX